# JUST CAN'T
# GET ENOUGH

# JUST CAN'T
# GET ENOUGH

THE MAKING OF **DEPECHE MODE**

*Simon Spence*

# JUST CAN'T GET ENOUGH
## THE MAKING OF **DEPECHE MODE**
*by Simon Spence*

A Jawbone Book
First Edition 2011
Published in the UK and the USA by Jawbone Press
2a Union Court,
20–22 Union Road,
London SW4 6JP,
England
www.jawbonepress.com

ISBN 978-1-906002-56-5

**EDITOR** Thomas Jerome Seabrook
**DESIGN** Paul Cooper Design

Printed by Everbest Printing Co. Ltd, China

1 2 3 4 5 15 14 13 12 11

# CONTENTS

CLOCKWISE FROM TOP LEFT: **an early-60s map of Basildon, showing the New Town's emergence between Laindon and Pitsea; Basildon town centre by night, 1964; an aerial view of the Fryerns estate; Shepeshall, the street in Lee Chapel North where Martin Gore grew up; Basildon town centre, 1962.**

CLOCKWISE FROM TOP LEFT: **a young Dave Gahan with pals Nikki Avery and Deb Danahay; Martin Gore, performing as Norman & The Worms in his parents' front room, 1979; The Vermin outside Woodlands, 1978; The Vandals, featuring Alison Moyet (centre), 1980; local punk fanzine** *Strange Stories*; **an** *Evening Echo* **article about the embryonic New Romantic scene at Croc's; Vince Clarke with friends Rob Andrews and Rob Marlow, 1979.**

# THE CULT WITH NO NAME

## Fine and dandy! Kids cut a dash

By SUE TAYLOR

# STRANGE STORIES

20p
ISH.19

NEW

## THE LIGHT AT THE END OF THE TUNNEL

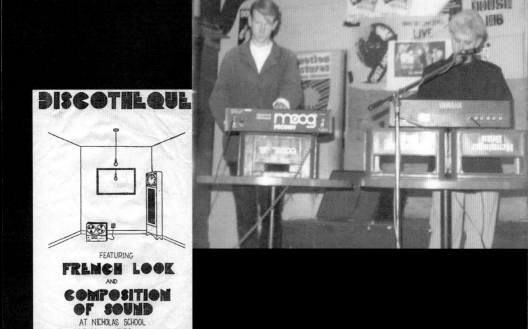

DISCOTHEQUE

FEATURING

FRENCH LOOK

AND

COMPOSITION
OF SOUND

AT NICHOLAS SCHOOL
JUNE 14 7:30

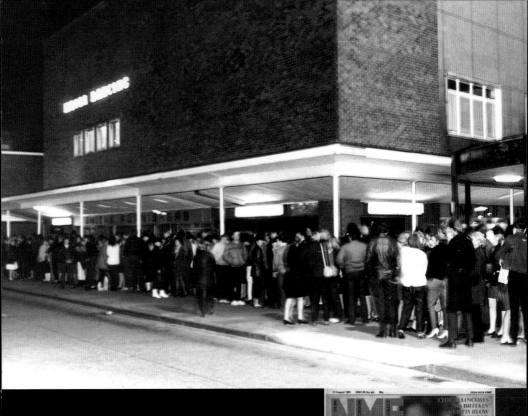

CLOCKWISE FROM TOP LEFT: **a flyer for the gig at St Nicholas Comprehensive that marked the first time the four original members of Depeche Mode performed together as Composition Of Sound, June 1980; Fletch and Martin at the Bridgehouse, late 1980; fans queuing outside Raquel's, Basildon, May 1981; the band's first *NME* cover, August 1981; the Raquel's audience; Depeche Mode at Raquel's.**

a career with authority

CLOCKWISE FROM TOP LEFT:
Fletch, Martin, and Dave at the Basildon careers exhibition at Pitsea Leisure Centre, 1983; early promo photos of Vince and Martin; Fletch, Dave, and Martin on the cover of *The Face*, January 1982; Anne Swindell and Martin at the Greenbelt festival, 1983.

THE FACE

NUMBER 21 JANUARY 1982 65p

DEPECHE MODE
A year in the life
FACE REVIEW OF '81 · SOFT CELL
VIC GODARD · AU PAIRS · JOHN COOPER CLARKE · 2000 AD
RICK MAYALL · WILLIE DEVILLE · MATERIAL · KENSINGTON MARKET · WHAT IS FUNK?

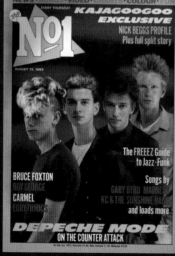

FAD GADGET

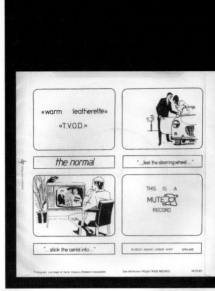

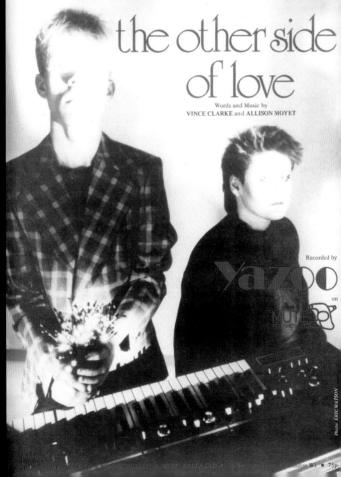

CLOCKWISE FROM TOP LEFT: **Alan Wilder (right) makes his** *Top Of The Pops* **debut for the band's performance of 'See You', 1982; Mute label-mate Fad Gadget; Daniel Miller's sole single as The Normal, 'Warm Leatherette' / 'T.V.O.D.'; sheet music for Yazoo's 1982 hit 'The Other Side Of Love'; Mute Records boss Daniel Miller; Depeche Mode on the cover of pop mag** *No 1*, **August 1983.**

ABOVE: **Martin, Dave, Alan, and Fletch in Berlin during the making of** *Some Great Reward*, **July 1984.**
LEFT: **Depeche Mode on the cover of** *Smash Hits*, **November 1984, with Martin front and centre, his fondness for bondage wear increasingly at odds with the band's pop audience.**

U2 **Smash**
LIMAHL **HITS**
SIOUXSIE
FRANKIE
WHAM!
**STRANGE TALES!**
**DEPECHE MODE**
THOMPSON TWINS
PRINCE
PREFAB SPROUT

# PREFACE

I can't recall when or why I first got into Depeche Mode, but by the time of *Black Celebration* in 1986 I had all their albums. No one else I knew liked them. I was 16.

I do know that by the time I joined the *NME* as a writer in 1989 I'd sold the lot, and it can't just have been to fund the drug habit. I can still remember selling my vinyl copy of *Speak & Spell*. I had handwritten what I thought were the song lyrics on a sheet of A4 paper, slipped it inside the sleeve, and forgotten all about it – until, after checking the vinyl, the record shop guy sneeringly handed back that relic of my teenage infatuation.

I had collected all the seven-inch singles, too, up to and including 'Shake The Disease'. All sold too, regrettably. I saw them live for the first and only time on the Black Celebration tour. I know what I wore. A girl at school I had a crush on loaned me her black leather trousers and I coupled them with some sort of black fake-leather belted overcoat bought in a charity shop. No doubt I was caked in make-up.

My most vivid memory of the band from this period was of the blonde candyfloss-haired Martin Gore, in a leather skirt and black diaphanous woman's slip, handcuffs dangling casually by his side, as he played a bicycle wheel on *Top Of The Pops* for 'Blasphemous

Rumours'. It was almost as sweet and as illicit a thrill as slipping into those leather trousers.

I liked Dave Gahan too. He wasn't as subversive as Gore but his hair was easier to copy: the flat-top with the blonde highlights at the front. It was a disaster on me. Maybe that was what brought an end to my Depeche Mode period.

Looking back, it was, in truth, about more than the hair (although I could never like a band with bad hair). Depeche Mode had never been perceived as cool – according to John McCready of *The Face*, they were "second only to the combined forces of Kylie, Cliff, and PWL when it comes to being subjected to the acid wit of the pop media" – and in my late teens I was desperately subsumed by the desire to be cool.

I don't know if I was embarrassed by them, but I certainly never mentioned my teen love for the band as I scribbled my way across the *NME*, *The Face*, and *i-D*, covering bands such as The Stone Roses, Happy Mondays, and Primal Scream. Not even when Vince Clarke remixed The Happy Mondays' 'Wrote For Luck' and transformed it into a classic.

As the 90s progressed I just forgot all about them. It seems I wasn't the only one. Ironically, the more famous they became in America and Europe during that decade, the lower their profile in the UK. It was only after I began research for this book that I realised just how well they had done without me.

Twelve studio albums, a handful of greatest-hits packages, four live albums, innumerable videos, and one great feature film; Depeche Mode are now officially one of the ten best-selling British acts of all time, sitting pretty alongside such exalted company as The Beatles, the Stones, Led Zeppelin, and David Bowie. And, after 30 years together, they continue to grow in popularity.

On their 2005–06 and 2009–10 world tours they played to over five million people in 32 countries. Their most recent studio album, 2009's *Sounds Of The Universe*, went to Number One in 21 countries. In America they are giants, playing stadiums, topping the *Billboard* charts, and winning Grammy nominations. In Europe they are closer to being Gods, revered from East to West by a devoted mass of 'alternative' youth, their own 'black swarm' cult. In 2006, the iTunes Music Store released *The Complete Depeche Mode* as its fourth ever digital boxed-set, following on from similar packages of music by U2, Stevie Wonder, and Bob Dylan. That's not bad company to keep.

In their homeland, however, Depeche Mode have never really won over the critical cognoscenti. Here, perhaps, is the biggest band in the world, certainly the most worshipped, and yet their achievements and significance go broadly unreported in the UK. People ask whether they are still going, or remember that they were once huge in Germany. This has, understandably, long troubled the band.

In the late 80s, Martin Gore pondered the question of why the band had not been given the respect they deserved in the UK. He thought the current crop of music journalists were too stuck in rock's past; it would take a new generation of writers to come along for his band to be truly, critically appreciated.

More than 20 years later, perhaps, there is a sense that the attitude toward Depeche Mode is softening in this country. Some new faces have begun to hold cultural currency in the UK media; reappraisal of the group is slowly beginning. Video artist Chris Cunningham, for instance, explicitly referenced *Speak & Spell* in one of his acclaimed artworks, while in 2008, Turner Prize winner Jeremy Deller co-directed a documentary about the band's fans, *The Pictures Came From The Walls.*

But Gore is still waiting for someone to truly capture and rapture the band in print. In a sense, Depeche Mode are still waiting to be truly discovered. Paul Morley, in his liner notes for *Depeche Mode: The Best Of Volume 1*, floated the idea that the band were the Rolling Stones of their generation. I'd say they were more like The Who – not just in the way Townshend writes for Daltrey as Gore writes for Gahan, but in the way both bands represent something else, something more than music. The Who started to dismantle rock with their 'we are art' stance, and Depeche Mode cast the parts to the wind with their mantra, reductive of punk's 'three chords is all you need': 'one finger is all you need'.

Pete Townshend once told me how he felt The Rolling Stones had built a "massive fucking wall" between one generation and the next – "no more singing silly love songs". Depeche Mode built another huge fucking wall. No more silly guitars.

Going back to them now, looking at those first five albums afresh, it's hard to understand their struggle for credibility. Maybe they were just too far ahead of their time, as Gore suggested. The line-up was easy to decipher – the bubblegum dream of four teenage kids – but everything else about them was like nothing that had been seen before.

Perhaps their attitude, so anti-rock in every way, was the barrier. They certainly did a lot of uncool pop TV – but never as anything but themselves. The tunes surpassed pop: 'Just Can't Get Enough' is virtually a national anthem, a terrace anthem for Celtic and Liverpool fans. 'Master & Servant' matches 'Venus In Furs' for lyrical and sonic subversion. Their second album, *A Broken Frame*, is wildly esoteric. *Some Great Reward* and *Black Celebration* broke electronic boundaries.

But it was that first album I initially returned to. The CD comes with a lyric sheet now. I still love it: it's camp, weird, catchy – a new world of sound. My idea was to reappraise 1981's *Speak & Spell* and hail it as one the greatest British albums of all time. In fact, I would argue that it was a landmark work, a game-changing album comparable to the first Velvet Underground LP.

Originally, the book would have covered the conception of their deeply influential hometown of Basildon, traced their youth and coming together as a band, and ended with the last note of that first album. Now, I'm glad to have continued to follow the band's journey until their massive 1986 Black Celebration world tour. That was five more years of ammunition to suggest that Depeche Mode broke ground in a way few other British acts before them had, maybe just The Shadows or Roxy Music, and that they were every bit as redolent of their times as Pink Floyd or the Sex Pistols.

True, they were not the first all-synth act (and they have since mellowed toward guitars) but in the words of Seymour Stein, the president of Sire Records who rushed to sign the group in 1981, and whose other discoveries include Madonna, Talking Heads, and The Ramones, Depeche Mode were the first electronic outfit that "fucking rocked".

But it was not just their music or live shows that made them unique: it was the way they approached making their music and the way they delivered and managed their output too. Everything about them was so ultra-modern, even their sexuality. They were the first word in post-modernism.

I wanted to exhume and re-evaluate the early career of Depeche Mode, to wallow in and celebrate it, elevate it to its true level, above what is commonly remembered, in John McCready's words, as "two parts jokes about leather skirts, one part references to their New Romantic tea-towel-wearing period, and several gratuitous references to Basildon".

In the period this book now covers, Depeche Mode conquered the world and put in place a team and a way of working that would provide the bedrock for the next two decades of their record-breaking career. This book explains how and why.

There was certainly no envisaging that places such as Argentina, Mexico, Israel, Colombia, Peru, Chile, Russia, Poland, Czechoslovakia, Germany, France, Italy, Sweden, Ukraine, Spain, Portugal, Austria, Croatia, Denmark, Hungary, Turkey, Finland, Romania, and on and on and on would all feature on the band's juggernaut, multi-million-dollar world tours when, in 1980, they first set up their cheap synths and an even cheaper drum machine on tables and beer crates and sang of feeling like a television set in front of their trendy clique of 50-odd fans in Basildon, Essex.

But the Depeche Mode story starts before that, with another black swarm: a black swarm of World War II German bombers and fighters, flying across the Channel, following the Thames estuary up to London and beginning their apocalyptic devastation of the capital.

The story starts with Basildon.

# PART 1
# GENESIS

# CHAPTER 1
# THE MASTER PLAN

To really understand Depeche Mode we need to really understand Basildon, the Petri dish in which the group were formed. It was the so-called city of the future, built from nothing out of the mud in the aftermath of World War II. This artificial settlement, intended for around 80,000 people, was created to provide homes for East London overspill and make good an area that was unfit for modern living. The broader consequences of what was from the outset described as a "bold social experiment" were unknowable.

The members of Depeche Mode were from the very first generation of kids to grow up in this experimental New Town. It seemed obvious that the kind of music Vince Clarke, Martin Gore, Andrew Fletcher, and Dave Gahan found fame playing – a brutal onslaught of processed newness – must have been informed by their Basildon childhoods, and none of the original band members have denied it.

Basildon was conceived as a kind of utopia for the working classes, with green open spaces, luxury housing, and a plentiful supply of jobs. Plastics, electronics, cars, and other things of the future would be made in modern factories by happy workers living a new, healthy, better life. Like the music of Depeche Mode, Basildon was all about innovation, modernism, and progress, and free of grime and ugliness.

The future was being reborn, and these four young men were lab rats in a truly alien landscape. It was no surprise that when they first made it out of Basildon, the London music press described the group as "half-Martian" – or that, when they first found their fame, it was as part of a movement called the Futurists.

To really understand Basildon, we really need to speak to Peter Lucas, whose three books on the subject provide the definitive historical word on the creation and development of the New Town. Unfortunately, his previous employers, Basildon council and the *Evening Echo*, the local newspaper, responded to my enquires with the news that in all likelihood Peter had passed away. He and his wife had lived in Portugal for a while before returning to the UK to retire in Dovercourt, Essex. But that was about ten years ago; nobody had heard from him since.

Judging by the author picture in *Basildon: Birth Of A City*, published in 1986, I'd guess the current age of Peter, if he were still living, to be just north of 80. After a little digging, I found an address for a Peter Lucas in Dovercourt. The age demographic matched; the house had been bought in 2001, but was sold in May 2010. The telephone number was ex-directory, so all I could do was write a letter to the present occupiers and wait.

Even Peter's three books on Basildon – *Basildon: Behind The Headlines* (1985), the aforementioned *Basildon: Birth Of A City*, and *Basildon* (1991) – are hard to find. The publishers have long since lost contact with the author. Reading these books, I was reminded of an early line from Dave Gahan describing Depeche Mode as "a new sort of band from a new sort of town". A similar theme was raised by Robert Marlow, a close friend of the band who came within a whisker of making it into the final band line-up. He described the sound of Basildon, the Depeche sound, as "coming out of the New Town bricks".

That very first New Town brick was laid by the Lord Lieutenant of Essex, Sir Francis Whitmore, in a ceremony held on November 10 1950. It was the foundation stone for the South East Essex Wholesale Dairies on the evocatively titled Industrial Estate Number One. The ceremony coincided with the publication of the first Basildon Master Plan, produced by the secretive Basildon Development Corporation; a plan catering for a proposed population of 83,700 in what was dubbed "the first City for the 21st century".

The New Towns Act had been introduced in 1946 by the newly elected Labour government. The Act was part of Clement Atlee's party's ambitious post-war vision for a better future for the country, alongside the creation of the welfare state and the NHS. Two years later, on May 25 1948, the Minister of Town and Planning, Lewis Silken, announced provisional approval for the setting of an 11th New Town, in the Basildon area, with a population of 50,000.

The country's leading town planner, Professor Sir Patrick Abercrombie, drew on the principles of the Garden City Movement and the modernist movement in proposing to reduce the population of London by moving over half a million people to New Towns located in an orbit around the capital, just beyond the green belt.

These New Towns were planned as self-contained communities with employment provided by tailor-made factories – places where businesses could be given the space to expand and where workers would benefit from being freed from the daily commute. The logic was persuasive, suggesting both that the UK was open for business and forward-looking, and that there was an alternative to rank, overcrowded inner-city conditions. This was the beginning of the modern age.

Introducing the New Towns Act, Silken said: "We may well produce in these New Towns a new type of citizen, a healthy, self-respecting dignified person with a sense of beauty, culture, and civic pride. I want to see New Towns gay and bright – they must be beautiful. Here is the grand chance for the creation of a new architecture. We must develop in those who live in the New Towns an appreciation of beauty. The New Towns can be an experiment in design as well as into living."

Between 1946 and 1950, eight satellite towns for London were designated: Stevenage, Hemel Hempstead, Hatfield, and Welwyn Garden City in Hertfordshire; Crawley in Sussex; Harlow and Basildon in Essex; and Bracknell in Berkshire. Six more were planned for the rest of the UK. It was reported that each one would cost around £10 million, and that their development would take 20 years. This was an inspired guess at best. In 1970, Silken admitted: "We had no real knowledge of the organisation and finance required [to create the New Towns] nor could we readily see the social problems that might emerge."

Each New Town was to be built by a specially appointed Development Corporation that had legal powers to compulsory-purchase land in the "designated areas" at agricultural value and to grant planning permission.

In effect we were talking about large-scale land nationalisation, and the largest public housing building programme of its kind.

The New Towns were heavily promoted as a giant leap into the future – a move away from polluted, unhealthy, and dysfunctional slums dominated by smokestack factories to an era defined by clean, walk-to-work neighbourhoods, zoned living, green spaces, and leisure. The image sold to the public was of modern, morale-raising, bright, clean, white, light, and airy apartment blocks, schools, and hospitals rising from bombed out Victorian slums.

"It is not enough in our handwork to avoid the mistakes and omissions of the past," announced Lord Reith, the former Director General of the BBC turned Chairman of the New Towns Committee. "Our responsibility, as we see it, is rather to conduct an essay on civilization, by seizing an opportunity to design, evolve, and carry into execution for the benefit of coming generations the means for a happy and gracious way of life."

The rhetoric of Silken and Reith fell on deaf ears in Stevenage, the first designated New Town. Here there was tough opposition from the existing 7,000 inhabitants, who strongly objected to the thought of having a further 70,000 people – urban slum-dwellers, no less – plonked on top of them. Local author E.M. Forster declared that the New Town would be "like a meteorite upon the ancient and delicate scenery of Hertfordshire". There were further legal challenges to block the creation of the proposed New Towns in Crawley, Hemel Hempstead, and Harlow.

In the media, Silken quickly acquired the nickname 'Silkengrad', in reference to Soviet authoritarianism. Others took a broader view. As the esteemed Frederick Osborn put it, with sound reason: "The urban many should outweigh the desires of rural few."

Osborn had been the right-hand man of Ebenezer Howard, the founder of the Garden City Movement, on which many of the ideals of the New Town Act were based. In fact, the success of Howard's Garden City of Letchworth, completed in 1926, had already impacted on town planning and the British landscape. In the aftermath of World War I, the government had interpreted part of Howard's thinking in the outward expansion of existing cities and the creation of vast new suburbs.

There were pockets of success for Howard's advocates. For instance,

Hampstead Garden Suburb – where the man behind early Depeche Mode, Mute record-label boss Daniel Miller, grew up – retained the spiritual undertones of the Garden City Movement with romantics and radicals living in co-operative idyll. But in essence, this inter-war suburbanisation was the antithesis of the Garden City Movement, the sprawl of a city the very thing Howard's original model sought to prevent. One of the final suburban estates to be created before the Green Belt Act of 1938 stopped city expansion without limit was Dagenham – home to and birthplace of Martin Gore before his family's move to Basildon in the early 60s.

Dagenham was made up of 18,000 homes built by London County Council in the east of the city. There was nothing 'Garden City' about it; there were few social amenities and no schools, hospitals, or shops. Families were left stranded, with a long, expensive commute to work. It became known as a 'non-place'.

The New Towns Programme held a greater respect for the Garden City Movement's core concept of the "best of town and country" in self-contained communities and coupled it with a new design for living that had risen to prominence in the 20s and 30s: the modernist movement. Spearheaded by Swiss architect Le Corbusier and symbolised by vast, brutal concrete, the modernist movement would come to have a huge bearing on the architecture and philosophy of the New Towns. Le Corbusier envisaged modernism in its extreme form as a city for three million composed of large mega-blocks separated by freeways and linear parks. The house, he famously said, was as a machine for living in.

Cost was at the forefront of government thinking, and the modernist movement rationalised – even celebrated – low-cost terraces constructed from mass-production panel systems: houses imagined as large structures and sub-divided. Streets, estates, and whole neighbourhoods could be built simultaneously and mass-produced. This was how many of the estates of Basildon were planned and constructed.

In Stevenage, a public enquiry ran for three years before the Court of Appeal and the House of Lords eventually ruled in favour of the New Town policy as being in the national interest. The first New Town neighbourhood was not created there until 1956. By then Basildon was well underway, with over 2,500 new homes and almost 10,000 residents.

Built on an area of 18 square-miles located between (and covering) the existing towns of Laindon and Pitsea in south-east Essex, not far from Southend-on-Sea, Basildon was where the future began. It may have been the penultimate London New Town to be designated but it was the first to begin construction.

The seat of the Urban District Council (UDC) and local authority for the whole of the area was the nearby small town of Billericay. The top brass there had been unusually keen, unlike Stevenage council, to have a New Town built on their doorstep. Billericay UDC looked after a population of 42,500, and 25,000 of them lived in Laindon and Pitsea, small settlements where the majority of homes had no sewers, electricity, or mains water. The massive task of providing these basic amenities and making good the unmade roads in the area fell to the council.

Billericay Town Clerk Mr Alma Hatt canvassed tirelessly to make Basildon New Town happen and put pressure on the influential Essex County Council and the government. He was keen to impress upon them the fact that strong ties already existed with East and West Ham, since many of the 'plot-land' residents of Laindon and Pitsea had originally come from that area. He foresaw not just the solution to the council's problems in Laindon and Pitsea but employment opportunities and a rise in council income from rates.

That sentiment was echoed in a letter written by Lewis Silken of provisional approval for the setting up of the New Town in Basildon, with "regard to the urgent need to find an outlet for the excess population and industry of the congested inner areas of East London". A delighted Hatt announced to the local press that Basildon would become the best town in Essex. Hatt goes down as the man who brought Basildon to life, and would later became known nationally when he oversaw a record turnaround of vote-counting for the Billericay constituency, which at the time still included Basildon, in the 1955 and 1959 general elections. The 1959 turnaround of 59 minutes has never been beaten. These results were said to be an indicator to which way the election would go. (In the late 70s and 80s, when 'Basildon Man' was talked about as a political phenomenon, the same idea re-emerged.)

Silken made clear that in selecting a name for the New Town he did not want reference to Laindon or Pitsea. He said the difficulties of those areas were best forgotten and dismissed the area as "not the brightest spot in the world". But the 'plot-landers' of Laindon and Pitsea and the connected areas of Langdon Hills and Vange, and the tiny village of Basildon sandwiched between them, did not share that view. They felt they'd been sold out. To them the area was not some hillbilly backwater to be wiped off the map, but a version of their own rural arcadia. It was a frontier sort of place that had sprung up over four decades in ad hoc fashion. The whole of this part of Essex had once been typical farming country. The building of a direct railway line between London and the nearby seaside town of Southend, via Laindon and Pitsea, had coincided with the virtual collapse of farming in the late 1800s and radically transformed the landscape. Farmers sold their fields to land speculators, who in turn sold it off to the newly mobile working classes in individual plots, commonly just 18 square feet each.

The sales of these plots were heavily and misleadingly advertised in suburban newspapers and London railway stations. "Mains water readily available" often meant a standpipe a mile away; Pitsea was said to be so healthy that it didn't even have a doctor. The water in Vange, it was claimed, was a cure for rickets, stomach disorders, rheumatism, lumbago, and nervous disorders. On special occasions, free rail tickets from East Ham to Pitsea were issued; travellers were given a free lunch with champagne before the plot sales. Some deed owners never built on their land. After the generous hospitality on the train, some owners did not even realise they had purchased plots, or tore up contracts and threw them out of the carriage window on the way home.

Even so, a slow trickle of better-off people from the East End began to migrate to the area, with some of them building substantial two-storey brick villas. Others followed, with the less well-off building their own wooden and asbestos Shangri-Las in their tiny plots and spending weekends or summers blissfully free of the London smog.

Most of the land where Basildon New Town would sit was offered for sale between 1885 and 1910, but the much-vaulted 'champagne sales' were not a huge success. Supply far exceeded demand. The plot-land sales boom came in the 20s and 30s; the area saw an influx of many thousands, mainly from London's East End. People with no agricultural experience dreamed of making a go of it on their own plots – a rag-tag bunch of returning soldiers, the newly retired, or young idealists glad to escape London.

In the winter, the plot-lands became a muddy nightmare, but people could live with that for the sense of open space and freedom. Many of the plot-land shacks that were originally planned as weekend getaways became full-time homes, with their owners either subsisting off the land or commuting to London. Between 1921 and 1941, the population of the Billericay UDC area almost trebled, with the greatest increase taking place in the plot-land areas of Laindon and Pitsea. The completion of the A127 arterial road between London and Southend, and the A13 through Vange and Pitsea, further opened up the area.

A sprawl of shops popped up in Laindon and Pitsea to serve the growing population. It was still a rough and ready existence, lacking basic amenities, but with a cohesive community spirit: candles in jam jars, horse-and-cart deliveries, a network of footpaths. People dug their own wells, grew their own vegetables, and kept rabbits, chickens, and goats. The idea of making way for a vast modernist New Town and the threat of compulsory purchase orders did not go down well. According to the Residents Protection Association, which dubbed the New Town 'the monster': "The loss of freehold would be a heartrending blow to those who have striven for years to acquire a small portion of their mother soil."

Then, on October 7 1948, the Minster of Town and Country Planning himself, the Rt Hon Mr Lewis Silken MP, came to the district to speak at Laindon High Road School – the school that Vince Clarke would later attend. Over 1,500 people turned up to hear Silken speak; many stood in the playground listening over loudspeakers. He invoked a sense of wider responsibility to the people of East and West Ham, "their own kith and kin", where, he said, one building in every four had been flattened by bombs and 20,000 people were on the waiting lists for homes.

He sympathised with those who built their own places at "great sacrifice" and who wanted to spend the rest of their days in "peace and quiet". His business, he said, was not to destroy but to build. He had no intention of pulling down (on a large-scale) buildings that already existed, but proposed to use the large area between Pitsea and Laindon to build the nucleus of a New Town.

"Basildon will become a city which people from all over the world will want to visit," he proclaimed. "It will be a place where all classes of the community can meet freely together on equal terms and enjoy common cultural and recreational facilities. Basildon will not be a place which is ugly, grimy, and full of paving stones, like many modern towns. It will be something that the people deserve – the best possible town that modern knowledge, commerce, science, and civilisation can produce."

It was a historic speech and a historic day – the one on which Basildon New Town was really born. The Designation order was passed on January 4 1949, just under six months after it was first mentioned to the Cabinet Committee. It was the quickest ascension of any of the New Towns.

□-□-□

This is where the Depeche Mode story truly begins. The land where this city of the future was to be built holds their deepest roots, their sap rising from this viscerally romantic and potently evocative plot-land area, all shacks, swamps, and scrubland. Laindon and Pitsea would never be eviscerated entirely, and to this day both are still commonly referred to as areas of Basildon. Vince, Martin, and Andy would all live and grow-up in Laindon; Dave called the other side of town, Pitsea, home.

The hillbilly Cockneys who had built their own homes from scavenged materials carted along muddy paths were outlaws and idealists. Their ramshackle way of life, their sweat and spirit, their strong sense of community, suggests a kind of British Mississippi. By extension, then, we can imagine Vince Clark as a kind of British Robert Johnson, Martin Gore as the British Bo Diddley.

Perhaps it is no coincidence that Depeche Mode's early music spoke a similar language to the socially and economically excluded blues pioneers, conveying the same sense of alienation and religious intensity. Did they unwittingly create the first original British Blues? Certainly, Depeche Mode were the first British group to enter the mainstream without displaying the influence of America blues. The Basildon Blues were a modern blues, born out of a feral heritage and the huge disconnect between the hopes and dreams for the New Town and the nightmare reality of becoming the capital city of Chavland.

In many ways we can all connect to that disconnection, which is perhaps one of the reasons Depeche Mode are loved by so many millions the word over. This is the story of our age: Basildon was the future, a socialist ideal that quickly became overwhelmed by the grey concrete facades of American consumer capitalism.

Peter Lucas talks about the 'Basildon blues' in his books, but in the context of the new mothers coming to live in the town in the early 50s and finding the place harsh and depressing. It was their sons who would set this disconnection from the new world to music. Vince, Martin, Fletch, and Dave would become the outriders of the future, messengers from the new modern metropolis – with just enough of the real God in them to put those feelings into song. Theirs were souls not yet surrendered to the shopping centre and the television, the concrete and the plastic. Their soul music was a new sort of soulless music, their blues a new form of blues, their spirituals a salvation – of sorts.

Basildon was a living experiment, a leap into the unknown. It was not just a New Town but a new way of life. In charge of it were seven members of the Development Corporation Board, with Sir Lancelot Keay KBE, a past president of the Royal Institute of British Architects, at the helm. Only one of the seven was a local man; from the onset, the Corporation projected aloofness, choosing a headquarters outside the designated area of the New Town in nearby Bowers Gifford, virtually out of reach. They paid little attention to public consultation. The Corporation was a very authoritarian body, with every aspect controlled tightly by the government.

In the Master Plan, Sir Lancelot called the project a "bold social experiment" and argued that "thousands living in grossly overcrowded conditions will benefit and many will be saved the fatigue and expense of travelling long distances to and from their places of work".

The Master Plan was to form the basis for Basildon's development over the next 35 years. This was construction on a hugely impressive scale. The document stated that Basildon covered the largest area yet designated for a New Town, and would hold the largest population of all of them: 83,700.

In total, Basildon was set to cover a 7,834-acre area six miles long from east to west and three miles across from north to south. Some 4,300 acres consisted of scattered development and 3,500 acres of farmland of "variable quality". One of the problems the Master Plan highlighted was that the land and buildings in the designated area came under 30,000 different ownerships. Of the 8,550 properties in the area, 6,000 were not connected to sewers. Only 3,000 of them came up to standards required by the Housing Acts of 1936. There were 78.2 miles of unmade roads.

The basic design for the town was also laid out in the Master Plan, with the vital function of the Town Centre at its core. If Basildon was to succeed commercially it needed to be the focus of town life. The Corporation stated that the placing of the town centre in a central position of the designated area "may well be regarded as the key to the problem of welding together the two existing towns of Laindon and Pitsea", which were three-and-a-half miles apart. Planning was made for two industrial areas, which were to be no more than 15 minutes by cycle or bus from homes and were expected to provide work for 16,000.

In terms of housing, there would be nine "neighbourhoods": three in new locations and six built in the existing areas of Laindon, Lee Chapel, Langdon Hills, Vange, Basildon, and Pitsea. Within these neighbourhoods, 15 vast housing estates were planned, with each to be provided with its own primary school, shops, and playing fields. Thirteen secondary schools were planned to break up the flow of housing and to be easily and safely accessible on foot.

Four sites were designated for "consumer industries and services" and expected to provide employment for 20,000. Three would be next to the railway stations at Laindon, Pitsea, and Basildon; the fourth, north of Laindon, would be used for immediate needs. There were also detailed plans for administration, commercial, and cultural and recreational buildings. There was, however, no guarantee of these social facilities – the Corporation would need to bid to the government for them.

Parking for 2,000 cars was planned: way ahead of other towns but still vastly inadequate as car ownership quadrupled over the next 15 years. The New Towns Programme architect, Sir Patrick Abercrombie, had allowed for 16 per cent car ownership. By 1966, over half of the adult population owned cars.

From the start, industrialists were not attracted to Basildon in sufficient numbers to satisfy the Corporation. Finding employers willing to come to Basildon was not the only problem. The site for the industrial estate had been farmland, and the purchase relatively straightforward – and cheap – at £200 an acre for 2,345 acres. The clearance of the so-called 'shack areas' would prove far more problematic.

People liked the country life, however primitive it was, and had no wish to leave it to live on a housing estate in a New Town. In February 1951, residents of Laindon, Vange, Pitsea, and Basildon marched outside the House of Commons. They had no wish to sell their plots and called the compulsory purchase orders "legalised robbery".

The Labour Party had lost the 1951 election, and the first Basildon New Town MP, Sir Bernard Braine, was a Conservative. Looking back on the plot-lander protests, he told Peter Lucas: "Basildon could not have got off to a worse start. There were already 25,000 people in Laindon and Pitsea; tough, independent-minded folk, who had escaped the smoke of London to build freehold homes on freehold plots. The Labour government got carried away with planning fervour and the idea of land nationalisation and asserted freehold ownership would go, so property was acquired for development at below true market price." According to Sir Bernard, the new Conservative government had agreed a deal to pay fair compensation for freeholds – a decision he said "put Basildon back on rails".

The New Town Programme had been developed by Labour – the 1951 Festival of Britain had showcased a future vision of towns full of modernist architecture and pedestrian-only precincts — but would be executed by the Conservatives, who had never been thrilled by an idea they saw as indicative of Labour's paternalist idealism. In a sign of how the New Towns Programme lacked firm direction or cross-party support, it seems amazing to note that while car ownership was being pushed as a policy of central government, only 14 per cent of Basildon homes were being built with garages.

The first New Town tenants moved in on June 15 1951, by which time six houses had been finished. Mr and Mrs John Walker and their two children, aged six and 15 months, had been on East Ham's housing list for five years. They had been living in a temporary Nissen Hut in the slums of

East London. Now they had a brand new house in the middle of the countryside, a proper kitchen, a bathroom, and a garden.

The Corporation builders moved swiftly. By the end of 1953, 1,000 new houses had been completed. Tenants were either workers on the industrial estate or building workers – mainly from East and West Ham and all complaining that rents were high in comparison to the rent-controlled tenancies in London. There were now nine new completed factories, occupied by companies such as Rotary Hoes, the Freedman Upholstery Company, Nufloor Limited, and Marconi Wireless Telegraph Company. By 1956 there would be over 4,000 people employed in 19 factories and 34 smaller units on what became known as the Marconi estate, with the proposed second industrial estate under construction.

A great deal of thought had gone into planning the new housing estates. They were all built on the 'neighbourhood units' principle, with an emphasis on the separation of traffic and pedestrians. Intended to provide a safe environment for children to play and walk to school, the estates were criss-crossed with a network of footpaths. Roads onto the estate would often lead to the back of a property, with walkways to the front and green areas linking the houses to other groups of similar houses. Each neighbourhood was intended to contain a small group of pantry shops, a school, a pub, a church, and a community hall to foster a sense of cohesion. The basic concept – based on an American model pioneered in Radburn, New Jersey, in the 20s – was sound, but the provision of amenities was slow.

Two hundred families were soon accommodated – with many houses going to building workers – but the more rural areas had hardly been touched. Outside their luxury new homes, the first inhabitants soon faced up to the appalling conditions and a lack of social amenities and shopping facilities within easy reach.

The first estate to be built – Fryerns, where Dave Gahan would later live – was marooned in a sea of mud, with a two-mile walk to the nearest shop, in Pitsea. Provision of schools was also way behind schedule. The existing primary schools were overcrowded, so newly arrived kids were ferried out of Basildon by bus to be schooled. Fryerns would not get its own primary school for a further three years.

The Conservative government imposed tough restrictions on capital expenditure when Basildon was in dire needs of amenities of every sort. The Corporation was focused on delivery but not on social development. The building of houses – the top priority – was not affected by the tightening of budgets.

Many new arrivals were of the same family model: young, with husband in the factory and wife looking after the newborn, eager to add more. Basildon became know as a 'pram town'. Many of these young mothers complained of being lonely and homesick, and when the Basildon Blues hit the national newspaper headlines, psychiatrists were called in. Living in a new estate in a rural area came in stark contrast to East Ham High Street with the convenience of shops and entertainment on the doorstep and relatives and friends nearby. The young mums felt isolated in the middle of these giant housing estates devoid of community life, away from their families.

For many of the early workers, wages were low and rents were high. Their houses were sparsely furnished, often with no carpets and furniture bought on HP agreements (hire-purchase, or credit). The men worked overtime to boost income and pay off debts, the women became even lonelier, and marriages fell apart. Families split, and many returned to London. Divorce and alcoholism, like depression, were quickly linked back to Basildon.

Meanwhile, the housing estates mushroomed westward across the fields and farmlands. During 1955–56, the Corporation built over 1,000 homes in a year for the first time. Fryerns was still the largest estate but was now rivalled by the vast Barstable. The number of newcomers was expected to soon top 15,000. The popular idea was that the majority came from East and West Ham; a quarter of them did, but others came from Dagenham, Ilford, Hackney, Romford, Hornchurch, Tottenham, Hendon, Walthamstow, Willesden, and Leyton.

Wherever they came from, they all recognised the fact that progress on social amenities was sickeningly slow. First came a post box, then a telephone box, then a pub (the Crane), then a primary school; the Co-op on Fryerns was joined by a hardware shop, a chemist, a newsagent, a grocery shop, and a fish and chip shop. Ironically, the lack of facilities fostered a sense of community in the Basildon pioneers. Volunteers built the first wooden community huts on the estates and started their own hobby groups.

The Corporation was now the principal land and property owner in Pitsea and Laindon, with both areas still relatively untouched by development. Compensation for freeholds had been set at an acceptable figure and many plot-landers were amenable to selling. In fact, land and property owners were now able to serve notice on the Corporation to buy ownerships. Despite this there were still incidents of the lone rebel stood with a shotgun on his roof with a Union Jack fluttering from the chimney, refusing to budge, and tragic stories of old people forcibly removed by a clumsy bureaucratic steamroller. The price paid for property often depended on the colour it was shaded on a map. If the land was needed for industry or housing, the owner was usually well compensated; if the colour denoted recreational or leisure use, the payoff was much smaller. Unscrupulous land dealers moved in, too, buying and selling plots for profit.

The first major development of a plot-land area came in Lee Chapel, Laindon, where 500 homes were demolished to make way for what was conceived as the Five Links Estate, a huge unit of five large, separate estates. Elsewhere, a series of setbacks had delayed the start of work on the town centre. In June 1957, the Duke and Duchess of Gloucester arrived at the muddy building site where the Duke cut a ribbon to open the centre's main road, Southernhay. A block of 41 shops was being built, with plans for two similar blocks. The Duke also named the town park Gloucester Park, although the only indication of its position was a banner strung up between two trees. The Royal couple finished their visit at Industrial Estate Number One, where they popped into the Marconi factory and were told that there were now 6,000 new homes in Basildon, with 70 per cent of tenants working on the industrial estate, where there were now 58 factories in operation.

The first shop was opened in Basildon town centre in August 1958 – a shocking seven years after the arrival of the first New Town resident. It was a tailors and outfitters, and soon there was a shoe shop next door. The market opened next, and within a year there were 28 shops in the town centre itself, including branches of WH Smith and Boots.

The Corporation's own administrative centre, Keay's House (named for town planner Sir Lancelot), was being built in the town square, as were two blocks of flats: the infamous Brooke House and Freedom House, designed by Sir Basil Spence. Brooke House is now a listed building and divides opinion to this day. Spence, who had designed the new Coventry Cathedral, was responsible for the whole look of the town centre, a major work of classic modernist architecture.

At the western end of the town centre, the famous Mother & Child water sculpture was unveiled. Made by William Lambert in bronze, it cost £4,000 and took a year to cast. It was said to symbolise the essential element of New Town life: the young mother and her child. It became a symbol of Basildon. (There was also a less famous sculpture of the Greek poet Homer.)

Soon there would be 200 shops in the centre, including a department store, Taylor's, and a pub, the Bullseye – a favourite, later, of Dave Gahan. It was Britain's first modernist pedestrian centre, and became a major draw. On one Saturday in the early 60s, 1,400 cars were counted arriving for a day of shopping. Plans were quickly altered to allow for a multi-storey car park for 5,000 cars (up from an original allowance of 500). Expanding the town centre outward was difficult, due to the close proximity of adjacent housing estates. It had been designed for a specific community right at the point when society was changing.

▭▬▭

By the end of the 50s, the population in Basildon was nearing 30,000. The town centre was finally starting to shape up, housing estates were plentiful, Industrial Estate Number One was all but full, and Number Two was operational, but there was still no hospital, post office, or train station, and social and recreation facilities were thin on the ground; fire, police, and ambulance stations had also failed to materialise.

There was, however, one welcome new addition to Basildon's social life, and it would become a focus of teen life for the next 30 years. The Church Commissioners' building in the town centre had been leased to Mecca Limited for a 1,000-capacity dance hall. The Mecca would later become Raquel's nightclub, the scene of a famous early Depeche Mode concert.

The Mecca produced Basildon's first pop star, the remarkable Graham Bonney. His family were typical of the early newcomers to the town. He had been born in Stratford, East London, and his family had moved to

Fryerns in 1954, when he was 11. "Everybody was bursting to get out from East London after the war," he told me. "We'd been playing on bombsites and all of a sudden we had this countryside. There were hardly any houses around. At the beginning Basildon was ... there's no better word than hope. It gave everyone hope that things were getting better. For an 11-year-old boy it was like paradise on earth."

Bonney shared a four-bed Corporation house – soon to be besieged by screaming girls – with his sister, parents, and grandparents. To Bonney, as to many New Town pioneers, the place seemed fantastical. "The fact we had an inside loo was just heaven," he recalled. "Having a bath inside was just unbelievable. In Stratford we'd had a bloody tin thing hanging up outside. Basildon went up at an incredible rate. When I think about what was there when I moved, and what was there five years later, it was just not to be believed: schools, a town centre, the Mecca, shops, community halls, new pubs."

Hooked on rock'n'roll, school-leaver Bonney roped in Peter Cackett, a face about town, and bricklayer Tommy Berry to form The Expresso Five. They rehearsed in the cinema in Pitsea and – in an echo of the early development of Depeche Mode some 25 years later – played local community halls and schools. "We made our own entertainment, as such," Bonney said.

The Expresso Five were the first Basildon band and also the first group to play a residency at the Mecca ballroom. "It was just kids at the Mecca," Bonney recalled. "Some mums and dads used to come as well but they'd go into the bar. It was kids in their Italian suits, mods."

There was a massive mod scene in Basildon in the early to mid 60s. For the London mods, the Basildon Mecca was a stop on the way to a Friday night out in Southend. They'd get on their scooters, go to the Mecca, and then drive off to Southend to spend the night on the beach.

The Expresso Five split in 1963 and were replaced for a brief time as the Basildon Mecca house band by The Dave Clark Five. (The Who and The Kinks also played one-off shows at the club.) Graham Bonney's subsequent solo career bore another uncanny echo of Depeche Mode when he became hugely popular in Germany. His 1966 UK smash 'Supergirl' went to Number One there, prompting him to sing the follow-up, 'Das Girl

Mit Dem La La La', in German. Bonney had had enough of struggling and turned now to what was known as Deutsche Schlager – catchy, middle-of-the-road pop. 'Das Girl' was another huge hit, and Bonney remains in high demand with German audiences to this day.

Another reason to believe that Basildon was on the up and up came with news that the Ford Motor Company wanted to develop a massive tractor-manufacturing plant in the area, creating jobs for 5,000 people. Ford had its eye on a 100-acre site between Industrial Estate Number One and Number Two. The government had wanted the plant to go to the North of England, but Henry Ford himself flew over to negotiate for the plant to stay in the South. Eventually, without consulting the Corporation, the government allocated a site of 250 acres to Ford, which was said to cost the company £10.5 million.

Ford would play a huge role in attracting many new workers to Basildon, including the Gore family. The company also announced plans to build an Engineering Research Centre that would employ a further 3,200 people, among them high-paid executives, graduate engineers, and technicians. These were the types of people the Corporation wanted in order to achieve a more balanced community in Basildon, and the sort who could afford the rents that were proving to be a stretch for unskilled workers.

Business was booming. There were now 31,000 people employed on the industrial estates, with more big firms arriving; Standard Telephones & Cables took a 24-acre site with plans to employ 2,500. Soap and perfume manufacturer Yardley & Co announced that it too would open a factory. The Duke of Edinburgh piloted his own helicopter for a flying visit to open the Carreras cigarette factory. He flicked a switch that made history, inaugurating the total automation of cigarette-making for the first time anywhere in the world. Other firms such as Ilford, Teleflex Products, Carson Ltd, and York Shipley Ltd all rolled in to town. York Shipley was a Nottingham-based refrigeration and cooling equipment manufacturer, and brought with it a few families from Nottingham – among them the Fletchers. After arriving in Basildon, Andrew Fletcher's father would go on to spend many years working for Carreras.

By the mid 60s, with the families of the future Depeche Mode members newly arrived in Basildon, the landscape of the town had completely changed: 12,000 new homes had been built, over 38 miles of new road had been constructed, and the population stood at 63,750. The Corporation had acquired 4,790 acres of land and buildings involving 7,400 ownerships at a cost of £7.9 million. Over 4,000 pre-New Town homes had been demolished, and the redevelopment of Laindon and Pitsea had transformed the former plot-land areas, with historic buildings such as Vange Hall and Laindon Hall (both 500 years old) demolished.

Laindon's I, II, and III estates – which covered the area of Lee Chapel North where Vince, Martin, and Fletch lived – were now completed. There was a science fiction aesthetic to many of these radical, brave, and imaginative designs on these monumental estates common across all the New Towns. (Stanley Kubrick's *A Clockwork Orange* was filmed in Harlow.) They were built to exact Radburn principles, and were places everyone wanted to come to: modern houses linked by pedestrian walkways, laid out in courtyard fashion, landscaped and family friendly. Young minds could envisage a future of getting about on jet packs or monorails.

Some of the earlier estates were already beginning to feel dated, however. The Corporation was forced to go back and add garages to many homes – a slow, frustrating process. It was also reported that many houses were already in need of remedial work due to leaking and dampness. This was the peak of the system-built housing boom, and these new, industrialised methods of construction had allowed the Corporation – under pressure from the government to improve national statistics – to build new homes at a rapid rate. But not everything they did would prove successful.

The 1,000-home Laindon V Estate, intended to bring to a close the successful and complete redevelopment of Laindon, would end up as a concrete slab disaster, dubbed 'Alcatraz' by locals. It cost £3 million and took 31 months to build. The Ghyllgrove estate, also in Lee Chapel North, was another embarrassment. It was built near the town centre, carved out of an area designated for Gloucester Park. The Ghyllgrove III scheme won first prize in the Ministry of Housing's Housing Design Competition – a first for Basildon. But a few weeks later it was disclosed that many of the flat roofs on the estate were leaking – and that it would cost £80,000 to repair. The award was taken back.

In 1964, the target population for Basildon was increased to 106,000. It was the first New Town to significantly increase its target. And it was about to get bigger. A 1965 technical study and draft new Master Plan showed how a population of 140,000 could be accommodated in Basildon without changing the size of the designated area. The aim was now to make Basildon a self-contained centre for the region, offering a full range of employment opportunities for all classes of workers. The idea of bringing more white-collar workers to Basildon became a recurring theme over the next 30 years. After a nine-day public enquiry, Basildon's development until the new century had in broad terms – and despite protestations from Essex County Council – been decided.

More families flooded into Basildon following news of this increased ambition but they were not of the broader demographic the Corporation had hoped would arrive. Instead they were young working-class parents with a toddler in tow. They would find work on the industrial estates and quickly have more children. The place was awash with them. There were now an incredible 34 primary schools in Basildon.

The disparity between the fast-growing population and the lack of major facilities, such as a hospital or railway station, remained stark. This was not what the forefront of sociological progress was supposed to look like. Basildon train station would not be operational until 1974. The hospital – seen by many as the town's greatest need in its first 20 years, and promised as far back as 1960 – opened in 1973, although the casualty department was closed until 1975 because of a shortage of staff. Up until then, the New Town relied on the run-down hospital in Billericay, two bus journeys away.

Furthermore, apart from the pubs or the Mecca, Basildon was a cultural desert. Small drama or poetry groups had sprung up, but the majority of the town's entertainment was provided by its chief employers. Marconi and Ford had their own thriving social clubs; Yardley often provided grandstand shows for its workers, clearing the huge canteen and hosting the London Philharmonic in one instance. In these companies one found a trace of the socialist Utopia the New Towns had aspired to. Otherwise? Plans for a sports centre had been scrapped. There was a new golf course, but the only two cinemas in the area were on the verge of closing down. Rumour had it that wife-swapping was a popular pastime. Then came the Arts Centre, which brought culture to Basildon and planted the seed for everything that was to follow.

Vin Harrop, who had previously managed the Empire Theatre in Liverpool and the London Palladium, arrived in 1967 to organise the launch of the Arts Centre, and would remain as director for four-and-a-half years following its opening in September 1968. "When I first arrived it was a bit of a culture-shock," he told me. "I came out of the Dartford Tunnel and there was just a huge cement works and all this low-lying scrubland and I thought: what have I let myself in for? Basildon was still only half-built. The kids used to occupy themselves by going around smashing up telephone kiosks. There was nothing for them to do. It was pretty dead, culture-wise."

The Arts Centre was a modernist, temporary, demountable building. It was intended to last for seven years but in fact stood for 14. It had a theatre and a cinema, rooms for pottery, photography, drama, band-rehearsal, and recording, and a space for outdoor sculpture. It was to prove a boon for the Depeche Mode generation. "Basildon had its own education department," Harrop recalled, "and the director of education was a very enlightened fellow. He encouraged all his schools to use the Arts Centre, so the children used to come along to the performances, the concerts and the plays, and films and everything else."

Many of the people I spoke to recalled school trips to see plays such as *Macbeth* or films such as *Lord Of The Flies* and *Kes* as part of English Literature studies at school. Others saw Sooty or Charles Hawtrey in pantomime.

"The most popular things were Saturday morning film shows," Harrop continued. "I introduced an entertainer between the films. We showed one film, then we'd bring on Uncle Willy during the interval to entertain the children, and then have a second film. I remember one little boy looking at Uncle Willy and saying to his mother: this is interesting television. He'd never seen a live show in his life. That actually brought it home to me. A lot of these kids had never seen anybody performing on a stage. I introduced them to live entertainment."

The Arts Centre also put on touring theatre and classical, jazz, opera, and pop concerts. Acts such as Oscar Peterson and The Barrow Poets performed there (but not, as local legend has it, David Bowie). "I would select acts that I thought would be good for Basildon, in the sense of introducing them to new experiences," Harrop said. "It was an eclectic programme. I thought: I've got to educate the people of Basildon as well as entertain them."

Many of the people I spoke to from the Depeche Mode generation recalled seeing acts such as Vivian Stanshall from the Bonzo Dog Doo-Dah Band, Curved Air, or Henry Cow at the Arts Centre in the 70s. Harrop recalled having many arguments with the council, which had provided funding for the Arts Centre to the tune of £100,000, over his choice of entertainment. "There were those among the council who wanted me to run it differently," he recalled. "The art exhibitions were criticised for being too bold and too radical, too contemporary for Basildon audiences – quite how they knew that I'll never know because the people who came in to see them thought they were wonderful."

Fortunately, Harrop resisted calls from the council to abandon the arts in favour of putting on all-in wrestling shows, and the Arts Centre became the key venue in the town's cultural development. It would later provide a sanctuary for Vince, Martin, and Fletch. But culture and the arts was not what brought together these three young boys who would go on to form Depeche Mode.

▱▱▱

To really understand Depeche Mode we need to really understand Basildon, and Peter Lucas was the Jacques Cousteau of its deeps. And finally he surfaced – the letter I posted to what I hoped was his old address in Dovercourt was passed on to him in his new luxury retirement home in Braintree, Essex. He sounded pleased to hear of my interest and happy for me to reference his books. He grew up in Laindon, he said, in "a lovely brick bungalow with delightful gardens" that was bought and demolished by the Corporation. He joined the local newspaper, then called the *Standard*, in the mid 50s, and worked there until he became the council's press-relations officer in 1970.

"A lot of people were very worried about the New Town," he said.

"Laindon was like a village in the early days, and to have a huge town of 100,000 people plonked on them was rather frightening. There was a lot of activity behind the scenes to try and stop it. There were a lot of anxious people. But, of course, you can't stand in the way of progress. There was an awfully long waiting list of housing from the London area, and Basildon did the job of providing a lot of that housing. It was not everyone's cup of tea but it served a wonderful purpose."

I already knew that, in 1983, Lucas had invited Depeche Mode to the annual Basildon careers exhibition at Pitsea Leisure Centre. They had come free of charge and showed genuine concern for the unemployment situation of the time – a curse to many young people their age.

Peter was tiring. He had not been well. But he was eager to tell me his Depeche Mode story. "As far as the early days of Depeche Mode, I only met them on one occasion," he continued. "I was the PRO for Basildon council and it was my idea to contact the band in the hope that their presence at our careers exhibition would attract the youngsters to the show.

"I will always remember the Depeche Mode boys; they came up to the first floor where we were entertaining them for lunch and looked out of the window, and of course every child around wanted to wave and cheer and shout and what have you. It was a tremendous opening for the careers exhibition. They came and had a bit of lunch with the town manager and myself. But they didn't eat much lunch – they were sort of hanging out of the window waving at their fans. After that I never heard from them again."

I had many other things to ask Peter, but he was fading. It was the shortest interview I did for this book, but I felt somehow as though he had blessed the project. I did manage to ask him about religion in the New Town, about the incredible number of churches that had sprung up in Basildon's early days. "The churches were pretty well the first lot in," he said. It was through them that Vince Clarke and Andy Fletcher first met.

# CHAPTER 2

# BORN AGAIN

Religion was everywhere in the early days of Basildon, and it was the Methodist Church that would bring together Vince Clarke and Andy Fletcher. Churches flourished in early New Towns, often appearing on the new estates ahead of schools and shops. Fryerns Baptist Church, for instance, opened in 1954 and was swiftly followed by the Church of England St Andrew's. In the early 60s, St Martin's, another Church of England, was consecrated in the town centre. It had as a focal point a controversial modernist sculpture of Christ. The Archbishop of Canterbury gave a famous speech at St Martin's in 1968 that caused uproar in the New Town. His message of all-inclusive race relations was met with shouts of "send them all back home" from parts of the congregation.

The Methodist Home Mission Society, whose job it was to look after Methodist interests in developing areas, had sent a missionary to Basildon as early as 1953. The Reverend Donald Shaw, on his first appointment straight out of Cambridge University, pioneered Methodism in Basildon. He first held services at the home of one of the Corporation's architects, attracting just seven or eight worshippers. He then converted an old empty bungalow called Hillview in the middle of a waterlogged field, laying paving stones in the mud so people could safely worship.

Shaw was a popular figure in the New Town. He later told Peter Lucas how, even back then, certain streets on the estates had developed a certain character, with some houses and gardens kept beautifully and others already showing signs of neglect. His pioneering work was continued by another dynamic figure, Reverend Ronald Gibbons, who became notorious when he campaigned to oppose the granting of drink licences to the Mecca. He invited The Beatles to open his Boys' Brigade youth club. The pop group did not come, but because of the publicity hundreds of youngsters did, Vince and Fletch among them.

St Paul's Methodist Church was built in 1968 in Ballard's Walk, Lee Chapel North. This was the church of Depeche Mode. "Ron Gibbons was instrumental in getting both Trinity and St Paul's built," Harold Swindell told me. "He used to organise a bus to go round the town to pick up the children. He was a livewire. He'd been in the RAF and I think he'd forgotten he was out."

Harold is the father of Anne Swindell, Martin Gore's first love, and was involved in the Methodist Church in Basildon from the very early days. In trying to track down Anne I found Harold through Basildon's Trinity Methodist Church, which was also built in the late 50s, and with which Harold is still involved. He was another typical Basildon man, originally from East Ham; his wife came from Canning Town. He took the opportunity to relocate when the company he worked for, Stability Radio Components, moved to Basildon. It was, he said, like a "frontier town".

"There was war-damage money that went to the London churches to help them rebuild," he recalled. "As Basildon was a New Town taking mainly Londoners, it was agreed that the money could be transferred and used to build replacement churches there."

Harold ran the senior youth club at Trinity church; his wife was the Girls' Brigade captain there. He had fond memories of another local Methodist minister, Reverend Daley, whom Vince Clarke would later cite as a childhood hero. "Malcolm Daley was the Minister for Langdon Hills and St Paul's Methodist Churches," Harold recalled. "He got a choir over from Sweden on one occasion. He was that sort of guy. He seemed to be able to organise things – some of them can and some just jog along.

"I knew all the Depeche Mode boys. They went to St Paul's Church and my daughter was the fan club secretary. A couple of them performed in a musical play that we put on at Trinity. It was about the founder of the Sunday school movement, Robert Raikes, to celebrate its 200th anniversary. Some of Depeche Mode played in the music group for the play, *A Grain Of Mustard Seed*. The one I remember was Andy Fletcher."

Steve Burton is Depeche Mode keyboard player Andrew Fletcher's oldest friend. His parents came to Basildon – to Woolmer Green in the northern part of the Lee Chapel North neighbourhood – in 1963, from poor-quality rented accommodation in South-east London. His father worked for the Post Office.

"Most of those parents who came to Basildon came with the firstborn," he recalled. "A lot of us firstborn were not born in Basildon, we came with mum and dad when we were babes in arms – our siblings were born in Basildon. Andy's family came from Nottingham, and he was the one born in Nottingham. His sisters, Susan and Karen, and his brother, Simon, were born in Basildon. Andy's dad, John, worked in the cigarette factory, Carreras, for a long time. I think he worked for Marconi and York Shipley as well. There were three families from Nottingham who came down together: a family called the Scotts, Andy's family, and Andy's aunt and uncle, and they all lived in Woolmer Green. We all lived almost next door to one another in the same row of houses."

The two boys became pals. Fletcher was born on July 8 1961, making him a year and a week older than Burton. "I've known Andy since he was four or five, and although he was older than me we did everything together," Burton said. "Basildon was an idyllic place to grow up as a child. If you speak to Andy, he'll tell you he had a great childhood. And we did."

Steve and Andy and most of the kids from the northern end of the Lee Chapel North neighbourhood went to the newly built Chowdhary Infants School, which opened in 1966 and was named after a well-loved local doctor, D.S. Chowdhary, who was born in the Punjab and died in 1959 after serving in Laindon for 30 years.

"We'd be with each other during the day at school, we'd come home and we'd be playing out on what we called 'the back' [in the Belstedes estate]," Burton recalled. "There was me, Fletch, Jamie [Scott], Gary [Turner], and Rob [Andrews] – a hard core of us, and we'd play until dark, even when it rained. We had a game we used to play called Wembley, a football board game. Fletch used to love that. Me, my brother, and Andy all wanted to be Chelsea FC. Rob was Spurs and Jamie was Notts County.

"In the summer we'd have what was called the BelGreen Sports, which was between Belstedes and Woolmer Green, and we'd create our own mini

Olympics. We'd have a five-a-side competition, cricket, tennis, and then we had a racing track and on our bikes we'd hurtle around what we called the ABC track. We all had Space Hoppers. We used to play Space Hopper bundles. We'd have a square of ten yards by ten and you'd try to bounce the other one off his Space Hopper. Then we'd do skids on our bikes and create a skid patch outside of Woolmer Green.

"The beauty of the estate was there were no main roads. We had no worries about roads whatsoever. Near the houses opposite, in Knights, 30 yards away, there was a little sandpit, and if you really ventured out, another 150 yards, there was the big sandpit, where there was a big frame to climb. We'd get on our bikes: where are we going to go today, the big sandpit or the little sandpit? But you never crossed a road because it was all paved, alleyways, things like that. There was never any traffic."

Reflecting on the young Andy Fletcher, Burton revealed the origins of an unusual early nickname. "Andy was a natural leader and always very, very confident as a child. No hesitation whatsoever. We did look up to him. That was his role in our group, as leader. When we got a little bit older Fletch used to like the board game Risk. That's when you get a little bit more on the diplomacy and strategy. And Andy and I used to play a game called Soccerama, a football game with dice and you'd move up the league tables. We changed the name of the game, created our own rules and called it 'Flusherama' because that was Andy's nickname: Flush.

"It's one of those nicknames that has always been there. You know how you'd knock for each other to come out to play, you're bouncing the ball and you'd be waiting? Well, when you'd knock for Andy, it was like: oh, Andy's in the toilet, we've got to wait. He had all these comics up there: *Whizzer & Chips* or whatever, *The Beano*, *The Dandy* – he used to sit there, just reading the comics on the loo while we're all waiting. We would just sit there in his garden, in the sunshine, waiting for him to come out to play, to just put the comic down and flush and come out to play. And in the end we called him Flush, because he never did. Andy was never Fletch – he was Flush to us for years, Flush Fletcher. That was his nickname."

In 1970, Burton joined the junior section of the local Boys' Brigade, organised by the new Methodist Church in St Paul's. "In the summer holidays they used to organise a thing called Play Leadership," he told me.

"We could borrow stilts and stuff to play with. The estate was growing: families had two, three, or four kids; there were kids everywhere. The Boys' Brigade was just another organisation that started up, another thing to be involved with, to keep the kids occupied.

"Jamie Scott's dad was an officer in the Boys' Brigade and Jamie asked me to go. I didn't have a clue what it was, but because one us went we all went. That's what used to happen. Andy and all the kids from the area went to Boys' Brigade. Vince was there, and so was Rob Marlow. We had a huge company of boys, 40 or 50. We used to go camping in the summer. And we used to play football as a Boys' Brigade. We were very good. We won the Harwood Copeland cup, a Boys' Brigade cup over five counties, two or three times. We played cricket, table tennis, handball – all the things that kids should be doing.

"If you were in the Boys' Brigade you had to go to Sunday school. It was part of the duty of going to the Boys' Brigade as a Christian organisation. There's this great misnomer that everybody went to the church because we were all religious. That was far from it. None of our families were religious."

The Fifth Basildon Boys' Brigade Juniors met at Janet Duke Infant School on Markhams Chase in Lee Chapel North, another new school built to serve the influx of children coming into the area. Vince Clarke's closest friend growing up was another early Boys' Brigade Junior, Rob Marlow, who like Steve Burton was also a pupil at Chowdhary.

"Vince and I get mixed up about whether we were eight or nine when we first met," Marlow told me. "We used to go to the Boys' Brigade on a Friday night, to Janet Duke with Mrs Chesterton, the woman in charge. We stayed for a long time. Fletch's dad was involved; he was like an officer, he wore a hat. He was a very mild-mannered man, lovely bloke. He used to come with us to the camps and run the football team."

Marlow was born in Basildon in 1961. His family had originally lived on the Ghyllgrove estate before moving to Falstones in 1969, to the southernmost road in the Lee Chapel North neighbourhood. His father worked for Mobil in nearby Grays, while his mother worked at the Carreras cigarette factory. Growing up in Basildon, he said, "wasn't like anything or anywhere else. It was like living in your own play world. It was all infused with this sense of newness. Growing up, the place was like a building site.

You would walk down the road and come home just covered in mud because there were still contractors working, and there would be bulldozers. Where we lived was the edge of the town then. The 'Alcatraz estate' went up just over the road from us. Before that it was all fields with adders, rabbits, foxes. We used to go and play in these old abandoned cottages where the plot-landers used to live.

"Alcatraz was completely pedestrianised, but they had to have spaces for cars and they were all put underground. We would roam these underground car parks. It was almost like this subterranean world – we would take a stick and bash the lights in. We weren't saints."

□-□-□

Vince went to a different school to the rest of the gang: Bluehouse Infants School, named after a local farm that had once stood nearby. It was the first infant school in the Laindon area, having opened in 1960 to serve the new estates being built in the Lee Chapel North area. It was within the same square-mile area as Janet Duke and Chowdhary but not as popular, and by 1968 its low pupil numbers had to be boosted by the transfer of pupils from Janet Duke.

The future founder of Depeche Mode was born on July 3 1960 in South Woodford, Essex. He only became a 'Clarke' during the early days of the band. Before that he was Vince Martin, the son of Dennis and Rose. The Martins – Vince, his two younger brothers, Michael and Rodney, and elder sister Carol – moved to Basildon in 1965 and settled in a four-bed Corporation house in Shepeshall, close to Falstones, at the southern end of Lee Chapel North. He lived at 44 Shepeshall; Martin Gore's family lived at number 16.

According to Rob Marlow, Vince's dad was "a bit of an Arthur Daley character. He and Vince's mum actually split up when the kids were quite young, in the early 70s. He didn't really have a lot of proper, stable work – he was a bit of a fly-by-night, always had some get-rich scheme. He was a tic-tac man [a bookmaker who used rhyming slang and hand movements] at the dog tracks in Rayleigh".

After Vince's parents split up, his mum took the kids to a new house in Mynchens, less than 100 yards from their previous home in Shepeshall. It was a three-storey townhouse with a garage on the ground floor. "That part of town was quite nice," Marlow recalled. "It was green; there were trees, gardens. His mum used to take in racing-car drivers' coats, the anoraks that the Formula One racing crews wore. She'd over-lock and stitch them. It was a job she could do at home so she was still there for the kids.

"She remarried this German, a silver-service waiter up in Southend – he was a very peculiar character. Vince didn't really get on with him. So during those days, Vince spent a lot of time round our house. He grew up round our house, really. He wasn't neglected, he had a family life with his mum, but they didn't have any of the little extras. Same with Fletch – I don't think there was a great deal of money floating about."

After leaving Bluehouse in 1971, Vince moved to Laindon High, formerly known as Laindon High Road Secondary Modern, where he would study from the ages of 11 to 16. His sister went there, and it was seen as the area's best school; along with Craylands Secondary, it had been the only school teaching at secondary level in the area when Basildon was designated in 1949. It was a well-kept, single-storey red brick building, dating back to the 20s, with its own open-air swimming pool.

In 1963, when Labour took over the running of the district council, it embraced the progressive ideals and liberal attitudes of the Comprehensive school system and promised to introduce it across the board within six months. Basildon's Chalvedon Comprehensive, which opened in 1965, was one of the first purpose-built Comprehensives in the county. Basildon's strongly left-wing council was happy to see an end to the divisive '11 Plus' exam, the result of which determined whether a child would be sent to Secondary Modern (if they failed) or a Grammar school (if they passed).

The school Dave Gahan attended, Barstable Comprehensive, felt the effects of 'downgrading' when in 1968 Timberlog Secondary Modern School merged with Barstable Grammar. In a similar move, Fryerns Grammar merged with Craylands to form Fryerns Comprehensive. Andy Fletcher and Martin Gore's school, St Nicholas Comprehensive (commonly referred to as Nicholas), newly built to accommodate kids from the Lee Chapel North area, also quickly adopted the Comprehensive system.

When Vince started at Laindon High it was still clinging to its old reputation and not that much further from home than Nicholas – a mile, maybe, as opposed to a few hundred yards. But the year after he arrived, Laindon became a Comprehensive too, making that extra distance feel pointless. (In the 90s, Nicholas and Laindon High were amalgamated, but back then there was an intense rivalry between the two sets of pupils.)

That Vince and Rob Marlow (now at Nicholas) didn't drift apart when they started at separate secondary schools could be put down chiefly to their continuing to attend Boys' Brigade together. The seniors met at St Paul's Methodist. "Malcolm Daley was the vicar there," Marlow recalled. "They moved the vicars round all the time but Malcolm was our favourite. He was a typical 'jolly hockey sticks' type of character."

Vince, Rob, and their network of friends were all involved in the Boys' Brigade. One of the loudest characters in that group – you couldn't miss him – was Andy Fletcher. "Fletcher was called 'big-head'," Marlow recalled with a laugh. "He used to brag that he was the best footballer – the best at everything really. We used to go away on Boys' Brigade camps together. Vince and I both had long greasy hair, and Fletch had long greasy ginger hair. We used to try and think of all these strategies for controlling the grease, which basically involved putting talcum powder in our hair. We were just spotty herberts."

Away from Boys' Brigade, Vince and Rob began to explore music. Rob was learning the piano; Vince had violin lessons. "Then I moved onto guitar and he started playing guitar as well," Marlow recalled. "We started having these little sessions. We had a piano and an organ in our house so he would come round on a Sunday afternoon and we'd play together. He was a massive Simon & Garfunkel fan – his all-time hero is Paul Simon. I was more Marc Bolan, David Bowie, glam-rock – crash, bang, wallop."

The pair shopped for their music at the Pop-Inn stall on Basildon market, with Marlow splashing out 45p every week for a new single. His first single was 'Coco' by The Sweet; Vince plumped for 'This Town Ain't Big Enough For The Both Of Us' by Sparks.

"We used to get *Disco45* magazine, which had all the lyrics in," Marlow recalled. "That magazine was a big thing. When I started hanging out with Martin Gore later, he used to collect that. Vince and I used to learn the words and try and learn the chords – not very successfully – but we used to play things like The Who.

54

"Vince was into Pink Floyd, really early Pink Floyd. *Ummagumma* was the album we used to play. We used to turn the lights off and listen to 'Set The Controls For The Heart Of The Sun' and 'Careful With That Axe, Eugene'. All a bit macabre, in a way, but atmospheric. Then one of the people at the Boys' Brigade lent me a Hawkwind album, *Space Ritual*, and I just loved that; all these weird noises. Vince with Pink Floyd and me with Hawkwind was the embryonic synthesizer thing. We loved those strange atmospheric and cinematic sounds, things that had a very visual sound.

"Vince and I went to see Hawkwind live later on, in Southend at the Kursaal, Christmas 1976. I was just blown away with the light show, the smoke and acid – even though we were too young to get the drug side of it. We started to experiment with out tastes, try things out with one another: what do you think of this and what do you think of that? We listened to a lot of stuff. Vince has always had an ear for a catchy tune and I like commercial music as well. We went through prog rock and pretty much rejected all of that, Rick Wakeman and all that stuff, it was just tedious."

Steve Burton and Andy Fletcher were also regulars at the Pop-Inn. "That was part of our routine," Burton recalled. "We would definitely buy a single every week. I think my first record was 'Son Of My Father' by Chicory Tip. Then one of Andy's was 'Whiter Shade Of Pale' by Procol Harum. I always remember that one because Fletch took the pee out of me because I went and asked for Procol Harum's 'Wintery Shade Of Green'. He would often bring that up. But that's where we really started to get into the music. Andy was a big fan of David Bowie, T.Rex as well. 'Ride A White Swan' is his favourite single of all time, along with '"Heroes"'. Don't dismiss his musical contribution to the band.

"I remember when Andy's dad bought a stereo – the first time anyone in the street had got a stereo system. I remember being called in by Andy, and his dad showing off his new Moog stereo system ... we listened to 'Popcorn' by Hot Butter with this absolutely stunning sound, amazement as it went from one speaker to another."

The pair worked to earn money to buy records by delivering the local evening newspaper. "Andy and I also used to clean floors," Burton told me. "Andy's mum and my neighbour had a cleaning job at the local Government Skills Centre, where people would go to learn a trade. They used to clean all the offices at night, and Andy and me used to sweep and mop the floors of this huge canteen. After we'd done our *Evening Echo* paper round on our bikes, we'd then come home, whoosh our tea down, and then get back on our bikes and cycle a few miles to one of the industrial estates, sweep all the floors, get a mop and bucket and mop all the floors clean. Andy and I did that for years; that's how we earned our pocket money and began to be independent."

The Boys' Brigade was still central to all of their lives. "As we got older the group met on a Sunday night," Burton recalled. "It wasn't so much Sunday school as when we were younger, but it seemed the most natural thing to do: to continue that friendship by going in the evening to the youth event, or the Youth Fellowship as it was called. On a Sunday night after the church service, there would be, at its peak, 40-odd kids. Friends of friends would come along, and sometimes you had the other churches that had Fellowships as well, so you got to know a wider range of kids across the town because of the church."

The Youth Fellowship meetings took place on Wednesday nights, too. "Andy was a central character in the Fellowship," Burton continued. "So was Vince – he was an integral part of it. I was 13 or 14, I'd just joined, and Vince was such a bright, happy, bubbly kid, he almost had this aura about him of being permanently happy and joyful."

"We became Christians there," Marlow recalled. "The Youth Fellowship group at St Paul's was run by Chris Briggs, a diamond fellow. Fletch, me, and Vince all made firm commitments to Christ."

"Chris Briggs was *the* leader at Youth Fellowship; a magnificent person," Burton added. "He had a band called Insight with a few of the older boys. He was a natural leader, and still is – a get-up-and-goer, a doer, always on every committee."

▭▭▭

Chris Briggs is now a Methodist minister. He was only three years older than Vince and was also a pupil at Nicholas. He had moved to the Lee Chapel North area of Basildon, close to St Paul's, when he was eight, and had been involved in the Fifth Basildon Boys' Brigade since it was founded in 1968.

"Youth Fellowship started off with half a dozen people huddled around a radiator in the church hall," he told me. "But soon the room could be packed with about 30 young people aged between 11 and 30. It was a large group for what was effectively a church youth group. It was not a youth club, although we did youth club-type stuff together on certain nights. We would sing, we would praise God, and we would pray together; we would read the Bible together and do talks for each other. We were already heavily involved in the church, but in terms of defining what a Christian is and Christian commitment – that was a conscious decision.

"One of the things our local church did – without us realising it at the time – they were pretty trailblazing because they gave us our heads. We pretty much ploughed our own furrow and the people that were leading – people like myself – there wasn't much separating us all in terms of age. Young people drove it. So from the age of 16 we were putting it together ourselves. That's probably one of the reasons it grew, because if you've got young people leading the charge, rather than older people, usually it's more attractive."

Briggs was modest about the band he formed at the Youth Fellowship, Insight, who had a profound impression on the young Vince Clarke and who played mainly covers versions of songs by Cream, The Beatles, Led Zeppelin, and their big favourite The Who. "We would meet together and almost pretend to play instruments," he said. "Then eventually we bought guitars and things. We still couldn't play them very much so we draped the leads into a record player and pretended to be playing along.

"Eventually we learnt some basic songs. We used the church hall to practise in. We did a few concerts – we scarily ended up playing at someone's wedding reception. I remember Vince saying that he'd love to play in Insight. Really, in those days, Vince was just learning the guitar as well, but he was a really good guitarist. He picked things up really quickly.

"Vince and Andy were very much a part of the fabric at St Paul's in terms of the Boys' Brigade and the Youth Fellowship through the years. They played a very major part in both; they were enthusiastic and committed, they were certainly part of that central core. And they were hugely popular. Vince and I would go back to his mum's place, often on Friday night after Boys' Brigade, and sit and chat for ages. We'd be there until one in the morning. It was tea and coffee and toast and a chat. It was all so innocent but it was also very deep. We'd be chatting about our faith, anything and everything really. Abstention from alcohol was very much part of the culture of the Methodist Church, but it was already a matter of individual conscience. We'd be putting the world to rights. Our faith was really central to what was going on."

As a group, the Youth Fellowship was exceedingly close, its members rarely apart. As well as the formal Sunday and Wednesday meetings, they would see each other on a Friday night at Boys' Brigade, on Tuesday for games night at Boys' Brigade, and would go to church together twice on a Sunday. They would also be involved in outreach events. They had a room at St Martin's Church in the town centre and on Saturday nights would go out on the streets preaching and trying to lure people in to what many secular kids called the 'BBC' – the 'Bible Basher's Club' – although that wouldn't stop them from popping in for tea and biscuits. It was a popular spot for a wide range of kids with nothing else to do on a Saturday night.

"We wanted to reach out to other people to convert them," said Briggs. "As a group, we were meeting to grow in the Christian faith but we were also there to reach out to others with the Christian faith as a mission movement. We did that in a variety of ways. We were born-again Christians. That's the language we would have used at the time. The language I would still use. That would be how we understand it. Not to be aloof, it was just the sense of: this is not just religious ritual; this is a real relationship with the Lord Jesus Christ."

There were also parties, cinema trips, and visits to big Christian events in London. "A number of us went on holiday together each year from the Youth Fellowship," Briggs recalled. "We went to many Christian events over the years – Larry Norman Concerts, special services in London; we would go to the Greenbelt Festival. We used to go to the Marquee club sometimes to see a Christian band called After The Fire."

Briggs also recalled Martin Gore coming along to some of the Youth Fellowship meetings. "Martin came from outside the church to interact with it at some level," he said, "but not at the level Vince and Andy would have done. They grew up from within it. Martin came along a bit later, more through his girlfriend at the time, Anne Swindell."

Anne Swindell and her family were members of the Trinity Methodist Church. She had two older brothers and attended Woodlands Girls School. She'd been involved in the Girls' Brigade since the age of four, her mum being the Captain of Second Basildon. "We had a Youth Fellowship at Trinity but the people running it went away for a while and during that time suggested we went over to St Paul's," she told me. "That's how we linked up with St Paul's, and that kick-started a whole chain of events that took us off in a completely different direction.

"The Youth Fellowship we had at Trinity was run by older people, so it was more traditional. When we went to St Paul's it was a bit of a shock; it felt less controlled. Chris Briggs was older than we were, but he wasn't that much older. At the same time it was good because it felt like the reins had been taken off and we were all a bit freer to do our own thing. St Paul's was more 'happy-clappy' than Trinity. It was also much more evangelical. It was stirring things us up."

Anne started attending St Paul's Youth fellowship with her pals Denise Jekyll and Gillian Towers when she was 14. She knew all the boys. "Rob's got a cheek saying Fletch was loud," she laughed. "He was loud himself. Fletcher was a real comic – very gregarious, playing tricks on people – he was always winding people up. He was a big personality. Him, Rob, and Vince were quite big personalities.

"My first ever memory of Vince is walking into St Paul's – he was there the first ever night we went over to St Paul's, and I was really nervous. I remember walking in the room and seeing Vince with this big bushy white hair and red face and a guitar and thinking: gosh, this isn't like it is at Trinity, but being really impressed with this image of this really very captivating guy.

"He and Martin were really very captivating: strong presences but much quieter than the others. Martin wasn't really a part of the Youth Fellowship. He was never really interested. He came into the scene through his friendship with Andy at school. He got to know Vince a bit through music, then he came to Greenbelt because of me. But in the Youth Fellowship scene he was very much on the periphery and not interested in religion. He might have come once or twice but it really wasn't his thing. If he came he would have come at the end or come and met us."

Anne's relationship with Martin deepened over time. "I would have been around 15, 16 when I started seeing Martin as boyfriend–girlfriend," she continued. "We'd gone to some event that mixed friendships from school with church and Martin pitched up with Andy. Somehow the music from *The Deer Hunter* [the theme song by Stanley Myers, 'Catavina', also known as 'He Was Beautiful' and performed by classical guitarist John Williams] was involved.

"If we ever went on Youth Fellowship walks, we'd be sitting in the woods as a group and Martin would be sitting under a tree, playing a guitar and singing. So he would do that, if we were out and about he would bring his guitar. We'd go to parties or we'd meet at the church. Martin was very quiet, shy, and studious, but then prone to bouts of extroversion. He would go between the two: he'd have moments of madness and then slink back into being quiet and considered.

"We shared relatively similar tastes in music. I grew up with a lot of what my brothers were listening to. My big thing was David Bowie. I had a phase of Bay City Rollers, The Sweet, Alice Cooper, but David Bowie and Bob Dylan were the two for me. Martin had quite a broad range of likes. Often we'd sit in of an evening and he'd play songs on his guitar, things like 'Wonderful World' and more bluesy stuff, blues and soul. Martin liked Sparks. He also really liked Talking Heads. He loved to play Talking Heads on guitar. He was always fiddling around with music."

Anne also remembered the Youth Fellowship going to Greenbelt, the annual Christian music festival held between 1975 and 1981 in the grounds of Odell Castle in Bedfordshire. "Through St Paul's, Martin and I got exposed to more of the Christian pop thing," she said. "We went to Greenbelt a few times and had a great time but it didn't really do it for me. It was too bizarre for me. I liked my pop bands to be pop bands and my Christians to be Christians. I didn't like to see them mixing, really.

"It was a bizarre mix at St Paul's. On the one hand it felt quite extreme and I was never that comfortable with Chris Briggs's take on religion. There was a lot of debate and discussion, questioning of things. For me, part of the confusion was that there were a lot of parties and a lot of things going on, and you'd sometimes think: how does that fit, then? It was very challenging, a time of exploration I guess."

Steve Burton also went out with Anne briefly. "At St Paul's you had a bunch of rowdy boys," he recalled. "There were so many people in our circle of friends, there would almost always be someone who would have a party on a Saturday night, because they were going to be 16 or something like that. Anne famously had a party and friends just came along. I suppose there was a bit of drink, but not like these days where kids go absolutely mental. We're talking about a bunch of good kids. The bad kids never came to our parties because we knew they would ruin it. If anything, the fear was that someone would turn up who would be one of the bad kids."

Burton also attended the Greenbelt festival. "Although it was a Christian event it was not inward-looking, so Martin would come along," he recalled. "It was a safe environment. If you went to other concerts, maybe it's a little bit scarier, a little bit more risky, but Greenbelt had that air of security about it because of the nature of the root of the event.

"The reason why the Fellowship met primarily was religion, but it created a social bond, it was friends together. So while there was definitely a Christian influence, you had the friendships. It was a really nice mix of cosiness and relationships and broken relationships and boys going out with girls in the same friendship set. You would get all the usual teenage angst thrown in for good measure – who fancies who, who's going out with who.

"We were all of that age when music became really important. Vince was a brilliant guitarist, what a talent when he was a young man. Just had that gift, you could tell from an early age – and the same with Martin. I love my music but I'm not musical. We all picked up a guitar; Fletch and me had a go playing it but I was never naturally a musician. Andy, by his own admission, is not a natural musician. I loved to listen to music but I was never going to make it as a musician because I knew what a musician was – that was always going to be Martin and Vince. Martin always had his guitar, he'd be bored not playing his guitar."

❖❖❖

Vince Clarke left Laindon High in 1976 with five O-levels. He then went to Basildon Further Education College, where he formed his first proper band, a Christian duo with former Insight drummer Kevin Walker. The band would continue for the next couple of years, from 1977 to 1979, and were managed by Walker's best pal, Chris Briggs, who described them as a gospel duo. "I don't know if we'd have used that term, but that is effectively what it was," he told me. "They called themselves Nathan, which means God's Gift. They were doing Christian concerts. A friend of mine, then and now, Billy Slatter, who is also now a Minister, said he'd be happy to try and fix some concerts up."

Nathan were played on Radio Basildon, where Briggs acted as deputy station manager, heading up the Religious Programmes Team. The station was beamed into around 25,000 New Town homes. "It was a really innovative thing," Briggs recalled. "It was at the time the third tier of broadcasting, directly licensed by the Home Office. So it was very experimental. It went through the television. It became, for a while, the most listened to station in Basildon, above Radio 1. It even broadcast the council meetings."

Vince's band-mate Kevin Walker came from Laindon. His family had lost their home – with fields and an orchard – to a Compulsory Purchase Order and moved into a council house in Falstones. He went to Nicholas School and was in the same year as Chris Briggs, making him three years older than Vince.

"When Insight fizzled out, Vince and I got together with the guitars and said: look, why don't we do a Simon & Garfunkel kind of duo?" he told me. "We were kind of good with the harmonies; Vince wrote a few songs but I wrote the majority of the songs.

"I remember practicing at Vince's house one day, and for whatever reason he decided to drill a hole through the floor – he wanted to see what was going on downstairs but he'd just drilled a hole through the floorboard. I said: you've got to drill it so it goes all the way through into the ceiling – which he didn't do. We used to practice at my house and also at his flat. He'd moved out of home at some point and his flat used to be above a kebab and Indian takeaway shop. Every time we practiced there it would stink of kebabs and Indian food.

"At the Youth Fellowship meetings, what generally used to happen was we'd have a short Bible study – or at least a topical discussion about something related to scripture – and we'd talk about it and share experiences," Walker continued. "Then we'd have a few songs – we used to call them choruses, the Christian choruses, the popular ones like 'Abba Father' – clapping of hands, bit of worship, then tea and coffee or soft drinks and a bit of chit-chat. I recall Vince being quite sincere and spiritual when we used to chat about things, when we were in that particular mood. I think Vince always had lots of questions from a spiritual point of view.

"The Methodist church was more evangelical. That was certainly the message when Vince and I were together – our music had a message. They weren't all about Christ, but they had a message.

"Our songs were a bit more thought-provoking in terms of life. I wrote a song, 'Nathan', about a loner drifting from place to place who didn't have any aim in his life. If you were talking in between the songs you could say to someone: maybe if that song spoke to you and you want to speak to us about what we've got, we'll talk to you afterward. It wasn't heavy duty but it was thought provoking, and then we'd put a funny song in, lighten the mood, then a Simon & Garfunkel song or a Joni Mitchell song. On 'Nathan' we used to sing alternate verses and do the chorus together."

According to Walker, the duo also played under the name Kev & Vince rather than Nathan. "Chris Briggs and Bill Slatter said this name, Nathan, is a name you should use," he recalled. "I didn't ever feel comfortable with it." Whatever the name, the duo proved popular. They took their 40-minute set around colleges, church venues, and community halls. "We did a lot of gigging, a lot of travelling," Walker added. "We were quite good friends. He was at college. He was quite into his art and other bits and pieces."

Nathan played gigs in Basildon and the surrounding areas, such as the Brentwood Centre, and then further afield in Staffordshire and Birmingham. "It was largely on the Christian scene," Walker said. "The gigs could be anything like the Arts Centre theatre to a church hall or a church itself, some community centres – we even did a few open-air things. We didn't mind what we did.

"We weren't full-time, we had jobs and college, so most of this was done at the weekend or a Friday night. On Sundays we'd be special guests in a service or something. We were getting fairly busy in terms of our popularity. We would often go in and do some numbers together live on Radio Basildon. Vince did have a good voice. When Vince and I were singing together, our harmonies were quite sharp. We did a song with a violin, quite a good song. I played a guitar, he played a violin; it was a good laugh, and we enjoyed it. It was like an Irish jig with a lot of rhythm guitar in the background, quite a foot-stomping, hand-clapping kind of thing."

The pair wrote a lot of songs together, and old reel-to-reel recordings of their songs still exist. "It was quite apparent to me that when Vince formed Yazoo, some of the tunes we'd written together came out in different forms," Walker said. "They were recognisable to me because I'd written them, especially the song 'Only You'. When he was just starting Yazoo, he invited me round to his new flat in Pitsea – he'd just bought a new computer, a Fairlight, and we were doing a few songs together. I was hoping we would have been able to take up what we used to have but it didn't happen. Anyway, he gave me a first pressing of 'Only You', and when I heard it I said: that sounds like one of my old songs. He just sort of laughed and said: no, it's not. But I recognised it straight away."

Walker was one of the most respected members of the Youth Fellowship, and the whole gang who would often congregate at his home. "We'd know each other from our teenage years into our early 20s," he said. "Andy I knew more through football for the Boys' Brigade and through church than through music. I was hanging out with Vince most of the time, and Vince wasn't particularly interested in football. We had a good Boys' Brigade football team, we won cups and tournaments – Andy played every week. I think it was a bit too physical for Vince.

"Martin Gore used to come along as a peripheral kind of person. He didn't say much, didn't do much, but he was pleasant. He had a lovely voice. When they would come round to my house, about 15 of them, we'd get the guitars out, and I'd always remember what a lovely voice he had. We'd sit in a corner and I'd share a song with Martin and he'd share a bit of a song with me. Or at the Greenbelt festival I'd go in his tent and I'd have a go of his guitar and say: this is a new song I'm working on, and he'd sing me one. It was quite nice, that time. I heard all about Martin's band, Norman & The Worms, but I never got engrossed. They had quite a following, but that was more the Anne Swindell crowd. Robert Marlow would float between the two groups."

Vince played in Nathan for two or three years. "Then one night he said to me: I'm thinking of joining a band, do you think you might want to be part of it?" Walker recalled. "I said: what sort of band is it? It was this electronic kind of band. I told him it wasn't really me. That's where we parted ways, in terms of musical interests. We went our own ways musically, and from a fashion point of view, he was into the clothes and stuff and I wasn't."

Walker stayed with the Christian side of things. His first cassette album, *There's Hope*, landed him a record contract; he then made a "jazzier, more contemporary" second album, *The Dusk*. "Vince and I didn't part on bad terms or anything like that," he told me. "It was just a natural progression: he wanted to join a band and I didn't see myself doing that. I recorded a couple of the songs we used to do together when I did my first album. The song that sounded like 'Only You' I recorded on my first album – I called it 'You And Me', and it's exactly the same kind of chord structure. I wrote a song about Vince after we went our separate ways on my second album, called 'Song For A Friend'."

# CHAPTER 3

# THE WORMS

**M**artin Gore was in the same year at St Nicholas Comprehensive as his pal Andy Fletcher. Just two weeks separated their birth dates. Gore was born July 23 1961 – both he and Fletch were a year younger than Vince. They both stayed on at Nicholas until 1979 to do their A-levels.

Gore's family came to Basildon from Dagenham and lived on Shepeshall, a little terraced street at the southern end of Lee Chapel North. Martin had two younger sisters, Karen and Jacqueline; mum Pamela and step-dad David both initially worked at Fords until Pamela took a job at an old people's home.

Martin was intelligent, shy, polite, kind-hearted: the sort of kid your mum and dad would have approved of if you brought him home. He liked things smart and kept his bedroom organised. It was hard to get much out of him but he was always happy, always smiling. Like Fletcher, he loved football, and was a big fan of Arsenal.

"Martin was slightly better off than Fletch and certainly Vince," said his girlfriend, Anne Swindell. "Martin's home life was stable. He always knew his dad wasn't his real dad, but not the details – nobody knew, there was no real detail about who his father was at the time. His step-dad was the girls' real dad. His sisters were quite a bit younger than him."

Gore was on the periphery of the Youth Fellowship scene, but there was another side to him. He had his own musical thing going on: a school band called Norman & The Worms, formed just as punk was hitting Basildon. The Worms weren't really a punk band but stumbled into a burgeoning local scene led by The Vandals, whose singer was one Alison Moyet, and

The Vermin, a band that Dave Gahan would later claim to have fronted.

Steve Burton saw Norman & The Worms play early on. "It was in Martin's living room," he said. "I always remember the big build-up to seeing them perform. I think Martin's mum and dad went out and we turned the settee round in his living room and they had it set up, him and Phil Burdett, and they just did a concert in his living room. Probably about ten of us sat in his front room, just enjoying a concert. I've still got a photograph of it: it was one of the first concerts I went to, really."

The Worms were essentially a duo. Gore formed the band with Nicholas classmate Phil Burdett in 1977, when they were both 16. Burdett lived on Jermayns in the centre of Lee Chapel North. He had nothing to do with the Youth Fellowship. "Martin's house was about half a mile from mine," he recalled. "His mum and dad were working class but decent people, same as my mum and dad really – we were similar in a lot of ways. Basildon was like the East End without romanticism. It was a very boring place, very regulated. The streets all looked the same, neatly planned – there were no winding back alleys, no old parts of town. There was conformity to the architecture and to people's attitudes."

Burdett had two older brothers who had taught him guitar and grounded him in the music of Bob Dylan, Van Morrison, and Jimmy Webb. Martin, Burdett said, liked the more interesting end of the pop stuff: Sparks, Kraftwerk. "We used to play each other records and he would constantly be trying to get me into David Bowie and I'd constantly be trying to get him into Bob Dylan."

The pair would listen to music in each other's bedrooms while Phil taught Martin the guitar. "He picked it up quite quickly," Burdett recalled. "I just showed him some chords and he was away. He would write songs quite prolifically. Looking back on it, he treated it like an exercise. He was diligent, as he was with his homework at school. I think that's how he does things. This is how you do this, so I will do this – you put these chords together and some words. He was always quite fastidious about the words. They didn't really say anything, though. I was looking, thinking surely there must be more to this. We had no equipment at all when we started. We had a guy called Martin Sage who used to hit his school satchel with an egg whisk as a drum. We used to tape stuff in our bedrooms."

JUST CAN'T GET ENOUGH

Although they found gigs on the nascent Basildon punk scene, The Worms stuck out as being defiantly odd. "I looked like a sort of Marc Bolan gone to seed," Burdett laughed. "I had long, wide hair, a tangled mess. Martin had what looked like a bubble perm. I used to say – and Martin agreed with me on this – that we were actually closer to the spirit of punk. The idea was it didn't matter what you looked like. We used to wear flares way before Kevin Rowland was advocating it. It was good in a way because it set us apart, we were more of a fifth column, a sort of insurgency in the Basildon punk scene."

The band, Burdett recalled, was named after his guitar. "That was Norman. We worked out that everyone would say: how can you be Norman & The Worms? So I said, well, the guitar is Norman – I had this terrible white guitar, a white Stratocaster copy, the worst guitar, no redeeming features, it was just shit. I said, well, that should be Norman. So Norman was the guitar and we were The Worms."

The name wasn't that serious – no names were, back then. "We used to be on the bill at gigs with bands like Hitler's Pyjamas," Burdett continued. "Any name that was stupid enough stuck. We thought Norman & The Worms fitted because of what we looked like as well – we didn't look like punks, we were the least threatening band, we weren't even a punk band, we weren't playing punk. It was nothing like it."

The Worms' first proper gig was in the sixth-form common room at Nicholas. There's a well-thumbed photo of Gore and Burdett up on stage; the only other person in the photo, sitting on a chair in the background, is Andy Fletcher. "We started out doing a few covers," Burdett said. "Then the last few gigs we played, which is where people in Basildon knew us from, I think it was pretty much all originals."

Among the songs in The Worms' set was future Depeche Mode single 'See You' as well as a track from the album *A Broken Frame*, 'Photograph Of You'. "I invented the riff for 'See You'," Burdett told me. "Martin sang 'American Pie' a few times. When we did the first Basildon Rock Festival in Gloucester Park [in 1978], we played the theme tune to *Skippy The Bush Kangaroo* – not ironically, not the way the Dead Kennedys would do it. I had one song we did called 'Saxophone Joe', which was probably a misguided stab at Steely Dan.

"People were mystified," he added. "We were usually about third on the bill of about six local punk bands, and we'd sound like The Carpenters by comparison. I don't know if it was balls or stupidity but we'd be playing a country song in the middle of a punk gig. We didn't fit in but we were tolerated. If was different to a city like London or Manchester, where things were really happening. Locally, in Basildon, everyone was just trying to help everyone else, no matter what you did."

The Worms stayed together for two years, gigging sporadically through 1978 at Basildon venues such as the Van Gogh pub and the Woodlands Youth Club. In 1979 they played a few benefit gigs for the local fanzine *Strange Stories* at the Basildon Arts Centre. They occasionally roped in a drummer, Peter Hobbs.

Originally from Pitsea, Hobbs lived in Lee Chapel North and had also attended Nicholas, although he was four years older than Burdett and Gore. He too was part of the Youth Fellowship at St Paul's. "Chris Briggs was my age at school and I just used to tag along to the Youth Fellowship meetings," he told me. "I think Chris taught Vince how to play guitar. He taught a few people how to play guitar. We used to go and watch his band, Insight; that's where I got my interest in playing the drums. They inspired us. Vince had long blonde hair right down past his shoulder, really long. Fletch was a character, an attention seeker, in the middle of everything. We went on a canal boat holiday once and we went to the Isle of Wight, a couple of big holidays with the church, and Andy was the main character. Martin wasn't very heavily involved but sometimes he used to visit."

Hobbs got involved with The Worms after his band The Neatelllls, who sang Monkees songs with their own words, supported The Worms at a school gig. "Martin and Phil came round and said: we've got a gig at Gloucester Park, will you drum for us?" Hobbs recalled. "They wanted bass and drums because it was an open-air gig. They didn't want to do an acoustic gig. When I used to go see After The Fire at the Marquee with the Youth Fellowship, they used to play the theme tune to *Thunderbirds* before they came on. I thought it was a fantastic entrance. I said: why don't we do one? So we did *Skippy*. We used to have the *Skippy* theme tune and then Norman & The Worms would come on and do *Skippy* and Martin would be doing kangaroo noises down the microphone.

"We were doing things like 'See You' – they had some great tunes. Some of them were like the Average White Band – every song seemed to remind me of another tune, like The Beatles. Some were even sort of country & western-type things, almost Steely Dan-type stuff. We did the Gloucester Park gig and we did a talent contest in Southend, at the Esplanade, a pub on the seafront, opposite [local amusement park] Peter Pan's Playground. A bloke from Radio Basildon liked Norman & The Worms and wanted us to go into this talent competition, to win £1,000 or whatever it was. He drove us down on the back of his van, with the drums.

"We were expecting all these people, all this talent, but there were just four acts, it was like a heat. There was some girl of about ten singing some song off the telly, a tap-dancer, us, and this other disco-type funk band who were all very young. We came third. It was just a disaster. It was probably my fault. The drum kit I had at the time was very cheap – when I played it the pedal turned round. I tried to fix it down as much as I could but it used to turn around – and at this talent contest it came off and I had to get down on the floor to try and put it back on. Burdett looked at me and saw me on the floor and burst out laughing."

o-o-o

According to Anne Swindell, Martin Gore had written 'See You' after returning from a school-exchange trip to Germany. "He met somebody there," she told me. "He was studying German at A-level. The school exchange with Germany was a common thing in Basildon: I had a pen pal in Germany and I went over and stayed with her for two weeks."

Gore went to Heiligenhaus, a small town near Düsseldorf in West Germany. The school exchange link between Heiligenhaus and Basildon was forged in the 60s through the efforts of then Town Manager David Taylor, who signed a Youth Exchange Charter between the two towns in 1972. It's interesting to note that at the time of Gore's visit, Düsseldorf was at the forefront of the just emerging Neue Deutsche Welle scene, with both DAF and Der Plan emanating from the city. Both bands would later become Gore favourites.

It was on one of these school-exchange trips that Gore first met Mark Crick. They became – and remain – firm friends. An emerging photographer, and later the author of *Kafka's Soup* and *Sartre's Sink*, Crick did the painting that graced the cover of the first ever Depeche Mode single, 'Dreaming Of Me'. He and Gore lived on the same street but Crick was a couple of years younger.

"We were on the ferry going to Germany with school when I first heard Martin play guitar," Crick told me. "People say Martin was an unassuming figure at school but he was a standout character for me because he was so intelligent and really talented. When you're 15, as I was, and one of your friends can pick up a guitar and play and sing beautifully, that's a standout, isn't it?"

Crick went to most of The Worms' early gigs in Basildon. "The thing that was exceptional was that they mostly did their own material," he said. "I remember seeing Martin singing a song called 'Green Grass' – for me it was a shiver-down-the-spine moment: my God, that's my friend up there and it's a fantastic performance, it's a great song, and it's their own creation. You didn't see that so often round the pubs in Basildon. Phil was a very funny bloke, very self-deprecating. If there was particularly nice applause, he would say thank you for your sympathy, that sort of thing. He was later known as the Bard of Basildon, there was a documentary about him."

Like Steve Burton and Fletch or Rob Marlow and Vince, Crick and Gore explored new music together, buying their records at the Pop-Inn stall on the market and venturing further afield to gigs by Kraftwerk, The Only Ones, and The Human League. "We also went to see Elvis Costello on Canvey Island, very early on," Crick recalled. "I do remember us going to see The Ramones but it's one of those where you think: is that a real memory?" (It was: the shows by Kraftwerk and The Ramones left a deep impression on Gore.)

"We'd go to record shops all the time," Crick continued. "Martin would be turning through these records incredibly quickly, just buying intuitively really, buying things he'd never heard of, often looking to see what studio it was produced at, who the session musician was. I remember him buying one because he saw on the back cover Robert Fripp was playing guitar, another because it had been recorded at Hansa. There was a process going on that you couldn't quite keep up with."

The Basildon branch of the electrical-goods shop Rumbelows was another regular stop-off. It had a good record department, importing music from America like the early Pere Ubu singles and more left-field independent stuff.

"I'd go round to Martin's and hear Fad Gadget, Cabaret Voltaire, Throbbing Gristle, Swell Maps, and Billy Bragg's first album," Crick said. "Even then I think he knew the lyrics to every single Beatles song, which is remarkable. I remember Martin having the Human League single 'Empire State Human'. He was a big fan of Sparks, the *Propaganda* album. Plus he's always been a fan of Robert Johnson, a lot of that early black spiritual stuff, a lot of the Delta blues, and a big fan of Elvis."

Gore taught Crick to play guitar and the pair hung out in each other's bedrooms trying out and taping new songs. "I'd always walk to school with Martin," Crick continued. "I'd be asking him what German books he was reading. *Der Richter Und Sein Henker* [*The Judge And His Hangman*, a 1950 novella by Swiss writer Friedrich Dürrenmatt] was one Martin studied for his A-level. He was reading quite a bit of German literature."

On the way to school the pair walked through an estate opposite Nicholas, Leinster Road, which had succumbed to the familiar faults of mid-60s construction. "They were pulled down," Crick said. "That whole area was decanted somewhere else. It was a bit of a ghost town. When I used to take people to Basildon I used to take them to see Alcatraz, which none of us realised was the name of a prison in San Francisco. We just thought it was the name of the estate. As young children we thought it was fantastic there because they had under-floor heating, split-level houses, a great adventure playground with a rope bridge and things and a few underground car parks. Most of it has been knocked down now.

"Apparently lots of the streets in Basildon were named after villages that died out during the Black Death. Strange street names – Capelston, Mynchens, Shepeshall, Pamplins – which would go along with the mud and the bleakness there."

Unlike many of the punks, Crick didn't think of Basildon as being culturally dead, although he did recall "the great excitement of taking the train with Martin to Southend so we could go to McDonald's for a milkshake. We did that more than once. Maybe we were desperate but I didn't feel like that, the library seemed pretty good and the Arts Centre was great. We saw our first Woody Allen films there; our first Rainer Werner Fassbinder films, such as *The Bitter Tears Of Petra Von Kant*. I think of us as living in this fantastically creative place and perhaps for me being slightly younger there was all this excitement to look up to. Maybe if you were a couple of years older you looked up and it seemed kind of desolate. It was a kind of communist state, where almost everybody, within reason ... their parents earned the same kind of money, they lived in the same kind of house, everybody pretty much had the same, there wasn't a rich part of town."

Crick went on to university after leaving Nicholas but he was the exception to the rule. "What was seen as a good outcome at Nicholas was if you went to work in a bank," he said. "That was probably the benchmark. That's what Martin did. That's what Fletch did. That would have been high-achieving results with the school's kind of ethos. I think they were quite pleased if anyone took an A-level. I think Martin was probably the only person doing the German A-level in his year. There were two in my French A-level class. Martin certainly had it in mind to go to university. I remember us going to a party, when we were still at school, and someone asking Martin what he wanted to do. He did say he wanted to be a pop star. Maybe he thought there was no point going to university. He may in his quiet way have had his eyes on a bigger prize."

Kim Forey was the guitarist in the most infamous of all the Basildon punk bands, The Vandals. She was in the same year as Martin Gore and Andy Fletcher at Nicholas, and was in Andy's class all the way through school. They were the original generation of comprehensive school kids. "At Nicholas, our year spelt 'AGINCOURT' – each form corresponded to a letter," she told me. "Andy and I were in G. We were in the top set of G. We did A-level politics together. Martin was in N. I remember Martin as this shy, sweet thing; he was obviously very good with a guitar because in the common room he would play sometimes. Norman & The Worms were lovely and they played such sweet songs. I always really liked Martin. I had a bit of a ... he was always shorter than me so I couldn't possibly have had a crush on him, but I always thought he was lovely and gentle and kind, and I needed to look after him. That's how I felt about Martin."

Forey described Nicholas as a "sink school" with about 1,500 pupils. "There was a general expectation that you went straight to work at 16," she said. "If you were stupid you went off to the industrial estate, but you still had a job. That was if, as a girl, you managed to get through without getting pregnant. There were lots of jobs on the industrial estate. If you were slightly better than that you could go work in the shops. And if you were clever you could go work in London. A few of my friends went off to Southend Technical College – that was the other alternative. University wasn't really talked about."

Forey gravitated toward the Arts Centre, where she watched French films and went through what she called her "pseudo-intellectual" stage. "That was the first time I ever realised there was this thing called culture or alternative culture," she laughed. "Bearing in mind at this time I didn't even know what a pizza was. We'd never have a pizza in our house. Stewed mince was what we had for tea. Mum would boil mince, skim off the fat, and give you that with some mash.

"The Vandals started out as just us three girls singing. We'd be walking to the town centre and we would make up our own songs. Alison would make up the songs and she'd teach us the harmonies, and we'd have to sing them and practise until we got it right. Then we'd also sing what was on the pop charts; we were singing all the time, a pain in the arse I should imagine. Then when we got the group, we did a song called 'Poseur', which Alison would just belt out and the whole room would go: fuck, what is this? It was a force to be reckoned with.

"Even at 17, Alison just had this presence. She was arsy, angry. She wasn't allowed to wear any of her punk clothes at her home, so she'd leave all her clothes at my house or come with her plastic bag, cycle on her Elswick Hopper, and get changed at my house. She'd come looking like a nice sweet girl and then put her make-up on, spike her hair."

Alison, The Vandals' singer, was Alison Moyet, future Yazoo and solo star. She was also in the same year as Martin and Fletch at Nicholas, and in the same class for quite a few subjects. "We were in the top maths set together, and because we were good at languages we started doing German together," she told me. "Fletcher and Martin were the perfect students, as far as you got perfect students at Nicholas. We never had any idea that any of us were destined for university, but were we to have candidates for that you would have imagined it was Fletcher and Martin; they were always the best presented, they had briefcases, they had blazers, and they were well-mannered. They were not really like the rest of us. They were just as straight as they came, just the straightest kids. Pleasant and really nice boys but they were probably the kids you wouldn't have remembered had their lives not turned out the way they did."

The Worms and The Vandals played a number of Basildon gigs together, but according to Moyet, Gore's group "would not have been that relevant for us at the time. There would have probably been too much musicianship going on. It wasn't about that for us. It wasn't about the music, it was all about the throb, the aggression, and getting wild together, so they would have been slightly out of step – probably a bit too earnest".

Moyet lived close to Laindon High, Vince's old school; her mother was a teacher there, and Moyet passed the school on the way to Nicholas in the morning. "There was a lot of problems between the two schools," she recalled. "It was a bit of a 'hide your tie' job. None of the schools were posh and none of us would have known what the performances of the schools were, but Laindon was a bit more of an established place, it was mildly better than Nicholas." After school, Moyet recalled, "You'd just be walking home in swathes. There's something really brilliant about that. Your best mates were in the next houses. All the families were young ones so there was a mass of kids everywhere."

Moyet played oboe in the school orchestra and went to the same Laindon High School Saturday-morning music club as Vince for years. "It was the weirdest school orchestra: two oboes, three violins, and a euphonium," she said. "It was just not part of what people expected for their kids. For me, what I learned best at school was avoidance – if you avoided getting into trouble, you thought you were being successful. I always get highly surprised when I find out someone from Nicholas did something; when you come across engineers or people who went to uni, my jaw drops. Everyone just seemed to be at the same level there. The only class you knew was different was the one who got to dig the garden – you knew that was the bottom class. I was in the top set for everything and I came out with one O-level. School felt like a holding centre."

After initially deciding to stay on to do A-levels at Nicholas, Moyet left after less than a month and enrolled at Southend Technical College. Her main passion was punk. "When punk started edging its nose, the first thing you did when you met someone was you always looked at his or her feet," she said. "You looked to see if their trousers were flared or straight-legged, whether their shoes were pointed or round-toed ... if you were a boy wearing pointed-toe shoes and you came across the market boys you could really get your head kicked in."

Before punk hit Basildon, during the long hot summer of 1976, Moyet, Forey, and the third Vandal girl, Sue Paget, would all go to the popular Monday youth night at the local disco, Raquel's, or – if they were feeling flush – to the infamous Goldmine club on nearby Canvey Island. The Basildon disco scene, populated by soul boys and soul girls, was the dominant youth culture in town.

"We realised we were never going to be fitting in with those kind of people," Moyet recalled. "There was a future designated for you: you were supposed to get a boyfriend, a job; see who's going to get engaged first, who's going to go out with someone with a car. We made a clan. We met up with other misfits.

"The Arts Centre became a focus in that it had a bar, it wasn't too hard to get into, and it was a place where, if you were a bit left of centre, you could avoid the market boys," she said. "We were like an island in Basildon – we might as well have been surrounded by water. There was no money for wandering. We had decent housing, families didn't need to migrate, there were lots of jobs there, but we were kind of isolated. None of us had anything, none of us expected to have anything, and I never felt bitter about having nothing. When I was in bands I never had any tapes because I never had a cassette player. I didn't buy lots of records. I didn't consume it – music was always more about making it than consuming it. It was always about what you could do to entertain yourself rather than what you could access to entertain yourself. It was very much about stuff we could organise ourselves as opposed to there being a live music scene.

"I loved growing up in Basildon," she continued. "The mixture between these new clean streets and loads and loads of green spaces was idyllic. Basildon wasn't an ugly place, it was clean and it was bright and it was low built. You saw all the sky and all the grass. The only downside was the lack of anything cultural, but at the same time that's what made people creative. You don't become a receiver – you have to put it out there, make it yourself."

Unlike many of her punk contemporaries, Moyet saw a rich vein of romanticism in Basildon. "You'd be going through these complete new-builds and find some little old shack that had just been there for ever," she recalled. "There'd be scrubland and just the traces and remnants of foundations of old houses, the overgrown flowers, the hollyhocks, that would have once have been part of a garden that you never quite knew. It was like this house built in another time that wasn't quite eradicated. You'd always have a sense of another life lived. You'd have these areas of houses waiting to be demolished but that seemed to stand for 20 years in a half state where you could go in through doors, it would have no roof, and still find the newspapers or an ornament on the sideboard. It was magical.

"I felt really bereft when I heard people saying: I can't fucking wait to get out of this place. I didn't get it at all. I had no antipathy toward the town at all and the only reason I ended up leaving there was because, being that recognisable, when I still lived there I was getting the milkman bringing people round my house, the taxi drivers bringing people round my house. It just got mad, and I was getting agoraphobic so I had to leave, but it was a great sadness to me to have to do so."

⌖⌖⌖

Playing guitar for The Vandals was another Nicholas pupil: Vince's best pal, Rob Marlow. He, like Martin and Fletch, was close with Gail Forey, Kim's younger sister. "Alison Moyet came up to me at school and said: you play guitar, don't yer?" he recalled. "I said yeah. She said they'd got a gig on Saturday. Alison, Kim, and Sue used to sing in the market place or the bus station. They had a penchant for ham-fisted harmonies; they'd be singing songs like 'Young Love' and stuff by The Crystals. Then when the punk thing came along we all bought drainpipe jeans and threw away our flares, tried to make our ties as thin as possible at school."

Marlow had a baptism of fire with The Vandals at their first gig at the Grand Hotel in Leigh-on-Sea in 1978. "I was so embarrassed, because we were a bit amateurish," he recalled. "I called myself The Guitarist With No Name – I didn't want anyone to know who I was. We played all original songs except for a cover of 'Walking In The Sand' by The Shangri-La's.

"After that we used to play all the local youth clubs in Basildon. We had a bit of a following at the Woodlands Youth Club. I had a tiny practice amp and I'd take it to rehearsal in my mum's tartan shopping trolley. We didn't have drums or any real equipment. That's why we often did gigs with The Opposition, a bunch of lovely but older hippie guys who used to do Bad Company covers. They would lend us all the gear. There was a local punk fanzine, called *Strange Stories*, and The Vandals featured in there quite a lot.

"As well as the punks, there was quite a skinhead movement in Basildon at that time, too," Marlow continued. "It was very provincial, racism as fashion accessory. I took a beating one night because someone had put up on a wall: all skins are wankers. All the skinheads came up to Woodlands and cornered me and Rik Wheatley [the singer in The Vermin]. Rik said: run, Rob, run. I said: why, I haven't done anything. I got the pasting of my life."

Once he'd joined The Vandals and been bitten by the punk bug, Marlow abandoned the St Paul's Youth Fellowship and grew apart from Vince. "The thing for me was the Christian music was really dull," he laughed. "We went to a couple of the Greenbelt festivals. The music was so boring. The only person I liked was Larry Norman. Vince and I both loved him. He died recently. He wrote a song called 'Why Should The Devil Have All The Good Music?' – it was proper rock'n'roll. He wrote very interesting songs, political songs, not just in-your-face 'praise Jesus'. Vince and I met him at Greenbelt, just wandering through the crowd, we told him we thought his music was great. He said: no, it's God's music.

"Vince and I just drifted away from one another. I was still at school and he'd gone on to Basildon Further Education College. He used to parade around in this big greatcoat, it was still part of the hippy wear. The Christian scene was quite hippie-orientated." Vince and Rob would come back together after the novelty of the punk scene faded, but for now Vince was out in the cold.

Sue Paget was the bass player in The Vandals and was also in the same year at Nicholas as Martin and Fletch. "None of us three girls could play very well," she said. "Kim never really did pick up a guitar. I think the very first time we played she pretended she'd broken her arm and bandaged it up so she had an excuse not to be able to play. We never had a permanent drummer; we had whoever was going at the time."

The Vandals progressed quickly from hanging out at the Seafarer chip shop near the bus station and singing harmonies in the disabled car park at the back of the town centre to becoming the central attraction on a Tuesday night at the Van Gogh pub and at regular gigs at the Woodlands Youth Club on the grounds of Woodlands school. Basildon didn't have a regular music venue, so these two small venues were where most of the Depeche Mode generation consumed their live music. Slowly, little huddles of 'weirdoes' started to form in the corners of the rough pubs in the town centre, the Highway and the Bullseye, which backed onto the market, with a burger bar outside it.

"The Arts Centre, where Martin, Vince and Fletch and their crowd would hang out, wasn't considered very punk," Paget recalled. "It was more political – the thinkers went there. Everybody met up at Woodlands. The bands would rehearse there. It was all very incestuous, everybody knew each other, everybody borrowed each other for bands, everyone went to the same places at the same time."

When the Arts Centre showed the punk film *Jubilee*, a whole crowd of the Basildon punks snuck in with beer for a night of raucous punk action. Punk poet John Cooper Clarke also played there. The more adventurous Basildon punks would often travel to nearby Chelmsford to see gigs by bands such as The Damned, X-Ray Spex, Buzzcocks, and The Undertones at the Chancellor Hall. "We would all pile on a double-decker bus and go to Chelmsford," Paget recalled. "We saw Siouxsie & The Banshees there. We would all go out in big contingencies, en masse."

The Queen's Hotel, a seedy old place in nearby Westcliff, was also a top punk spot for a short period. Generation X, Slaughter & The Dogs, The Damned, and The Adverts all played there, and the venue provided a lot of Basildon kids with their first exposure to proper punk acts.

Paget recalled playing gigs with Norman & The Worms. "Martin and

Phil Burdett were a very odd couple," she laughed. "Martin was really, really small and shy and quiet, whereas Phil was quite a lot taller and had a big shock of curly hair. They used to walk around school with white coats on, like what you'd wear in a science lab, with 'Norman & The Worms' painted on the backs. They weren't so much in with the punks. They had these mops of curly hair. They didn't quite fit in with the punk scene, but they were around."

Paget had similar memories of Fletch. "I lived next door to his grandparents in Capelston," she said. "They were all such unlikely candidates to be what they became. They were just real geeky, heads down, shy, churchy boys. You wouldn't really be able to equate what they were then to what they are now."

ㅁ-ㅁ-ㅁ

The Basildon punk scene was an eclectic, fluid mixture of people and a very large network. "That's where we met people like Jo Fox [soon to be engaged to Dave Gahan] and Paul Redmond," The Vandals' Kim Forey recalled. "We all liked Paul Redmond and Doug White; they were like the first punks in Basildon. We used to go to a lot of gigs with them. I think all of us were reacting against Basildon. We thought it was a shit-hole, the worst place on earth. We were all destined to be cooler and better than living in Basildon allowed us to be. And we didn't want to be our mums and dads. Punk gave me a way of really marking my life – it was going to different from my parents'."

The Vermin were the other great Basildon punk band. They formed at Barstable Comprehensive School, where Dave Gahan was a pupil, and were famed for having a drummer, Tony Burgess, who played biscuit tins. Tony was in the same year and class as Gahan, and The Vermin would have a big influence on the future Depeche Mode singer.

Gary Harsent was the group's bassist. "Basildon was a great place to grow up in," he told me. "But when we got to the age of 15 or 16, all you could do at night was go out and hang in the street, and that was where you'd fall into trouble. Smashing windows on the new estates they were building, just getting up to mischief, not really wanting to. It wasn't through being bad; there was just nothing else there for you, for excitement."

At Barstable, Harsent was good friends with fellow Vermin Russell 'Jods' Jordan, who was already infamous for doing lunchtime concerts at the school. "He'd do posters and everything, dress up in a boiler suit and sing songs completely out of key," Harsent recalled. "It was a bizarre thing but he was quite famous for doing these. He'd do them unaccompanied, no music; he'd just sing old Elvis Presley songs or The Who. Teachers would come and watch. He used to fill a classroom out and hop on a desk."

Harsent recalled being influenced by a particular sub-cult – unique to Essex – that he saw going to Raquel's on Sunday nights. "We were too young to get in, but we used to go down and have a look," he said. "We called them smoothies but they were really soul boys. It was where this kind of punky influence was coming in, because these people would turn up and wear these big mohair jumpers, peg-bottom trousers, and plastic sandals; they would have like big feather earrings and their hair would be dyed in really bright colours."

When the Sex Pistols' 'Anarchy In The UK' single came out, Harsent and Jordan were hooked. "We started turning up at school in all these bizarre clothes," Harsent recalled. "Nobody really knew what punk rock was then or anything. We were just completely laughed at. In the early days of punk, Jods and I would walk to town and we'd run home – we'd always have someone chasing after us just because we looked different."

The Vermin — Harsent, his cousin Allan Johnson, Jordan, and Tony Burgess, who was in the year below the others — soon hooked up with the other Basildon punks. Harsent knew Paul Redmond, who would become a key figure later on in bringing Dave Gahan into the orbit of Vince, Martin, and Fletch.

"Paul was a year older than us, which made all the difference at the time," Harsent recalled. "He got his picture in the *Evening Echo* as the first punk in Basildon. What happened was, we went to the Chancellor Hall to see a gig – The Clash, Buzzcocks, and The Slits – and Paul did the whole punk-rocker thing. He made himself a suit out of bin bags and stapled them together. He stuck a safety pin in his ear. We had to get the bus from Basildon to Chelmsford. By the time we got there, his trousers were in shreds. I think his dad kicked him out, wouldn't have him in the house, and he had to stay in the shed."

The Vermin and The Vandals hooked up at the Double Six pub. "There was a gig billed as being The Only Ones but it ended up being a band called The Young Ones, a kind of plastic punk band," said Harsent. "We went, thinking we were the only punks in Basildon, and there was this group of people stood at the back – and that was basically The Vandals. They said they were in a band and we said: oh, we've got this band. Then I got up on the stage and said: V is for The Vandals, V is for The Vermin, first we'll take Basildon, then England, and then world."

The Double Six was the rock pub in Basildon, famous locally as the place where The Rezillos had once played. The mainstay at the venue was a band called Dog Watch, who had put out an album on the Bridgehouse label. Many of the acts who played the Double Six were also regulars at the Bridgehouse venue in Canning Town in London's East End, where Depeche Mode would later make their name. Apart from the Wednesday 'jam night' – where basically anyone could turn up and get a couple of numbers in before the people who wanted to hear Fleetwood Mac threw their beer glasses at you – the Double Six was enemy territory for the Basildon punks.

The Vermin played their first and only proper gig at Woodlands Youth Club with The Vandals and Norman & The Worms. "Martin Gore wasn't going to concerts or going to the pub and hanging out in the train station with the punks," Harsent recalled, "but he knew everybody." After the gig at Woodlands, The Vermin played only in front of whoever came down to the Barstable School to watch them rehearse. "People would come down and sit there while we was playing and mucking about," Harsent said. "That's where Dave Gahan came down to watch. I played bass a bit. Tony was good at playing drums but didn't have any so he used to bang the biscuit tins. Jods couldn't play a guitar at all, he would just play whatever he wanted to play at the time, and it was never the same twice. Then a friend of Alison Moyet's, Rik Wheatley, said he'd sing."

A combination of being heavily featured in the local punk fanzine *Strange Stories* and the novelty of having a drummer who played biscuit tins brought The Vermin to the attention of Virgin Records. "An A&R scout approached us at a Siouxsie & The Banshees gig and said: we want you to come down into the studios," Harsent recalled. "I said I wouldn't, because we couldn't really play. There was a little bit of infamy around Tony playing the biscuit tins. We even had a song called 'Life In A Biscuit Tin'. We were rebelling against Basildon. One of the songs I wrote was called 'Basildon New Town' and it was like: 'Sunday, Monday nothing to do / Tuesday, Wednesday nothing to do / Thursday, Friday nothing to do ...'"

By now, The Vermin's singer was Rik Wheatley. "Someone once said Basildon was a concrete jungle full of shoe shops and skinheads," he told me. "That sums it up in the mid 70s – what it had become. The Vermin were inspired by The Vandals. The punk thing was DIY, and we didn't have any money; we didn't have any instruments. We probably were the punkiest of the lot because we just played in a playground at night in the dark. We managed eventually to blag our way into getting a classroom at Barstable by chatting up a sympathetic caretaker so we could practice in the warm, and we came up with a couple of songs. We were more like Subway Sect; we wanted more that sort of vibe. We didn't just want to be a carbon copy of the Pistols or The Clash. We had a song called 'Robot' and one called 'Sunday Crimes', about the newspapers. We were really into it and we tried really hard but we had a good sense of humour as well.

"The Arts Centre was where all the misfits would go," Wheatley continued. "The Van Gogh was a room above the pub in the middle of the industrial estate, very hard to get to. We would walk there, in the middle of snowstorms in January, and we would go on a Tuesday night no matter what. Norman & The Worms played there. It was not just with their image and the hair and everything, but they were more like Simon & Garfunkel. It was that type of music. But they did their own songs that had a little Basildon slant, or they had some funny lyrics.

"The great thing was that you would get at the Van Gogh on a Tuesday night, for 50p, about five acts. Mik Bostik would open – he was like our version of Billy Bragg but five years earlier. Norman & the Worms would do 20 minutes, and then you'd have a horrible rock band, The Opposition – someone like that who were kind of fourth division Status Quo – then you'd have maybe The Vandals. But we'd all go purely because it was live music and there was nothing else to do. And you didn't mind sitting through the acts you didn't like, like Norman & The Worms, because we were all there together. We were very supportive of one another; everyone would use the same equipment and cheer everybody on. But Norman & The Worms were a strange duo, very bizarre, to be in the middle of 50 hard-core punks and getting cheered. That's how boring it was, you were so glad to be out on a Tuesday night watching live music."

The rumour was that Cream had played The Woodlands Youth Club in the dim and distant past. It really took over from the Van Gogh as the key punk venue in Basildon. It was on the school grounds but independently run. "The Bullseye pub was another good meeting place," Wheatley added. "It was right next to the train station, very central, tolerant landlord; during the week it was very quiet. I used to meet The Vandals in there almost every night and we would just have £4 between the four of us all night, clutching one drink with four straws, just to get out of the house." There was also the Highway pub, about which Wheatley recalled: "You wouldn't go near it for fear of violence. But I guess we got braver, because on a Saturday lunchtime we went there to sell *Strange Stories*. We'd all meet down the Highway at 12 o'clock, all these hard-core punks sitting in corners reading this fanzine from cover to cover."

For many in Basildon, the big band was The Damned – they were a particular favourite of Dave Gahan's. "They were probably the band we saw the most in the early days," Wheatley recalled. "We probably saw them about a dozen times. They were one of the biggest bands for everybody in Basildon: The Vandals, The Vermin, and Perry Bamonte's band, The Spurts. I saw The Damned quite early on at the Queen's Hotel in Westcliff: early 1977 they played, and it was like one of those life-changing nights."

Richard Seager ran *Strange Stories* between 1977 and 1979. "The only time I can remember The Vermin performing was in a children's play area, and we did review it," he recalled. "You can look back and think there was a lot going on – and to an extent there was and it seemed very important – but if you looked at the amount of gigs the bands did it probably wasn't a lot. *Strange Stories* was very, very local, so we covered The Vandals, The Vermin, and a band I managed from Southend called The Machines."

*Strange Stories* was more or less monthly. "We wanted to operate as a newspaper for a certain section of the community, rather than a fanzine," Seager said. "The emphasis was always on local bands and getting people to have their own opinions and to write to us and get in touch. Norman

& The Worms didn't fit in with the scene but because they were there we had them in the fanzine. I think they became part of the scene because they were happy to play for nothing even though their music was totally at odds with what you could call the sound of the scene. Disparate groups – if they feel alienated from the mainstream – will come together with other disparate groups even if they're not the same. I think Martin and Phil felt as out of sync with the general mainstream of Basildon as people who went round showing it more by dressing and sounding differently than they did.

"I felt I was rebelling against Basildon," he continued. "I absolutely loathed Basildon at that time. The National Front had a very strong presence. In the run up to the 1979 general election, London ITV news did a feature on Woodlands School, which had run a mock general election – which the National Front had won. A lot of us in the early punk days aligned ourselves with Rock Against Racism and the Anti-Nazi League. You couldn't walk through any subway in Basildon without seeing the letters SBK: 'Skins Back Klan'. That was a very real threat, and there was a lot of tension and aggression. We stopped doing gigs at Woodlands because loads of skinheads would turn up. It was dodgy. When the electronic thing started, a lot of the skinheads started talking acid and became New Romantics. Certainly, in 1979, there was a lot of acid and a lot of Tuinal [barbiturate] use."

Mik Bostik was another key Basildon punk performer. He played alongside The Vermin, The Vandals, The Spurts, The Machines, and The Worms. "It was a very pure development initially," he told me. "No one talked about 'making it' as such. We weren't on the first step of the ladder. At Woodlands Youth Club we just found a place where we could express ourselves. We were as shocked as anyone when we could get up and play and it kind of worked. It didn't matter. No one judged us. Everything was great. It was our own world. It was a tiny, tiny place with a stage. We seemed to have a free hand there. It was quite possible there were just a caretaker and a set of keys and then 200 crazy kids.

"Norman & The Worms were brilliant. They were like Simon & Garfunkel – they certainly looked liked them. Phil is kind of the Van Morrison of Basildon. It was great that that could happen. There was never any question of: is this right? I could have gone up and done a clog dance and someone would have thought it was the best clog dance anyone had ever done.

"The town in general was very aggressive, very unfriendly," Bostik continued. "There was a disco scene we were desperate to avoid. The burger bar outside Raquel's in the market area was a no-go zone. You've got these empty market stalls, people sitting on the frames, boy-racers everywhere, revving up, and there's going to be a fight. You didn't want to hang around, certainly didn't want a burger. I remember thinking this is like *Apocalypse Now*.

"A point that linked us all in the punk scene in Basildon was that we were trying to avoid what was expected of us; a job in the factory and slippers on in the evenings. Our parents had fought in the war, or certainly experienced a part of that: that was a generation who wanted to settle down and saw Basildon as a dream and a dream with a future. But for our generation, for kids our age, there was no future there at all. We thought we were all doomed and we needed to express that. We didn't feel any connection ... there wasn't really a generation in Basildon before us we could connect with, because they'd all moved from elsewhere. We were the first generation that had grown up there through primary school and senior school."

"We had almost a hatred of the town," Phil Burdett recalled. "It was weird because we had a sense of pride that something like this scene had come out of Basildon. We saw ourselves as the vanguard of this banality. All those neighbourhood ideas – aspects they designed to create a community – began to work against it. They work very well in Hampstead, where people interact socially, but basically in Basildon you started to get little cabals of lunatics. There was poverty going on and they were prey – the BNP would go straight to these estates."

Rather than stay on to do A-levels, Phil left school and became more politicised. By 1979 The Worms – like The Vermin and The Vandals – had fizzled out. "Martin had a few friends in every camp," Burdett recalled. "He would drift about. He was always a vague person to talk to. Never seemed to focus. He would suddenly become passionate about a Sparks B-side, and you'd think he was talking about the Spanish Civil War or something. This is a classic example of Martin Gore the invisible man: I didn't actually know if he was working or doing his A-levels. His life was a mystery to me. We didn't particularly care, beyond: have you got any money for this weekend? OK, you're paying.

"There was a group of us who would hang out at the Arts Centre and mainly get animated about Thatcher, politics. Rob Marlow and Alison Moyet would be involved in that. Martin would never be involved. He was not political. He would turn up at the Arts Centre occasionally. I remember him only drinking lager – he used to get drunk quickly but maintain a level of drunkenness for a long time. The Arts Centre became the left-wing HQ of Basildon; we used to sell the [Communist/Socialist newspaper] *Morning Star* in the bar. Anyone who had any aspiration to not go and work in a factory, to not have the 'prole' life, would go to the Arts Centre. Of course, the rest of the town just thought that was where all the weirdoes go."

# CHAPTER 4
# SOUL BOY

The 16-year-old Dave Gahan was, at best, on the very fringes of the Basildon punk scene of 1978. The gang he ran with was part of the prevalent soul-boy scene: trendies, casuals, beer boys, market boys, geezers, wide-boys, Ford Capri with furry dice sort of guys. More Raquel's than the Arts Centre, more Bullseye than Woodlands Youth Club – a bit of a rogue, a bit of a disco kid, up to a few naughty things; one of the bad boys the Youth Fellowship crowd worried might wreck their parties.

Dave Gahan was born in Epping, Essex, on May 9 1962. His family moved to Basildon in the mid 60s when he was three. His stepfather Jack worked for Shell Oil and his mum Sylvia was a ticket inspector on the buses. He had an older sister, Sue, and two young brothers, Philip and Peter. They lived on Bonnygate on the Fryerns estate at the Pitsea end of town – the older end of town, away from the Lee Chapel North crowd.

Dave's dad played sax and liked jazz, big sister Sue dug soul, and mum had a thing for the Salvation Army. His world was turned upside down when Jack died when Dave was seven. It was turned upside down again at the age of ten when his real father, Len, showed up on the doorstep. Unlike Martin Gore, Dave had always presumed his stepfather was his real dad.

Len didn't stick around for long, but the chaos and confusion he brought into Dave's young life did. Dave went to Barstable Comprehensive on Timberlog Lane, the school formed from the merger of Barstable Grammar and Timberlog Secondary Modern. Most of his pals on the estate went to Fryerns Comprehensive, but Dave lived in the southern part of Fryerns and crossed Broadmayne, the main road that bisected the two mammoth estates, to attend Barstable. However he got there, he didn't like it very much.

Dave's mum didn't remarry. The Gahans were poor but close; Dave later said he got a taste for drugs after he started nicking his mum's barbiturates, which were prescribed for her epilepsy. He later bragged of working on a fairground as a young teen and getting his first tattoo at the age of 14.

Like his future band-mates, Dave would buy his 45s from the Pop Inn stall at the market – glam-era stuff like T.Rex – but he had other things on his mind. He'd started bunking off school and getting into mischief. He said he ended up in Juvenile Court on three occasions for offences ranging from joyriding and graffiti to criminal damage and theft. He enjoyed the dumb thrill of stealing cars, driving them around for a bit, and then just setting fire to them.

In his final year at school, Dave's criminal record hindered his chances of getting an apprenticeship as a gas fitter with North Thames Gas. This rejection, he claimed, led to him trashing his probation officer's office. His punishment was weekend custody at "a sub-Borstal in Romford" for a year. He left Barstable in 1978 with one O-level, in art, and little prospect of any work except in the factories on the industrial estate. He enrolled at Southend Technical College on a window-dressing course and did a stint packing at Yardley, where summer joys were always readily available. Along the line he also found temporary work stacking shelves in supermarkets, and as a labourer, although his slim, girl-like frame would surely have counted against him when it came to hod-carrying.

The Vermin's biscuit-tin drummer, Tony Burgess, was in the same class as Dave at Barstable Comprehensive. "Dave mucked around a lot at school, same as we all did," he told me. "He knew a lot of kids from Fryerns School as well, the hard boys. Dave had a bit of a temper – his situation at home toughened him and he had to look after himself. I was in a similar situation as him so I knew what it was like. We knew a couple of families that had a bit of money but most of us struggled.

"I remember when he went to Borstal," Burgess continued. "There was a lot of that then, Youth Magistrates – the joke was you were going to get a 'basin cut'. They'd put a bowl on your head and cut round your hair.

That's what they all used to say: 'you're going to have a basin' meant you were going to Borstal."

Barstable Comprehensive had quite a good reputation. "If you wanted to learn there, you could," Burgess recalled – not that he and Dave did. "We used to have a good laugh in class. Teachers were dishing out backhanders and you'd have a few kids who'd hit a teacher. Then you'd get the cane and you'd put a couple of textbooks down your pants so you couldn't feel it. Quite a few used to bunk off school; it was the normal sort of thing, really."

Dave's best friend at Barstable was Mark Longmuir, who still has a wild reputation in Basildon. "Dave did the joyriding with Mark when they were 14, 15," Burgess continued. "It was trouble, but it was light-hearted in a way. Dave was trouble but he also had morals. His nickname was Dave Joon. We all used to do silly names like that, and no one knew where they came from. I called him that."

Burgess worked at the fairground with Gahan and frequented the same tattooist in Southend. "When the fairground came to Basildon we used to get jobs there," he said. "It was the time of Skins and Teds: on Whitmore Way, which is Dave's side of Broadmayne, there was a club called Four O'clock Rock – the teddy boys used to go there. The skinheads would go up there looking for a fight. The fairground came every year and we all used to meet down there and have a few fights. We'd be wearing high-waisted flared trousers, scarves around our wrists.

"We all used to go down the clubs in town, Sweeney's and Raquel's. All the market boys used to drink in the Bullseye. There were a few fights in there – there was a lot of fighting going on in Basildon – outside Raquel's by the burger bar something always kicked off." When it came to drugs, Burgess recalled, "Dave would try anything, like us all."

Burgess was 15 when he joined The Vermin. "I was the first in my year as a punk," he told me. "We were the early punks, the first in Basildon. Dave and his mates were still in flares. Going to the town centre, you had to duck and dive because there were always people who wanted to give you a kicking. It was Ford Capris and baseball bats. You'd have grown men trying to kick the crap out of us.

"I came up with the name The Vermin; I wrote the three songs we had and I taped all Tupperware and biscuit tins together for drums. When we did the Woodlands gig we had blood capsules in our mouths to soup it up. There was a big buzz around Basildon about The Vermin."

Burgess refuted the rumours about Gahan joining The Vermin as singer. "There was a youth club on the grounds of Barstable School," he recalled. "We had people like Dave come and watch us rehearse – they'd look in the window or come inside. I remember Dave just had a dog collar on and his normal clothes and his hair was normal. I think he had it in him – it was just waiting to burst out."

"The Dave Gahan thing was funny," Vermin founder Gary Harsent added. "Dave was on the fringes. He wasn't really in the punk thing; his friends at the time were casuals, beer boys. There was Dave and Mark Longmuir and another guy, Steve Saunders, a bit of a rogue really. Dave's little crew did have a reputation. He was gearing toward getting into trouble, doing a few naughty things. But at that time he was more into the soul-boy thing than punk. I think he had it in him, but his mates were sort of holding him back. Dave only started getting into the punk thing as it became fashionable; he wasn't in it at the beginning. When it became fashionable Dave and Mark Longmuir went up to the Sex shop and bought the T-shirt, the tartan trousers, and everything. But they were the ones who used to ridicule us in the beginning."

Dave was present, however, when The Vermin went to see The Clash, X-Ray Spex, Steel Pulse, and Tom Robinson at the first Anti-Nazi League Carnival in Victoria Park, London. "A load of big skinheads took all our money," Burgess laughed, "and we had nothing to drink or eat all day."

After punk, Burgess went 'electric' when Gary Numan's first album came out. "We were flitting between the fashions," he said. "When you went electric and started bleaching your hair, wearing eyeliner and shiny trousers, you had to get around Basildon without getting a kicking. It was hard."

Burgess also recalled the problem many school leavers were having in Basildon: finding a decent job. The population had reached 93,000 by 1979 and the children of the first migrants to the area were starting to leave school. The Corporation was right to worry about a lack of office development to absorb school leavers. There was a real shortage of white-collar jobs. The Station office block, which the Corporation hoped would provide office employment for young people in town, was let to Ford as its European truck division, but Ford imported skilled staff from outside. There were 41,000 people employed on the industrial estates but an above-average level of unemployment: from 514 in 1960 and 940 in 1974 to 5,060 in 1979. Life was becoming increasingly bleak, with phrases such as 'suburb of nowhere' starting to be bandied about.

"As soon as you left school everyone was drifting in and out of those factories," Burgess said. "Everyone went through Yardley – Yardley, Rothmans, and Fords were the main employers. They'd lose staff and you'd have some work for a couple of weeks and then leave.

"Dave could have gone to a life of crime easily. But he must have had his head screwed on a little bit as he was trying to get an apprenticeship. He would have got knocked back and knocked back – you can understand his frustration. There were the jobs on the industrial estate, but if you wanted to better yourself, those sorts of jobs were hard to get. You ended up in dead-end jobs until you found your feet and got out of it somehow."

After Dave left school and went to Southend Tech, Burgess didn't see him around until much later, when he asked Burgess if he wanted to be the drummer for Depeche Mode. "I was meant to meet him in town," Burgess recalled. "I did eventually meet him, and he said: we don't need a drummer now because we're going to use synthesizers. I said oh, that's OK then, thinking nothing of it, and then a month later he had a single in Kelly's Records. After that I used to see him because he did a little bit of fishing. I'd see him at the tackle shop."

▭▬▭

At Southend Tech, Gahan mingled with a whole new crowd of people – very different to his beer-boy mates in Basildon – and lived a weird sort of double life. Southend was something of a mecca for many Basildon kids. There was the buzz of the seaside resort, with its arcades and fairground, plus the lure of trendy, independent clothes shops such as Graffiti and Nasty's, and several venues including Shrimpers, the social club of Southend United FC, which was popular with The Vandals; the Top Alex, a hippie, druggy, biker pub; and the Kursaal, where bands such as Thin Lizzy, Dr Feelgood, and Stiff Little Fingers played. The area had a thriving pub-rock scene, led by The Blockheads and Canvey Island's Dr Feelgood, who had played one of their first gigs at the Railway Hotel in Pitsea, but there was also a strong punk movement. At Southend Tech, meanwhile, there was the beginnings of a new scene. When Gahan started his course there, Stephen Linard, the most celebrated fashion designer of the New Romantic era, had just completed his time at the college. Linard and his pal Boy George were both faces on the Southend scene, where Gary Turner was the lead player.

Turner is one of the unsung heroes in the Depeche Mode story. He is the man who started the Saturday night Glamour Club at Croc's, in Rayleigh, where Depeche Mode got their first break via a residency in the late summer of 1980. Before Croc's, Turner ran two of the area's most influential 'electro' nights, first at Baron's at the Elms pub in Leigh-on-Sea and then at the Cliff in Southend. He also ran his own hip clothes shop, Pin-Ups, which sold gear made by Southend Tech students and the odd bit from Malcolm McLaren's Sex store.

Turner was a couple of years older than Dave: he had gone through his Ziggy Stardust phase and was now a hardened clubber and soul boy extraordinaire. He started clubbing aged 14 at the Intercom in Southend, which played funky stuff: Al Green, The Memphis Horns. It wasn't as influential as the Goldmine on Canvey Island but it got him on the right road. He was 15 or 16 when he started going to the Goldmine in 1975. He was a regular at the famous Monday soul night with DJ Chris Hill. The soul-boy crowd adopted a look that had a strong influence on punk – and on Dave Gahan.

"The Goldmine was good for that in the early days," Turner told me. "Music, dance, and fashion, all combined. The movie *The Great Gatsby* was an influence on the look: flat caps, double-breasted suits, reporter shoes." Everything was fluid but precise. "We went from wearing high-waisted baggy trousers, the Kid Creole type look, into peg-top trousers with eight-inch bottoms on the ankle, sometimes with a turn-up and two or three pleats. You have to consider the look of what we referred to as the straight people back then – long hair, flared trousers. We'd gone the opposite way: we were very distinct as a group."

There were probably about a couple of hundred people involved in the scene, with a wide mix of ethnicities. Sometimes a good half of the people at the Goldmine were black: they'd come up from Tottenham and Brixton and it really added to the flavour of the night – what they were wearing, how they were dancing. As they got older, Turner and his pals got more mobile and would travel around in their old bangers. The Atlantis in Margate was the top spot for Bank Holiday weekenders. It was a real hot, sweaty, grimy venue, great for dancers. There were some real characters emerging. This was the start of the Essex soul-boy fashion scene that would have such an influence on the early punks, including John Lydon.

"In 1975, '76, Tommy Mack and several of his other mates would come on to the dance floor," Turner recalled. "Tommy had a cropped hairstyle coloured in the hexagonal pattern you get on a football. He had a whole range of odd hairstyles, blue on one side, red on the other. Outrageous styling. He and his mates would go along the seafront on roller skates – leather trousers, specs, Lurex tops – and just be totally outrageous. We were all really starting to push the envelope."

When DJ Chris Hill moved from the now extremely popular Goldmine to the Lacy Lady club up in Ilford, Turner and his mates followed. "It was brilliant," he recalled. "That was a very seedy club. People like Steve Severin from the Banshees, some of the Pistols used to go there in the early days, members of The Clash … fashion-wise you saw all the elements of punk creeping in: plastic trousers, rubberised T-shirts, leather jackets.

"When the soul scene evolved it got quite tacky in our eyes," Turner added. "There were 'tribes'; it was too cheesy for us. I certainly didn't go to Caister [Caravan Holiday Park, famed for its soul weekenders] because it was completely against what I was into at that time. I was into punk, out of punk, into something different; I'd moved on. We'd go to the Global Village in Charing Cross, where Heaven is now. They'd do half and half, a soul thing and a punk thing. We used to go down there as punks and throw each other around, pogo, do all that sort of stuff. It got us into a lot of the tunes that were around at the time: The Damned, 999, X-Ray Spex."

For Turner and his crowd, the two scenes were not so separate. "We liked things that were different; we found things like a Brass Construction track or Roy Ayers interesting, and in the same way the new punk tracks were very different and interesting to us. It just seemed a natural evolution – we were trying something new."

By 1979, Turner and Stephen Linard were regulars at the Blitz in London, which inspired Turner to start his own club nights. He took over Tuesday nights at Baron's in Leigh-on-Sea and launched his own electro club playing Kraftwerk and other German electro bands, plus "a lot of Bowie". After that he decided to do something above a pub in Southend called the Cliff. "We did it because we were going to lots of things," he recalled. "We saw The Human League, one of their first gigs, and bands like The Normal. Lots of odd little records coming out – we just wanted to play them. They had that quirkiness to them but they had that dance-ability as well."

Turner's night at the Cliff was on a Friday, with Dave Gahan often in attendance. "It was a gay pub and that was quite good for us, bearing in mind some of the outrageous things people were wearing," he recalled. "There were a lot of people wearing the 'leather man' look: leather trousers and leather chaps and leather jackets and leather caps and studded belts. I'm not sure why that masochistic look took off, particularly in our area, but it just sort of clicked. But then there were other fads such as when people got into the cowboy look and went overboard with the whole kit. It was dressing-up time."

Turner's next club night was the infamous Saturday night Glamour Club at Croc's in nearby Rayleigh, which was already building a solid reputation as a live venue, having hosted acts such as The Damned and Wayne County. At the Glamour Club, Turner did the late-night DJ slot as well as promoting and working the door. "I would stand alongside the bouncers, do the meet-and-greet, but also more importantly not let people in," he recalled. "It was important for me to ensure that the right people were there. There's always that danger of people feeling uncomfortable, threatened, fights erupting. That sort of 'you're in, you're out' function was important to me – it helped bolster our reputation." At the time, Croc's was owned by Anton Johnson, the former chairman of Rotherham United Football Club. "He was the one who got the live crocodiles in there," Turner recalled. "That's what football chairmen did back in the days of sheepskin coats and big cigars."

Once Croc's started to put on live music, and then the Glamour Club, its reputation spread quickly. Rayleigh was easily accessible from London by train and the club was right by the station, but it was a bit of a backwater, so it was a real testament to Turner that it started to pick up a reputation that spread to the capital.

"Virtually everyone who used to come to the Cliff night came with us to Croc's," he recalled. "Dave was very much part of the scene. A group of us used to team up with the Basildon crew. We all knew each other very well."

The Basildon punk contingent included Paul Redmond; Paul's girlfriend Fran Healy, who went to school with Dave; and Fran's friend Jo Fox. Dave and Jo met on January 12 1979 on the way to a gig by The Damned. For a while, Dave and Jo would double-date with Paul and Fran. By November, Dave and Jo were engaged.

It was the hook-up with Paul Redmond that would lead Dave to the door of Depeche Mode. "Punk went off in factions," Gary Harsent of The Vermin recalled. "You got the mod thing and the ska thing – Dave's pal Mark Longmuir got into that – and then you had this big rockabilly thing. Paul Redmond originally got into the rockabilly thing and he had a crew of mates with him, including Dave; then, when the electro thing started, Paul was bang into it. I met Dave and he said: you've got to come to this club in London, Studio 21 – they just play all Gary Numan and it's all electro, all David Bowie. Paul Redmond got a synthesizer and they were toying around with what they were going to do, band-wise."

▱▬▱

Alison Moyet was at Southend Tech at the same time as Dave. She'd left The Vandals and was now playing with "that whole Canvey Island scene, Dr Feelgood and people like that". She didn't share Dave's newfound fascination for the electro scene. "I was a bit horrified when the New Romantic thing came in," she said. "I thought on the whole they were wankers. I was in dirtier places. To me it was more of a natural progression to punk; Southend R&B was more akin to banging punk music than electro-led stuff. You went one way or the other: either the pub rock route, with Costello and Dury, or into this far poncier area.

"I'd known Vince since I was 11 and we both went to the Laindon High School Saturday-morning music club. We were like Venn diagrams – we were on the wrong circles but we knew people in the middle. I knew Martin and Fletcher better than him. In fact, I knew Dave Gahan better than him because when I was at Southend Tech he used to do a nice little shoplifting service for everyone. Vince was the one I knew less well. He seemed a bit more aloof and odd because of the Christian thing, and he had his big overcoat with 'Jesus Loves' on the back.

"Dave was lovely, really friendly, really warm, and yet at the same time he'd been part of this whole market-boy crowd. I never came across the side of him that was a bit more of a geezer: I came across the side of him that was always smiling and happy and a little bit high."

Rik Wheatley, the singer in The Vermin, was also at Southend Tech studying a two-year fine art course. "Dave was definitely a 'Jack the lad'," he recalled. "He disappeared one lunchtime with his mate and they came back with their jackets zipped up in the middle of an art lesson, the lecturer was there and everything, and they were giggling their heads off, came back from lunch stinking of booze. They'd been to a really bad lunchtime strip pub, and they unzipped their jackets and about a thousand packets of condoms just fell out all over the classroom. They'd just done over this condom machine in a pub.

"If people wanted to be really disparaging they used to call all Dave's art-school friends 'clotheshorses'. They were like the real trendies – the people who used to go up to London and bring down all the latest gear. None of them did me any harm but I couldn't hack any of that going to parties, standing in the corner, speaking loudly with cigarette holders.

"Everyone knew everyone in Basildon," Wheatley continued. "It was very incestuous. All the soul boys and all the guys who had the Ford Capris with the fluffy dice, all the disco kids – they all knew the 25 punks who became 50, then 100. When certain people had parties, like Dave Gahan's mates, you knew where you could go, and who with, and still be safe. At the same time you knew the places to avoid. We used to get beaten up quite a lot. Dave and his mates didn't go and see West Ham every second week and get into fights but they were certainly all tasty if there was any trouble – they would always back each other up. There were one or two psychos on the fringes of that kind of crowd.

"When I left Basildon I heard Dave had joined The Vermin but they didn't do anything. It was one of those things that lasted for ten minutes.

It was only: I'm in The Vermin – they didn't actually get it together to get any gigs. Three weeks later they were all doing something else – it happened that quickly. I got Dave a job at the fruit-and-veg shop, Peaches, in Basildon, just around the corner from the market by the bus station."

Gahan also found part-time work at the Sainsbury's supermarket at the newly opened SavaCentre in Basildon town centre, as did Vince Clarke. Based on the Corporation's study of American shopping malls, the SavaCentre was the most advanced regional shopping-centre complex in the South of England. A second phase was already under way: a covered shopping mall called the Eastgate, funded by £24 million from the Norwich Union building society. It was the largest building contract ever agreed in Basildon. Dave and Vince would also find work at a giant Tesco superstore built on a site in Pitsea that had been sold to the retailer by the Corporation for £2.8 million.

The Corporation was concerned that the town had not attracted enough incomers from higher socio-economic backgrounds, and that Basildon remained too predominantly working class. There was a reversal of the national trend in the balance between those working in manufacturing and service industry, with 60 per cent of Basildon residents working on the industrial estates.

Until Margaret Thatcher's Conservative Party won the 1979 general election, Basildon had been a resolutely left-wing place. It had had a Labour MP from 1974–79 and a fervent Labour-led council for almost the entire 70s, with Joe Morgan at the helm. Morgan was brought up as one of 13 children in a Canning Town slum; he saw Basildon as a way for the working class to enjoy decent housing and conditions. It was during his reign that Basildon gained its reputation as a 'Little Moscow on the Thames'. Morgan had clashed with the Corporation many times; in many New Towns, the transfer of Corporation housing to the district council had begun, but not in Basildon, where the cost of putting right unsatisfactory housing estates was considered by Morgan to be a deal-breaker.

Under Morgan, the council had revived Gloucester Park, held open-to-all meetings on council estates, funded a stunning swimming pool in Pitsea, and now planned to turn the Pitsea marshes into a recreational park. The idea became a reality in 1982 with the opening of Wat Tyler

Country Park, named in memory of the people of Essex and Kent who, in the cause of liberty, took part in the Peasants Revolt in 1381. This was quite a boon for Pitsea, once dubbed the 'anus of Britain' and home to the 'tip of death', where up to 200 lorries a day would dump millions of gallons of toxic waste throughout the mid 70s.

The newly elected Conservatives ordered the Corporation to stop building new homes to rent. No new starts at all would be permitted. It was the end of the Corporation's rented-housing programme, and the sale of Corporation homes began again. Between 1968 and 1974, the Corporation had offered its Standard II houses (most of which were semi-detached) to existing tenants with 101 per cent mortgages. About 5,000 tenants had taken up this deal, but spiralling interest rates had brought financial hardship for many. As a result, there was a high incidence of marital problems. The impact intensified in Thatcher's wake. The estates began to disintegrate, the Corporation no longer responsible for their upkeep. The decline in community was exacerbated by the architecture.

"The selling off of the council housing was one of the most devastating things to happen to Basildon," Alison Moyet told me. "My family still live there, and I go quite often and just see how it's fallen apart and become unloved. The great thing about living in council housing was it was looked after; it was well maintained. Growing up on a council estate in the 70s was a brilliant thing. You don't match the quality of life that comes from that."

In the late 70s, the Distillers Company built a huge gin-bottling plant on a 25-acre plot. Carreras merged with Rothmans. Gin and cigarettes were now, appropriately, the New Town's new flagships. Basildon was producing an exceptionally high number of school leavers, and there was nowhere for them to go but the factories. Unemployment would soon hit crisis levels of 12.4 per cent, with 5,000 unemployed – much too high a figure for a supposedly thriving New Town. For many, Basildon became the perfect representation of the emerging consumerist society, the perfect expression of the Thatcher reforms; business was everything, communities became fragmented. Many areas would soon become sink estates.

By 1979, Basildon was on the path to ruin. Profound social decay began to set in. The idea that the Corporation would pass on its assets to the local authority was reversed. Basildon's assets were stripped. The

Conservative government sold off the Corporation's land – not for houses to rent but for low-density private development.

Basildon girl Angela Hogg also attended Southend Technical College. She went on to study graphic design at Chelsea School of Art and illustration at the Royal College of Art and has enjoyed a highly successful career in the field. She recalled the fast-fading socialist Utopian ideals Basildon had been founded on. Her mum worked at Carreras, just as Andy Fletcher's dad had done. "She had a huge social life, lots of dinner dances in her social club at work where she would put on long evening gowns, going to these dances," Hogg said. "My mother loved Carreras – she had all her friends there, and wanted me to go into the factory. I got a job at the factory opposite. I was on the dole but, as they did in those days, they said: no, here's a job for you – and I worked taking plastic bottles off the end of a line and putting them in cardboard boxes, which was complete and utter purgatory. But to my mum that was a success."

Hogg went to Woodlands school and, with her straight-legged jeans and multiple ear-piercings, was one of the first punks there. She went to the Highway pub on a Saturday with the *Strange Stories* crowd. "Basildon was such a dreary, heavy-handed mono-culture, which made these things such a sweet thrill," she told me. "All the girls would wear one shade of tights, the only tights you could be seen in. Every year a different colour scheme would come in, like it would be maroon and cream one year, or this particular sort of coat would come on the market and everybody would buy that coat. It was really limited. You either dressed that way or you were naff, so it was very easy to turn against that.

"It was such a limited culture. If you went into a pub dressed in a slightly different way you'd have to be prepared for comments from the soul boys. I went in the Highway once with a tight cap-sleeved T-shirt and I didn't have a bra on and all these soul boys kind of turned on me. One of them picked me up and said: here you are love, put 'em on the bar love. That sort of grotesque sexism was very common.

"I remember seeing the Depeche boys up at the Highway," she said. "Fletch was very introverted and in a funny sort of way I was interested in him because of that. He would sit there very quietly; you never caught his eye. He never looked your way, or at you. I always wanted to go and talk to him but I never plucked up the courage because he looked like he didn't want anyone to talk to him. I think I was interested in him because he was clearly an awkward bloke. Dave looked much more neurotic, if you like – a frenetic sort of person and a bit vulnerable as well. He'd grown up in the thick of the Basildon estates. The soul boys were the enemies of everybody, really, because they constituted the core of Basildon."

At Southend Tech Hogg, like Gahan, met different people from different backgrounds, including people who lived in big Victorian houses. "Southend was completely different," she recalled. "It's our nearest neighbour, half an hour on the railway. A lot of people used to go to a workingmen's club there to see Dr Feelgood. Southend always had a strong teddy-boy element to do with the seafront and the Kursaal, a place inside the fairground. There were a fair amount of rockabilly types."

Hogg was also a regular at Gary Turner's Saturday night Glamour Club at Croc's. "It was a bit of a mecca for us," she said. "It was mainly a Southend crowd. I think Basildon people started to frequent it a bit later. It was more people like Stephen Linard. It was fantastic because people dressed in a very individual way depending on what they were interested in. I was into vintage 40s clothes. I used to go to Kensington Market and buy all these beautiful vintage clothes and then suddenly everybody started wearing this pirate stuff from Vivienne Westwood, and to me it was over then. It just became another uniform. And then you had the awful Spandau Ballet, who were just a horrendous manifestation of what was a really interesting period, and then it became a joke. Before that it was a real exciting expression of individuality."

◻-◻-◻

Tracey Rivers was another local figure who knew Dave during this period. She came from Basildon originally but had been booted out of home at 16 and since 1978 had been living in London squats with Boy George and Stephen Linard in Great Titchfield Street and then Carburton Street. They were all Blitz regulars. Rivers rhapsodised over Dave's new pal, Paul Redmond, who she dubbed the original Basildon punk. "He was very high end," she said. "In Basildon we cut our own hair and made our own earrings. I can't imagine what we must have looked like, but we thought we were cool."

Rivers recalled the punk nights at Woodlands Youth Club and the importance of Turner's club nights at Baron's. "Baron's was one of the first 'alternative' club nights in Essex," she said. "Everyone used to go to the Goldmine, but there was a group of slightly subversive people who didn't really have anywhere to go. That's why Baron's and the Cliff were so good. There was certainly nothing in Basildon. Raquel's was palm trees and glitter balls, and there was Sweeney's, which was much more upmarket – it might have been over-21s only."

Rivers, Gahan, and a few other members of the Basildon crowd also started to frequent Studio 21 on London's Tottenham Court Road. "Studio 21 was for Blitz rejects," she laughed, "but I used to go there, Dave used to go there, his mate Paul Valentine, Doug White; Stewart and Laurence, who used to drive for Depeche Mode in the early days. Paul Valentine was another dude – he was the first boy I knew who had a mohair jumper, and he also looked like Johnny Rotten, a dead ringer. Pete Burns used to go to Studio 21. That scene was very cliquey, it was all about who was in and who was out; what club you went to gave you your status and kudos.

"When he started the Blitz, Steve Strange was only 19, but we thought he was so old. Gary Numan was seen as so naff – 'Are Friends Electric?' is absolutely genius but you couldn't say that at the time. David Bowie was so hip and that's what you were into. There were a lot of leather boys at the Cliff, and at Blitz too. It was seen as a kind of androgynous thing, it was totally asexual. It was different and refreshing.

"Before that you'd go to Raquel's and it was about the girls dancing around their handbags. The boys used to stand in the corner, and you might get chatted up. In Basildon a lot of my friends got beaten up for being gay – even if some of them weren't – just because they had mohair jumpers on. It was quite aggressive. The burger van is where you always got beaten up. I remember Dave Gahan so admired Sid Vicious – he had the look, the leather jacket. He came out of the Bullseye and he went: I think I'm hungry. And everyone went: Dave's hungry, quick, let's go and buy him a burger. Dicing with death to get Dave to eat something. He was incredibly thin at one point, but it was all part of the look. That leather-boy look was Dave's look, a kind of fallout from his love of Sid Vicious and Joe Strummer. He was also hanging around with the soul boys but he was always slightly more subversive – he had something like a look. Dave had a pair of silver Bowie trousers that were really cool. The high-waisted pleat trousers – it was almost an extension of that soul-boy look but taken to extreme."

Rivers also remembered this small crew – including Gahan – appearing as extras in the film *Breaking Glass*. "Me, Dave, and our friend Phil Gurry did a crowd scene at the Rainbow in London, the end crowd scene of *Breaking Glass*," she recalled. "Philip Salon, George, Marilyn, Princess Julia – all those people were there. They scoured all the electro punk clubs and said: would you like to be an extra in the movie? It brought together people from Blitz, Studio 21, and the Cliff, all in one place. I think that's where a lot of people merged, because they went to all those clubs when they were scouting for extras in the movie."

Deb Danahay, Vince Clarke's future girlfriend, went to the same school as Dave and was in the year above him at Southend Tech. Her parents, like Martin Gore's, had moved to Basildon from Dagenham. "Barstable School had been a grammar school," she told me. "It was a very good school then. The head teacher used to wear a cape and we all used to whisper 'Batman' under our breath. Back then it was probably the best school in Basildon.

"Dave lived in Fryerns," she continued. "He should have gone to Fryerns but he crossed the road to go to Barstable. The thing is, nobody had any money. All the people I knew, their parents came and had council houses; your dad went to work, your mum stayed at home. My dad was a self-employed carpenter, very frugal. In terms of Dave being poor, that's how it was for everyone. We used to go out and nurse one beer all night. We all had Saturday jobs."

Deb was 'pubbing it' at 14 and 15, part of the soul-boy crowd – an original 'soul girl'. She was a regular at The Goldmine and the Lacy Lady, and at the Caister soul weekenders. "I knew Dave before he got together with Depeche," she said. "He was a year below me in school. The Sherwood Bar in the Bullseye was where Dave and his group of friends, very macho lads, would drink. I actually went out with the brother of Dave's best pal, Mark Longmuir. The Sherwood bar was sort of the trendy place and then when I went into being an electro it was the Highway. There were so many people in different cliques up there. Dave was in the it-crowd." Danahay quickly found her way onto the emerging electro scene. "Baron's was brilliant," she recalled. "It was here that I first heard Fad Gadget's 'The Box' [the B-side to his Mute Records debut single 'Back To Nature'] and that just blew my mind."

Danahay's best pal was a girl called Nikki Avery, from Nicholas, who was in the same year as Fletch and Martin. Her parents were also from Dagenham; her dad worked for Fords.

"Dave lived about a five minute walk away," she recalled. "He lived on one side of Whitmore Way and I lived on the other side. I was in the same A-level politics class as Fletcher. There were only four of us. He was A-stream, same as Martin. I didn't really know them until I went into the sixth form. My group of friends weren't their group of friends, probably because they were involved in the church. I remember Martin and Phil playing in the sixth form, but you didn't really think anything of it. These things didn't seem significant at the time. I remember sitting in the common room doing my homework when Alison [Moyet] started, and she used to be playing her guitar.

"Deb and I started our going-out days, going to places like the Goldmine. We were in a crowd of girls and that's what we did, and then Deb and I drifted away from that and got more into other music. I think we got disillusioned, or we wanted something more than the soul-boy/soul-girl scene offered. I knew Dave outside of school around the same time I got to know Martin and Andy at school. He was definitely part of that crowd going to the Goldmine, the soul weekenders at Caisters, the Lacy Lady."

Avery and Danahay flitted between the scenes. They knew the punks, the soul boys, and the electro boys; they were always at Woodlands Youth Club gigs or drinking at the Highway. They were among the few Basildon kids to frequent Turner's nights at the Cliff and part of the crowd that went down to Rayleigh for the early Glamour Nights at Croc's.

"We were all in a very different situation, growing up in Basildon," Avery recalled. "When we became teenagers it really had no history. We had no rulebook. No one had really done anything before; we had no famous people or anything. You can walk around most big cities or towns and there might have been a writer or a painter, but Basildon wasn't like that because it was new. The year Margaret Thatcher got in was the year we were taking our A-levels. Basildon had always been very left wing and for the first time there was a massive swing over to the right. It deeply affected Basildon.

"When we left school, there were no jobs for us in Basildon, so we all worked in London," she continued. "That's why we could explore London. We didn't think anything of coming home from work, getting changed, and getting back on the train. I would get home from work at 6 o'clock and be back on the 7:30 train. We'd meet at the station to get back on the train to go to London. The last train home was at quarter past eleven, so we were always running to get it.

"Every morning there would be loads of us catching the early morning train to work, about quarter past eight. Most of us started work at nine. You would get to the station in the morning and get on the train with eight or nine other people you knew. Basildon was such a commuter town. The city was just there and you just went and did it. The money was pretty good and you had this season ticket on the train – that was a lifeline for most of us. It saved us a fortune."

# CHAPTER 5
# COMPOSITION OF SOUND

I n June 1979, a month short of turning 19, Vince Clarke formed a band with former Norman & The Worms drummer Pete Hobbs and Vandals guitarist Sue Paget. He called the band No Romance In China.

"Vince changed," Hobbs told me. "Although he wasn't into the punk thing at the time, I remember when he turned because he actually went to a punk festival in Chelmsford. He had his hair all chopped off and it went all curly – he had a blonde Afro. He got this leather jacket and he had these winkle-picker shoes and he just completely changed."

Vince quit the Christian circuit he'd been playing with his former band, Nathan, and appeared to have left the church behind entirely. He'd also finished at Basildon Further Education College and was working his way through a variety of jobs on the industrial estates at companies such as Kodak and Yardley – the usual. His family life was still unsettled and he seemed always to be moving out of home and back in again.

"He was very much into The Cure," Hobbs continued. "No Romance In China was like a cross between The Police and The Cure. It was different to the folky stuff he'd been into: Simon & Garfunkel and all that gospel, folky acoustic stuff."

According to Hobbs, the No Romance In China set would comprise just three or four songs, including 'Tuesday', which ended up on the first Yazoo album, *Upstairs At Eric's*, and 'Television Set', which was written by Jason Knott from Hobbs's first band, The Neatelllls. There had until now been much mystery over who wrote 'Television Set', a song Depeche Mode would later open their live sets with. It became a fan favourite but was never recorded. "I think Vince dropped it because he realised he might have to pay Jason royalties," Hobbs laughed.

No Romance In China played the Double Six pub in Basildon and picked up a small following. Malcolm Leigh, who worked at the same factory in Basildon as Hobbs and would later marry Alison Moyet, was a fan; so too was Andy Fletcher, who would regularly watch the band rehearse at Woodlands Youth Club. Fletcher would later claim to have played in No Romance In China – a fact disputed by Hobbs and Sue Paget.

"What can you say?" Hobbs said. "Good luck to him – I don't know what he remembers. He might have picked a guitar up once but he didn't play, never did. It was just the three of us: Vince, Sue, and me. I was a mate of Fletch; even though he supported Chelsea, we'd go see West Ham together."

After The Vandals fizzled out, Sue Paget had played in another shortlived Basildon punk band, Hitler's Pyjamas, with Rik Wheatley, until Vince came knocking. "I was very surprised when he turned up at my door on a Sunday afternoon because I'd seen him in the church preaching, singing with a guitar, and that's the only thing I knew about him," she told me. "He used to hang around trying to press 'Jesus Loves You' badges onto people. He was a very active Christian.

"Then one Sunday afternoon he turned up at my door – I didn't even know how he knew where I lived or anything about me really. He and Pete came to my door and asked if I'd go and rehearse with them at Woodlands. So I went along, but I was very wary because I only knew of Vincent as a real dedicated Christian and I wasn't like that. And I didn't know Peter at all.

"I thought he was going to sing gospel-type things – after the evening had finished and they said we'd really like you to join our band, I said: I thought you were all into God and everything. I can't remember his actual words but I think he said: we don't believe in God anymore. Something along those lines. I don't know if he had a complete transformation within himself or whether he was still very religious and he was hiding it under the surface. It just seemed like overnight he changed from one person to another person."

No Romance In China had a short but eventful lifespan. "We only played one, possibly two gigs," Paget recalled. "It was a guitar, bass, drums setup. We were a really good band, actually. Vincent and I would hang around in each other's bedrooms rehearsing constantly and Pete used to come along when we went out to Woodlands to rehearse. It was the first band I'd been in that had proper coherent songs … it was very much like The Cure. Vincent was obsessed with the first Cure album [*Three Imaginary Boys*] and used to sneak it out of my room sometimes. He didn't have any records of his own so he used to nick that one. It would go missing out of my room and I'd find it in his room. And he pretty much modelled himself on the Robert Smith sound.

"I've got a tape of one of our rehearsals in his room. Apart from 'Television Set', the other songs are all named after days of the week. I think he gave them the name of whatever day he had written them on. So we had 'Tuesday', 'Wednesday', 'Thursday', 'Friday', and '2nd Tuesday'. The song 'Tuesday' that appears on the first Yazoo album was actually called 'Thursday' when we played it. There's an amusing moment on the tape where we had a bit of a laugh with a violin and snare drum, basically making a terrible racket, and you can hear his mum screaming 'Vincent!' from downstairs."

Vince may have had more than music on his mind when he recruited Sue to play bass in his new band. "All the boys had a thing for Sue," Kim Forey told me. "It was a chemistry to behold. She could get them to do anything. Not in a nasty way. She had a charisma, and girl players as attractive as her were few and far between. One time she had a boyfriend in Southampton and she got Vince to drive us there in his car. I'm not even sure it was his car. I don't think he even had a licence at that point. We drove on the M3 and he made me hold the windscreen all the way there because he was a bit worried about a stone hitting the windscreen and cracking it. We did 50mph all the way on the motorway to Southampton from Basildon on a Friday night. When we got there we had to sleep on the floor. We never saw Sue, so Vince and me hung out for the weekend."

Vince moved into Peter Hobbs's one-bedroom flat in Pitsea on a new-build estate called Felmores. Rob Marlow moved in as well shortly afterward, and the friendship between Vince and Rob, which had cooled during the Basildon punk year of 1978, was rekindled. It was a wild time: people moved in and out; drugs were commonplace.

"I went away for a couple of months and when I came back Vince was just there, he'd moved in," Hobbs recalled. "Then Rob moved in and for a while Vince and Rob were inseparable. They were like brothers. It was a love-hate thing between them. Rob was the better musician, in my opinion. He always was. Brilliant pianist. He used to play the piano at the church. They loved each other but they'd fall out – there was a lot of up and down with them. One minute they were best friends, the next minute they weren't talking."

"Vince and I diverged for a little bit," Marlow recalled. "Up until the punk thing we'd been inseparable really. Best mates. I remember Vince sort of changed when he went to the Chelmsford Punk Festival. I didn't go. I think he saw someone like Stiff Little Fingers, The Vibrators – that sort of thing. Then he cut his hair and got with the programme a little bit, really."

According to Hobbs, Vince had been deeply affected by his parents' split. "He was very moody," Hobbs said. "He was either up or really down. You'd ask what the matter was but he wouldn't talk. Rob and I would look at each other and laugh. Vince would walk in and he wouldn't say anything and it'd be like: oh dear. He had a step-dad and I don't think they got on well. I remember one Christmas he'd been round there and he brought back this Christmas present and he stuck it in the drawer because he wasn't talking to them and he didn't open it until February. He was a bit of a strange one sometimes."

Marlow recalled Vince having "various arguments" with both parents. "His real dad lived on the Craylands estate," he said. "I think Vince lived with him for a little while, then he moved back with his mum and that didn't work out. The Craylands estate was recently up in a European study as one of the most deprived areas in Europe. It's pretty notorious. It was pretty much at one point a no-go area."

Rob had done his first year of A-levels at Nicholas, dropped out, and moved to live on his own in Southend while doing a drama course at Southend Tech. He bought his clothes at Nasty's and hung around in the refectory with Alison Moyet, who was doing a piano-tuning course, and Dave Gahan, who was doing window dressing. Then he got kicked off of the course and moved back to Basildon.

"Pete's flat was a bedsit right up at the back end of beyond, you couldn't get to anywhere from there," Marlow recalled. "They hadn't built shops; it was just an estate, you had to catch a bus to go anywhere. There was about four or five of us in this place. It just had the one room, a bathroom, and a little kitchen. For about two years I slept on the sofa. We used to give Pete rent when we could. We used to live on chapattis – flour and water concoctions and all that."

▭▬▭

No Romance In China lasted about as long as most of Vince's jobs. "One of his jobs was working for the payroll at Fenchurch Street station in London," Marlow recalled. "He walked out of that and went missing. A policeman even turned up on the door asking if we'd seen him. Apparently someone had pissed him off at work and he'd walked home. Another time he worked for a delivery factory and he turned up and said: I've packed it in, I've crashed a vehicle, that's it. I don't have to do it and I'm not going to – whereas most of us go: oh well, it's a job, we have to keep it."

Another job came via Vince's old mate Andy Fletcher. "Fletcher's dad worked for a cleaning company at Southend Airport, and he got me and Vince a job," Marlow recalled. "Vince's job was terrible. All these propeller planes used to come in – huge, bulbous-nosed planes with four propellers – and they carried cars on them to the continent. Vince would drive his car onto the plane and collect the chemical toilets, basically. He had this estate car – he drove illegally, he only had a provisional licence. He'd drive in, collect them, and have to empty and clean out these things. He's different to me. I wouldn't go near that with a barge pole."

Marlow had explored the electronic scene while he was at Southend Tech and was now something of a Gary Numan clone. "Up in Southend I'd mixed with the Gary Turner contingent," he recalled. "They had more money, so they were better dressed. In Basildon we would still be a bit DIY, whereas they were buying Vivienne Westwood. I used to go to Baron's in Leigh-on-Sea. We'd hear stuff like The Normal, Fad Gadget, and OMD at Baron's. At the Cliff we all started taking speed.

"Vince didn't go out a lot. I think he came a couple of times with me to Baron's. I'm not sure about that even. We did go and see Ultravox with

110

John Foxx. I loved their *Systems Of Romance* album but Vince hated them. Kraftwerk and Giorgio Moroder stuff such as Donna Summer's 'I Feel Love' – that was kind of the spirit of the age. The John Foxx album that came out, *Metamatic* – that blew everyone's mind. Vince loved that."

Back in Basildon, Marlow was something of a scene-maker. He remained loyal to his old crowd, including Andy Fletcher, who was still part of the Youth Fellowship. "Fletch had no sense of cool," Marlow recalled. "He had no side to him. He would say what was on his mind. We went up to see The Damned at the Electric Ballroom, and he went up wearing this British Rail coat from Oxfam. There were a couple of cool punk girls from Basildon on the bus, and all of a sudden Fletch burst into talking about how it was good at Fellowship the other night. I'm sitting there cringing. When we got to the gig it was full of skinheads, and by that time I was sporting my bleached-blonde hair and eyeliner and I thought: I'm going to get my head kicked in. He was looking around like: what's the matter? He wasn't intimidated by anyone."

By now, Marlow, Clarke, Fletcher, and Gore were all regulars at the Arts Centre. "That was the pub of choice because it was a bit artistic, a bit bohemian," Marlow recalled. "We were a bit pussy, really. I like to think we were a bit more sensitive. We were quite happy to sit down the pub and talk about albums. Girls figured, too, but it wasn't going out on a Friday night and pulling. You'd have to be careful in Basildon, looking the way we did. We were wearing make-up. You kind of went around together and went to the places that were safe."

After No Romance In China came to end, Vince and Rob formed a band called The Plan with Perry Bamonte and Paul Langwith from Basildon punk outfit The Spurts. "The Plan were like an Ultravox rip-off," Marlow told me. "Guitar, drums, bass, and making funny noises with a synth. Vince played electric guitar. I played keyboards. Perry played bass."

Paul Langwith was just 17. He was part of a small contingent of Rayleigh punks who had discovered the Van Gogh – "the mecca for punks in the area" – and got in with the Basildon crew. The Spurts had been active on the Woodlands/Van Gogh punk scene. Langwith's parents had an old bungalow in Rayleigh on an industrial unit that had once been a POW camp. When they moved out, Paul carried on renting it. It became a notorious hangout for the Basildon punks. "It was just sex, drugs, and rock'n'roll," he laughed. "That became our weekend party place. Everybody headed down to Rayleigh and 'the Bungalow'. It was like a big family. I played with The Spurts but I would jump up and play with The Vandals. We would support each other."

Langwith already knew Marlow as The Vandals' guitarist. He remembered Vince playing keyboards, not guitar, in The Plan. "We were all into the electro-pop scene, bands like Kraftwerk; we wanted to form an Ultravox/Kraftwerk kind of a band," he recalled. "When I had the Bungalow, I also had a rehearsal room of my own on this industrial estate. All the equipment was set up 24/7 so we used to just go up there day or night and rehearse.

"The Plan was supposed to be a serious thing. Vince was the most serious and the rest of us saw it as a bit of a laugh – any excuse to jump on the instruments and have a bash around. We had a cassette recorder in the middle of the room. We actually made quite a few good recordings like that. We had some really good tracks. There was one track we did called 'The Day They Shot The President Down' – Vince was on keyboards and I think Rob had his guitar and keyboards.

"Vince was the same as Alison Moyet: you could tell Alison was a cut above everybody else with her vocals and presence. It was the same with Vince. You could tell he was going places, and that we weren't going to go along with him. Perry and I were happy to get rat-arsed and have a jolly-up. We'd come from a three-chord thrash-punk band, then all of a sudden we were playing electro-pop songs that were very well structured, organised. Vince was writing all the songs for The Plan. They were very good songs; you could see where he was going with the music. They were so catchy, so poppy. If you'd taken them to a producer you could have had hits with them.

"For Vince music was a way out of his dead end job. He was a grafter – all the equipment that he had, he worked bloody damn hard to get it. He had that single-mindedness. Vince was a little bit older than us and he'd grown up a lot more than we had, got off his arse and decided if you want something in life you've got to do it yourself – financially and musically. He'd already had this vision. He knew what he wanted."

The Plan hung out and took in the new music scene. "We used to go out in Rob's mum's car up to London with Vince sitting beside Rob as his mentor," Langwith recalled. "We would go to these clubs and crazy places with Rob driving and Vince telling him what to do. We would go over to Vince's and he would play albums, things like the early Human League stuff and Kraftwerk, and we were trying to find places where you could listen to that sort of music and meet likeminded people. Just four guys, none of us had any ties to women, just going out and having a good time. Fletcher was a good mate of Vince's so he used to tag along to rehearsals of The Plan. He used to come up to London with us to the Music Machine in Camden."

The Plan were due to make their live debut at Gary Turner's electro night, Baron's, in Leigh-on-Sea. "It was a bit of a fickle crowd," Langwith recalled. "Sometimes it was so full people were falling out of the doors; other times there'd be about a dozen of you rattling around. Anyway, we were going to do this gig – I think we'd even hired dry ice machines, strobe lights; it was going to be a real event. But I think somebody got bottled the week before and they closed the club down. That was the demise of the band, because we'd all put our hands in our pockets to hire equipment and things. We didn't get the money back, and we'd sort of blown all our enthusiasm at that one gig. And I think Vince had seen through us in the end. He knew what he wanted to do wasn't going to be with Perry and me."

There were all sorts of recriminations after The Plan went kaput, and Vince and Rob had their usual falling-out. "Everyone got the idea we were going to go grape-picking – go travel and do something," Marlow recalled. "Of course, no one did. We pissed it up down the pub. That's when Vince was harbouring his secret plan for world domination."

Both Rob and Vince wanted to form new bands, and they both wanted to feature synthesizers. Rob had one; Vince didn't. But they both knew someone else in Basildon who did.

▱▰▱

Martin Gore had left St Nicholas Comprehensive in the summer of 1979 and got himself a job working for NatWest bank on Fenchurch Street in the City of London. He used his wages to buy a Yamaha synth, which he was keen to put to use, accepting offers to join two new bands: Rob Marlow's

French Look Mk II and Vince Clarke's Composition Of Sound. (Gore had also played guitar in the shortlived French Look Mk I, and appeared with them at Focus Youth Centre in Southend.)

Composition Of Sound also featured Vince's best pal, Andy Fletcher, who had left Nicholas after taking his A-levels and was, like Gore, working in London, at Sun Life Insurance over the river in Borough. Vince, Martin, and Fletch started to rehearse together in each other's front rooms and in what was effectively a prototype Depeche Mode.

Vince and Rob were still living at Peter Hobbs's place in Pitsea. "Martin was very into The Human League," Hobbs recalled. "I went round to his house once and he had all the electronic stuff. They were all getting into the electronic stuff and I was more into Led Zep. I didn't mind The Human League but I couldn't get into some of the other stuff. Rob used to play it all the time and it'd drive me up the wall. And they'd all dress up and I'd be in my jeans and sweatshirt, completely different – it was like I was in a different era. They were moving in a different direction.

"Once Vince got into keyboards and then started off with Martin, there was a bit of jealousy, rivalry between him and Rob," Hobbs continued. "Fletch couldn't play, and from my point of view it was really weird because you've got Rob with all this talent, but who Vince didn't want in the band, yet Fletch who couldn't even play a guitar was in the band. But Fletch was such a character – I think his character pulled him into that. I think with the way Vince and Martin were, very shy people, you needed that. Fletcher made them laugh. He just bound them together in the sense of personality rather than musical talent. You needed someone like that, whereas I think if Rob had been in there, lot of egos flying around ... they didn't need that."

Martin's school friend Mark Crick was also on hand as the early Composition Of Sound began to gel. "The place we'd always go for a drink, pretty standard on a Friday night, was the Arts Centre bar," he recalled. "It was quite a big thing. They had these big tables with benches either side – you could sit about 12 of you there, and there'd always be Vince Clarke – Vince Martin, as he was – maybe Alison Moyet's brother Clifford, Rob Marlow, Gail Forey, maybe Jane Forey, Andy Fletcher, me, and Martin – there was always this regular crowd there. And on the other tables would be many of our teachers from Nicholas, funnily enough.

"Fletch was the most outgoing by far. He still is larger than life. Always makes me laugh. We had dinner over Christmas this past year, about 16 of us, and Fletch would be the one who quite happily speaks to someone at the far end of the table, whereas Vince and Martin – I don't imagine them doing that at all. Fletch is a larger-than-life character, lives up to his red hair, sociable bloke. He's perhaps the most ordinary of them all, but at the same time also the most extraordinary; he's got an eccentric side to him."

Another place they would all go was the local bowling alley. "There was a jukebox which would always be playing 'Albatross' by Fleetwood Mac," Crick recalled. "It was a popular place to go for a date because from the age of 15 you could probably get served. I remember Martin and I going on a double date there one time."

Crick got close to Vince after setting up a photography dark room in Vince's mum's garage in Mynchens. "I think there was a period of about a year when I was very close to Vince, I probably saw more of him than anybody else," he told me. "Vince had two records in his collection at that point: the Buggles album and *Bridge Over Trouble Water*. He loaned the garage to me. Before that I had my dark room in a garden shed.

"Vince was experimenting a lot with music. He had a reclusive side to him as well. He started doing some songwriting with a guy who came up from Godalming in Surrey. I remember this guy writing a song that was called 'Godalming'. Vince was always working on something."

After The Plan split Vince quickly cut a demo tape on his own, possibly including a song he wrote called 'Let's Get Together'. "He didn't really like to sing himself," Crick recalled. "He would even ask me: can you come and do the voice on this? I'd say well, have you got any lyrics? And he'd say: no, no lyrics, can you just use … and he'd have four key words. He'd say: can you just use those four words and improvise … and with a bit of a German accent? Both Martin and Vince had that ability. I'd go along, and not thinking of myself as musical, I'd follow the instructions – and I'd participate in making a piece of music with them.

"I remember very early on the three of us – Martin, Vince, and I – going on holiday camping. It was a complete disaster. I don't think we could find anywhere to camp. Three guys with two guitars, no campsite would have us. We were around Clacton, Holland-on-Sea. I think we'd made a big deal of setting off the night before in the Arts Centre. At some point on that trip, we'd eventually climbed over a fence and put our tent up in a field in the dark only to find the following morning we were on a school field – school children coming to school around us. We then abandoned the trip and came home, but we didn't want anyone to see us, because we didn't want people to know we'd given up so quickly. We did a series of photos around Basildon pretending we were camping. Vince could be very playful, and again – like Martin – had lots of creative energy around him. Martin and Vince weren't so interested in going out to clubs. They're very creative, and they were happy just to sit at home and create their stuff."

Crick was around to see the first tentative steps of Vince's new band. "When Composition Of Sound started I remember them playing in Martin's front room," he recalled. "There'd have been a small crowd watch: me, Fletch's pal Rob Andrews; Martin's sisters, Martin's mum."

Martin's girlfriend, Anne Swindell, who was still a member of the Youth Fellowship, also recalled this early period of Composition Of Sound. "Vince went through a bit of a weird time when he was coming away from the church," she told me. "He had a few bizarre episodes when we went on various holidays with the Youth Fellowship. Vince dropped away before Fletch – he dropped away quite dramatically, really. He turned his back on it and then he was gone. Fletcher was in it for a bit longer.

"In the beginning, with Composition Of Sound, Vince would make them keep working on something until it was perfect. I watched a lot of the creative process. Martin would make recordings in the bedroom. He'd be fiddling around just recording bits. We used to have lots of recordings of him on cassette tape just plinking around on the little keyboard and guitar, trying things out.

"I've got some photos of one the first Composition Of Sound gigs in Fletcher's front room, with Vince singing," Anne continued. "It was more for rehearsal really – to get a sense of what it would be like to be lined up and feeling like there was an audience. Vince was absolutely determined, totally driven. This is what he wanted to do with his life. Vince once walked to Southend to just look at a guitar before he saved up for it, just to make sure it was still there. He was completely committed that this was what he wanted to do with his life. He worked all sorts of crazy jobs to get enough money to buy equipment and be able to do this. That's what he wanted more than anything: he just wanted to be able to make music.

"Vince would have been quite controlling over the music. He did have a vision. The others were a bit more … it was all a bit of a laugh and a bit of fun. Vince knew that Martin was incredibly talented but I don't think Martin knew really how talented he was. He didn't have the same drive as Vince. He loved music and he loved doing music but I don't think he realised just how capable he was. He wouldn't challenge Vince much at the time. I think it was still Vince's thing and Martin would go along with that."

Sadly, although they would undoubtedly have been taped, none of these front-room gigs have ever surfaced. The earliest verifiable recording from this period is by Rob Marlow's band, French Look, featuring Martin on backing vocals and guitar: an accomplished, gloomy, and almost acoustic version of a song called 'Will The New Baby Grow'.

As well as Gore, Marlow had recruited the infamous Paul Redmond for French Look. "Once The Plan ended and Vince started up Composition Of Sound, I thought: I'm not going to leave it," Marlow recalled. "So I recruited the cool man about town, Paul Redmond – he was the ace face."

Basildon's first punk, Redmond was "two or three years above" Marlow at Nicholas. "He was tall, big, a fantastic fighter," Marlow recalled. "He was working as a brickie." Ever the trendsetter, Redmond was now firmly in the electro camp. He was a regular at London clubs such as Studio 21 and Blitz. To French Look he brought a Korg synth, a drum machine, and his new best pal: Dave Gahan.

"Dave Gahan was a mate of Paul's," Marlow recalled. "I remember Paul having all his gear in this kind of trunk – he used to carry it on his shoulder, like a hod-carrier. He used to march along. He was very tall. Dave was our sound engineer. I say sound engineer – he twiddled the knobs, turned the volume up and down.

"Vince spotted Dave's potential almost immediately. We used to rehearse up at Woodlands school, and Composition Of Sound had the classroom next door. They used to rent out the classrooms to rehearse in. The caretaker would let you in and you set up. Dave was with Paul Redmond one time and he got on the mike and was singing '"Heroes"'. It turned out he could hold a tune. Of course, I should have asked him to sing in French Look, but ego being what it is, there was no chance.

"Dave knew people; he was more gregarious than we were," Marlow continued. "If I was being cruel I'd say he was a Basildon beer boy – bit of a soul boy. He wasn't particularly part of our set. He was seeing Jo, who I'd first seen on the back of the bus going to Chancellor Hall in the punk days. She lived in Billericay. She used to knock around with Fran, who was seeing Paul Redmond. Paul had a Korg MS10 synth. He couldn't play it. My mum had bought me a Korg 700 on HP [hire purchase, or credit]. I only used it with one sound. Martin didn't bring any songs to French Look but he was great at adding things to it, little lines. He was getting quite accomplished on the keyboards and he had a consummate ear for pop music.

"Composition Of Sound were playing gigs in people's front rooms – each other's front rooms, basically. I seem to remember a memorable Composition Of Sound gig where the audience was made up of Martin's sisters' teddy bears. There'd be people like Anne, Denise [Jekyll], Steve Burton, and Rob Andrews there. We would come round and join the teddy bears. Fletch played a bass guitar, Vince played guitar, and Martin played the Yamaha CS synth he'd bought. They were a bit like the early Cure: all the songs were in place, the ones in the early Depeche Mode set."

By now, Vince and Rob had made up, and the rivalry between the two bands was friendly. At the same time, Alison Moyet was also putting her various post-Vandals bands – including The Screamin' Ab Dabs and The Vicars – through their paces at Woodlands school, in the classrooms that had once hosted The Vermin. "We'd be in opposite rooms," she recalled. She could see the logic that the sound of Vince's new band was inspired by (and seemed to match) the futuristic New Town environment, and saw the link between the social context of Basildon, which was in the vanguard of a new sense of aspiration among the working classes, and the band. She just didn't agree with it.

"When that Composition Of Sound first came up and the New Romantics first happened, there was this prettiness going on that I didn't get at all," she said. "There was something about the cleanliness of the sound that was odd. We were living in this New Town where no one had anything, and we celebrated having nothing. To see these young lads together – so clean-cut, thoughtfully dressed, with all their equipment – was just alien. Everything we had before had been things we'd made or purloined, or stolen or regenerated. Here were people who were starting to accumulate, and that was odd. The New Town was built, everything was fixed, nothing needed to be done up. In my mind you didn't have to build on it or aspire to build a new wall because it was already new. You had this thing made and it was there for you to play with; you didn't need to aspire beyond it because you had it."

Both French Look and Composition Of Sound made their live debut at the same event: a party for Deb Danahay at the Paddock, a community centre in Basildon, on May 30 1980. "The Paddock party was a bit of a surprise do," Danahay's best pal, Nikki Avery, told me. "I think Rob rang me up, because Rob was going to be playing, and said: can Vince and his band play as well? I said yeah, why not. Let's go for it. Probably if half a dozen bands had rung up, we'd have said yeah, all right, play. We just loved live bands.

"I'd seen Composition Of Sound play at Martin's house. They would play in each other's front rooms on a Sunday afternoon or something. It was like that. I did always think Vince had something. I don't know if it was Vince's charisma – which is a strange word to use for Vince because he's so quiet, but there was always something interesting about him. The other thing with Vince was he did seem to take it all so very seriously. That with his dogged determination drove him on. In a very quiet and subtle way, I think his determination was always evident.

"There were really not many places that would have bands playing, so people were always putting on parties," Avery continued. "That's what they were really: parties with a band playing. It was a case of if there was a reason to do it and we could get enough people, sell enough tickets to pay for the night, it was somewhere to go. Even if it wasn't bands, at least it was music we wanted to listen to. We weren't going to a disco where it was dominated by disco music. The Paddock thing was a full house – I got in trouble because there were too many people there."

"I was going off to work at Butlins so it was a sort of going away party,"

Danahay recalled. "Any excuse for a party." She remembered another crucial detail relating to that night at the Paddock: Vince asking Dave to join Composition Of Sound prior to the gig.

"We were at a house party somewhere, way before the gig," she told me. "Dave walked me home from there, purely as a friend. He came in and we had a coffee, we were chatting about everything. He said to me: I've been asked by Vince to join his band and be the singer. He said: I don't know what to do, I don't know whether I should do it or not. I can still see us sitting at my parent's kitchen table and me saying yeah, you should do it, it'll be a laugh – never dreaming what it would become, just imagining it'd be a five minute wonder, a good laugh around Basildon."

Vince had spotted Gahan's potential: not particularly as a singer, but more as someone who knew people in Southend and London. French Look were the headline act at the Paddock. "I think me and Vince made an arrangement where if we headlined at Deb's do they could headline at the Nicholas gig, which was a couple of weeks away," Marlow recalled. "Composition Of Sound had morphed into becoming more electronic. I think they had a drummer at one point. French Look, I would say, were ahead of Composition Of Sound by the time we came head to head at this thing at the Paddock.

"I think there was some kind of trouble with Paul Redmond at the gig. He was very into his personal image and I might have said something wrong there. There'd been some sort of tussle over Martin – both Vince and I wanted Martin to make a commitment to our bands. The sound of both bands was similar, but they were much more organised, in terms of arrangements. Vince was ... I hate to use the phrase 'control freak' but he had an idea of what he wanted it to sound like."

At the Paddock gig, Composition Of Sound was still Vince and Martin on keyboards, Fletch on bass guitar, and a drum machine. They played a version of 'Then I Kissed Her', the Phil Spector classic as reworded by The Beach Boys. French Look, with Gore, played for an hour. They played a couple of Rob's songs – 'Face Of Dorian Gray' and 'No Heart' – as well as an Ultravox cover and a version of the Sparks track 'Amateur Hour'.

Between then and the gig at Nicholas School on June 14 1980 – Dave Gahan's debut – Composition Of Sound played two gigs. The first was at Scamps in Southend, supporting The School Bullies, which was Perry Bamonte and Paul Langwith's new band. "They didn't go down particularly well but they were brilliant," Langwith told me. "We were loving the style of music but not everyone was into their thing. I remember they did an absolutely fantastic version of 'The Price Of Love', the Everly Brothers song."

The reception wasn't great, however. "A few of the punk/new wave crowd came to see the Bullies and they didn't appreciate what Composition Of Sound were doing," Langwith recalled. "But they were so fantastic: they were miles ahead of anything else. We were just playing for the fun of it, but you could tell from that moment that Composition Of Sound were really going to be something. Vince was taking a real serious note of it all. At that gig Dave was there just to help them lug their gear around."

Composition Of Sound played their final gig as a three-piece at the Woodlands Youth Club. They would have been a four-piece but Gore's girlfriend, Anne Swindell, freaked out before hitting the stage. "I was supposed to be playing saxophone on 'Tora! Tora! Tora!'" she recalled. "I'd been practising and practising and practising, and then we turned up for rehearsal at the school and Paul Redmond was there and Dave Gahan was there, and it completely flummoxed me: oh my God, I don't know these people and they're totally good looking and everybody knows them, they're really 'in' in Basildon! They were very sweet and I still did the rehearsal and everything, but when it came to the gig I couldn't do it. I couldn't go on stage.

"Dave had a lot of friends. Martin, Vince, and Andy were very … well, Andy was very outgoing, but Martin and Vince weren't really so outgoing. They were music boffs, basically. They weren't party animals as such. Martin wasn't really into clubbing at that stage. I wasn't either. It wasn't in my culture; in the early days with Martin I didn't drink at all. Dave was a much more sociable person, it seemed. He had a lot of friends, knew a lot of people. Suddenly, once Dave came along, there were a lot more people at the gigs, a lot more people to be exposed to. Dave was definitely cooler."

Fletch's pal Steve Burton was also part of the small, original Composition Of Sound crowd. "I remember the concert at Woodlands," he told me. "I used to help with the drum machine. Not being musical at all, I had to turn a knob on this machine to try and get the beat going, and I think Vince was a bit frustrated at my inability. At the time Andy was into rhythm & blues, and during that phase he went to see Graham Parker & The Rumour somewhere, I think at Hammersmith. As a gang we'd go to various concerts. We went to see The Human League at the Hammersmith Palais, this was with the slide show – and the *Travelogue* album was very important for us all. Also, I remember going to see Ultravox in Camden."

Burton remembered Gahan coming into the mix. "Dave was from the other side of town so we didn't know him from Adam," he said. "But he had something about him. You wouldn't mess with Dave. He was a different kettle of fish. It was strange, really, because those guys from the cool part of the music scene meeting us – Andy and Martin, very shy, well behaved – Dave's crowd had all the New Romantic gear, they were very much linked to the Blitz scene in London, and for us that was like: whoa – you only read about that in the newspapers."

Gahan would probably have preferred to have become the singer in French Look with his pal Paul Redmond but Marlow was having none of it. Composition Of Sound were certainly the less cool band. Their setlist included cover versions of songs such as 'The Price Of Love', 'Then I Kissed Her', 'I Like It' by Gerry & The Pacemakers, and even 'Mouldy Old Dough' by Lieutenant Pigeon. There was also the Jason Knott-penned 'Television Set' and various Clarke originals: 'Reason Man', 'Ice Machine', 'Tomorrow's Dance', and 'Ghost Of Modern Times' (also known as 'Addiction'). Gore's contributions to the set included 'Tora! Tora! Tora!' and an epic instrumental entitled 'Big Muff' – the only two songs from the original setlist to make it onto Depeche Mode's debut album.

The threesome may have seemed twee but they were far from it. "The first time I met Dave he was perhaps more considered in what he wore," Gore's pal Mark Crick recalled. "He was dressed as he still dresses now: he was incredibly slim, almost girl-like, I suppose, dressed in a black waistcoat. He had an awareness of fashion in a way the others probably didn't."

Did Dave really know what he was letting himself in for? It seemed more than coincidence that both Clarke and Gore should have emerged at the same time – and from virtually the same street – both shy and introverted but soon to develop into towering songwriters. In 1964 a ghostly crimson-gowned figure had been spotted in the 600-year-old Holy Cross Churchyard. The sightings attracted the television cameras and national newspapers. For many old Basildonians, the red-hooded ghost who haunted the crossroads at the southern end of Church Road remained a famous figure.

"Maybe they did sell their souls in return for musical talent," Crick said. "Another remarkable thing is that the band are still in touch with all those friends from that time. Martin's sister still lives next door to my sister in Basildon. His brother-in-law works at the Ford tractor plant in Basildon. Despite all their success they've kept their feet on the ground and not forgotten where they come from."

Dave Gahan's first live appearance with Composition Of Sound – the first time the four members of Depeche Mode played on stage together – was at the St Nicholas Comprehensive school gig, only two weeks after their live debut at the Paddock. They were supported by French Look, with Gore still playing in both bands.

The show had been organised by Steve Burton. "Chris Briggs had left Nicholas school and he wanted to maintain one of these old pupils associations," he told me. "I'd left the school in July 1979 and Chris wanted me to be involved with this Nicholas Old Pupils Association, NOPA. It was a little committee of about five former pupils, one of whom was Cliff Moyet, Alison Moyet's older brother, and they wanted to maintain this community, maintain the friendship. The guys said to me: oh, you're on this Nicholas old pupils thing, we'd like to play a concert. I said I'd take it to the committee.

"They played in the locker room in the school," Burton continued. "French Look played too, and I was the DJ. It was a ticket-only do, and a load of the local yobbos who couldn't get in got a load of stones and went around smashing a load of school windows. The caretaker came running in doing his nut. It was nothing to do with us – it was all the usual guys that would be out causing trouble who couldn't get in. That's the downside of

Basildon, of course. Always the bad apples who spoil it. So we were not allowed to replicate that. But that was a night, that was."

"We still talk about the Nicholas gig even now," Rob Marlow told me. "There were these spurious rumours: Vince accused me of altering all the settings for their songs, so that when they went on they were all playing funny sounds on their synths, but that isn't true. Even their synths became unplugged. There were accusations flying everywhere of skulduggery, and we had a real proper falling out. There was obviously this rivalry, but at the heart of it was this on-going thing about Martin. Martin sat on the fence. After the gig Vince and I saw each other in the street a couple of days later and we just started laughing – everything was back to normal. Vince never had a meeting with the devil at the crossroads but he did have a few dodgy things happen in underpasses."

"They'd moved the lockers and everything like that out, but it was our old cloakroom," Nikki Avery recalled. "We knew Dave was going to be doing it. It was strange, the fact that the soul-boy Dave we'd known before had moved into a whole new area. I remember when we first heard he'd joined them it seemed a bit of a strange choice, although the way he looked and everything else you could totally understand why. We didn't know if he could sing but we would still go along and support him and the band. There would never be any doubt about that."

When Gahan stepped on stage with Composition Of Sound it put them into a different world. They needed a face, and Gahan was a very cool guy: he knew the right people, he was well liked, and he looked the part. It was another very smart move by Vince: he knew what the band was lacking, so why not bring in one of the coolest guys in town?

"Dave brought that Southend crowd to the gig," Avery continued. "About 50 or 60 people. I think Dave made Composition Of Sound cool, for want of a better word. Before Dave joined they were just a bit of a geeky band."

# PART 2

# REVELATIONS

# CHAPTER 6
# FUTURISTS

A week after 18-year-old Dave Gahan made his live debut at St Nicholas Comprehensive, Composition Of Sound played at the Top Alex, the greasy Southend biker pub now hosting anything from heavy metal to new wave. Then, for the next two months, the fledgling band worked on their songs and sound.

Unemployed Vince provided the impetus, drive, and determination. He took the band to record a demo in a four-track studio in Barking, Essex, called Lower Wapping Conker Company – the same studio he'd used to record his solo material. There, using a primitive drum machine and perhaps even a bass guitar, Composition Of Sound cut Vince's 'Ice Machine' and two new songs he'd written, 'Photographic' and 'Radio News'.

Vince intended to tout the tape around London to help land gigs or even a record deal. For many years the demo was thought to be long lost, until an authentic-sounding version of the three songs surfaced in February 2011.

The structure, words, and melody of 'Ice Machine' are identical on the demo to the version that would subsequently appear on the B-side to Depeche Mode's debut single, 'Dreaming Of Me'. 'Photographic', an early live favourite, was also structurally, lyrically, and melodically complete, but the rhythm machine on the demo sounds pathetic. The band would have been better off using biscuit tins. Dave's vocals are solid enough but more hesitant, less confident than they would become. 'Radio News' was forgotten almost as soon as it was recorded, which is a shame; its simple, catchy melody sounds like the background music to an early video arcade game.

Rehearsals had to fit around Martin and Fletch's day jobs in London, and to a lesser extent Dave's college hours. "When Composition Of Sound were beginning to rehearse I used to go round to see them at Vince's mum's house," Rob Marlow told me. "She was at home all the time and Vince used to rehearse the band with their drum machine in the garage. You opened up the garage door and there'd be these four guys standing round with headphones on, clicking away."

During this period Vince was writing some of the band's most famous early songs, such as 'Dreaming Of Me' and 'New Life', and formulating a new setlist for the residency Dave had landed them at the Saturday night Glamour Club at Croc's. Composition Of Sound would play at Croc's on alternate Saturdays from August 16 1980 until the end of the year. It was here that they would first be noticed by the New Romantic crowd, at a time concurrent with Spandau Ballet's emergence at the Blitz.

Dubbed "Southend's premier freak club" by Boy George – even though it was actually in the relative backwater of Rayleigh – Gary Turner's Glamour Club attracted attention from hip London scene makers such as Blitz club founders Rusty Egan and Steve Strange, 'Futurist' DJ Stevo, and Spandau Ballet, all of whom were keen to suss it out to see if it was up to their standards. Egan was among the first to spot the potential in Composition Of Sound and was an early champion of the band. The Essex wave that had started at Turner's mobbed club at the Cliff kicked over to Croc's and became monumental. The atmosphere inside Croc's was electric; the place was packed with New Romantics, leather boys, rockabillies, skinheads, funk/soul dandies in their Kid Creole suits, two-tone fans, and mods. On some nights there would be trouble, including fights in the car park, but never when Composition Of Sound played. Even though the sound was aggressively alien, loud, and piercing, the band's non-macho stance seemed to lift rather than raise the tension.

"We knew Fletch, Martin, and Vince, but Dave was one of our mates," Gary Turner explained. "We'd be going out to all the clubs together. My crowd supported Depeche Mode at some of their early gigs – a couple of community centres they played in Basildon. We'd go down to their early band practices, first gigs at Barstable Youth Centre, whatever – those early places we'd go along and give them some support.

"It was a natural progression for them to play at Croc's. It was sort of like: if we're going to play anywhere, we're going to play on our home ground. Certainly, for Dave, Croc's was his home ground. They were perfect for the night I was putting on. That scene really started to explode from that point onward. On stage in the early days at Croc's you could tell by Dave's persona that he was enjoying it just as much as the crowd, and I think that was a big part of it. They wanted to get people dancing, not just sitting back and listening. That was the key, really."

Croc's held about 450 people but Turner had no trouble filling it. "We'd be turning people away on many nights," he told me. "We'd get lots of people coming down. On one particular night I remember a lot of the Spandau Ballet boys coming down; Steve Strange, Midge Ure, and Rusty Egan, people like that; they'd heard about us, and they'd just pop in for a drink.

"We had a good thing going. It was really buzzy. Obviously there was a lot of posing going on, lots of dressing up and people doing a whole range of things, but there was still a lot of people just enjoying a good Saturday night out and having a good dance. There was a lot of fun to be had but it was not a druggy crowd. Speed and pills wasn't the norm. It wasn't like the early Blackpool or Wigan Casino nights going on until six in the morning. Most of these things were done and dusted by two o'clock at the latest. Croc's closed at two. Alcohol was prevalent. I suspect some people would be into cannabis, but it certainly wasn't my cup of tea."

While Dave had got Composition Of Sound in with the trendy New Romantic crowd, it was Vince who landed them their first residency in London, at the Bridgehouse – a mock-Tudor pub in Canning Town, an unsavoury, distressed part of the East End – after taking a demo tape to the owner, former boxer Terry Murphy.

The Bridgehouse was an established spot on the London live circuit. Vince had taken the band's demo tape to the pub's owner, former boxer Terry Murphy. The venue had become synonymous with 'oi!' punk but Murphy had a wider musical remit, putting on anything from heavy rock to funk, blues, and psychedelia – but not yet electronic music. Nonetheless, he was impressed by Vince's bravery in presenting this music to a 'rock' pub, and he liked the name of the band.

Vince was confident that Composition Of Sound would bring a crowd with them to the Bridgehouse and Murphy took him at his word, figuring that Basildon was straight down the A13 from Canning Town. The pub was capable of holding 1,000 people, but according to Murphy only 20 showed up to Composition Of Sound's first gig, for which he paid them a fee of £15. He liked them, though – there was even talk of them signing to his Bridgehouse record label – so he decided to build them up via a series of support slots at the venue.

The first band Composition Of Sound supported at the Bridgehouse was The Comsat Angels, an arty guitar-band from Yorkshire named after a J.G. Ballard novel and signed to Polydor. Their 'Independence Day' single was highly rated, and they left enough of an impression on Martin Gore for him to record their song 'Gone' for his first solo release, an album of cover versions, in the late 80s.

After the Comsats gig, Composition Of Sound were given a regular Wednesday night slot at the Bridgehouse. Murphy was serious about signing the band; he talked about recording and publishing deals and continued to make efforts to build their live following. Murphy's son Darren played in Wasted Youth, a band that Dave and his girlfriend Jo were keen on, and who were playing venues such as the Marquee, the Lyceum, and the Rainbow. Darren would give out free tickets for Composition Of Sound gigs at The Bridgehouse.

Going to Canning Town was almost like coming home for Martin's girlfriend, Anne Swindell. It was where her mum was born. "Martin and I never went out in Basildon to clubs or pubs or anything," she recalled. "I didn't really start going out until the band started taking off and then we started going to things like Croc's. The Croc's crowd was quite wild. It was a whole new world for me. I remember Soft Cell supporting them."

Swindell was just finishing the second year of her A-levels; Martin refused to allow her to attend concerts when she was studying. Despite Gore's good intentions, Swindell didn't do very well in her exams. "I would sit at home thinking: this isn't working, because I'm still thinking about him," she said. "I'd be wondering what everyone else was up to while I was supposed to be studying. I managed to pass but not with good grades."

The band became her life. She laughed at the thought of the

"journeys up to the Bridgehouse in the van with the gear falling out of the back. At the Bridgehouse, Denise [Jekyll] and myself would dance on stage to try to encourage people. I'd be up there at the front dancing, trying to get people up".

Basildon trendies Deb Danahay and Nikki Avery were also part of the crowd of early supporters. "They never had a bad gig at Croc's," Avery recalled. "Maybe it was the places they played but it was always people who wanted to see them. Croc's would be packed out for those shows. They weren't exactly doing Northern clubs where people were saying: what the hell is this?

"The Bridgehouse always seemed very dark but it had a great atmosphere. It was quite moody and it fitted the band. By that time they had quite a good following. The Bridgehouse was never empty. Just the fact they were playing – quite a lot of people would have made the effort to go."

The band remained resolutely grounded during this early period of initial excitement. "They could be on stage one minute and they could be in the pub down the road the next," Avery recalled. "It wasn't: we're in a band now. That carried on when success came. I don't think the people around them would have tolerated any other attitude."

Deb Danahay had missed out on the very early gigs at Croc's because she'd been away working at Butlins in Clacton. "When I came back they'd started the Bridgehouse gigs," she recalled. She was impressed – particularly with Vince, who became her boyfriend.

"I met Vince up at the Highway pub," she told me. "He'd already turned away from the church. He was still respectful of the church but he was no longer practising. He never told me why he'd left and I never asked." Vince was still living with Rob Marlow at Peter Hobbs's flat in Pitsea and "never had any money"; Deb used to pay when they went out.

"Vince used to take speed for inspiration," she recalled. "If we went out to clubs, he wasn't comfortable, so he'd take speed." Beyond that, however, Danahay remembered life being relatively naive and innocent. "It wasn't sex, drugs, and rock'n'roll," she said. "Martin was with Anne, who was very vivacious, naturally sexy. Dave was going out with Jo, who was from Billericay. She was a true punk – she was squatting up in London."

130

Martin and Dave were always keen to include their girlfriends in what they were doing but Vince had a different attitude. He wasn't keen on anybody's girlfriend interfering with business – including his own. "He wasn't comfortable with me being there a lot of the time, which used to break my heart," Danahay recalled. "He was very work-orientated. It was a business. That's what he wanted, and it didn't matter if I was upset at times because that's how it was: business."

Danahay had met Vince through French Look's Rob Marlow, with whom she had also enjoyed a shortlived romance. "It was a bit of a pattern," Marlow told me. "I would go out with somebody and then later Vince would. He's very shy and wasn't very good at chatting up girls – nor was I, really."

Marlow was now resigned to losing Martin from French Look. "Composition Of Sound soared ahead of French Look," he recalled. "Croc's had all the elements. It was a dive with this poor lonely crocodile in a tank in the corner. It was dark. There was the drug culture – it was all amphetamine. You didn't know who you might see. You might get Boy George one weekend, or Rusty Egan; it was a place to go. Composition Of Sound made it even more popular, massively popular, you couldn't get in."

As the early New Romantic scene took hold, emboldened by the launch earlier in the year of a new magazine called *The Face*, bands such as Visage (founded by Blitz founder Steve Strange and Rusty Egan) and Spandau Ballet began to attract wider attention. Spandau Ballet were snapped up by Chrysalis Records and Visage landed a deal with Polydor. Both bands' debut singles charted in late 1980. There was also talk of a band from Birmingham: Duran Duran. Composition Of Sound always seemed one step removed from this scene, largely because of their Basildon roots.

"Basildon had a profound influence on the band," Marlow told me. "It was what made them different to Spandau Ballet and a hundred other bands, without a shred of a doubt. That's what sold it. That's what they were. It was the sound of Basildon in 1980. The sound of Basildon came from the bricks and the glass. We were used to the modern. Everything was modern in Basildon – and concrete; everywhere was concrete. Spandau Ballet always seemed naff, even though they had some nice tunes; they were bigger and had much more credibility with Robert Elms and *The Face*, but they were thin and reedy compared to the early Depeche sound. They were a bit corporate – same with Duran Duran. Of that slew of New Romantic bands, the Basildon boys were head and shoulders above.

"The Depeche songs were better, they reflected something," Marlow said. "The imagery in Vince's early stuff was so right for the times. The actual image – the guy in the know on that – was Dave. Ivor Craig and Stephen Linard made his clothes, and I think Jo was a bit handy with the old sewing machine." In 1981, Linard's final-year fashion collection at St Martin's School of Art, *The Reluctant Émigrés*, brought him fame overnight. He was the most influential London fashion designer of the early 80s, especially among clubbers.

"Dave had an influence on the 40s high-waisted suit thing they were into," Marlow continued. "It was very Essex – the same with the leather look. It was a pandering to a local level, sort of saying: we're with you. There was a gay element in Southend, but we didn't know anybody who was openly gay in Basildon. It was not allowed. Basildon was a very homophobic place. That leather look was a reflection of people going to gay clubs, more worldly-wise; the San Fran imagery was filtering in. Vince bought a leather cap, and at one point they were all leather boys."

As Composition Of Sound emerged from the New Town cocoon, Basildon itself was at the centre of much political and sociological debate. "At that time Basildon became known as a Little Moscow down the Thames," Marlow recalled. "We were always on the news as being the median point; whichever way Basildon voted that was the way the general election was going to. We'd had a very left-wing council and of course Basildon was sort of a socialist ideal. But following Thatcher's election, things were changing very quickly."

"They were toying with image," Nikki Avery recalled. "I always thought Dave could carry anything, really, but the others – when they started to use the leather boy look, everyone knew they were too soft. They didn't have the hardness about them. It was too strong a look for them."

"Dave inspired the look of the band," Deb Danahay told me. "The pale-coloured suits they wore at one point in the early days were made by Vince's mum, but Vince, Andy, and Martin were never ever trendy back then."

o-o-o

After five Saturday nights at Croc's and three Wednesday night gigs at the
Bridgehouse, Composition Of Sound performed their first central London
gig Upstairs at Ronnie Scott's in Soho, with Boy George watching on. This
was the night the band changed their name. Composition Of Sound was
no more: now they were Depeche Mode, a name suggested by Dave and
famously taken from the title of a French fashion magazine.

Dave's pal Tracey Rivers was at Ronnie Scott's that night. "I went with
Boy George," she told me. "I said to George: you've got to come and see
my mate Dave play. It was a tiny little room at the top of Ronnie Scott's and
there weren't many people there. I remember Dave coming over afterward
and saying: what do you think, Trace? And I said: oh, brilliant, I think
you're going to be stars. And the next minute they were … . It happened
really quickly – a big overnight success."

The following night, October 30 1980, Depeche Mode played at the
Bridgehouse. The set was recorded for posterity (and can now be found on
YouTube). They opened with a Martin Gore instrumental, 'Big Muff', and
then played 'Ice Machine', 'The Price Of Love', 'Dreaming Of Me', 'New
Life', 'Television Set', 'Tomorrow's Dance', and 'Reason Man' before
climaxing with 'Photographic'.

It was this same set that caught the attention of the owner of Mute
Records, Daniel Miller, when he saw Depeche Mode support one of his
acts, Fad Gadget, at the Bridgehouse in early November. Terry Murphy
had put Depeche Mode on the bill thinking that they would be a good fit
with the crowd coming to watch Mute's young, hip act. He remembered
Dave screaming with delight at the news. 'Back To Nature', Fad Gadget's
1979 Mute debut, was a big favourite with the Essex crowd – as was Miller's
own debut single as The Normal, 'Warm Leatherette'.

Vince and Dave had hawked the band's early demo around a bunch of
record labels in London – including Beggars Banquet, DinDisc, Stiff, and
Rough Trade, where Miller more or less worked – but with no luck. In fact,
Miller had dismissed the pair with a look and had not even bothered to
listen to the tape. But the band had developed since then, and their set
now included several new Clarke songs that were more powerful, more

instant, more pop, and right on the button of now – which in 1980 meant the future. Vince remained resolutely in charge of band affairs, having rebuffed offers of management from Dave's pal Paul Redmond and Croc's owner Anton Johnson.

Miller was wildly impressed by the show. He approached the band after their set and talked about making a single with them, vowing to return to the Bridgehouse the following week to see them again. Miller was 29. He'd started a small independent label, Mute, on the back of his own debut single in 1978, and had subsequently released music by his "imaginary teen electronic" band, The Silicon Teens. At the time of the Bridgehouse show, he was working with Fad Gadget and the controversial American musician Boyd Rice. Crucially, his heart had recently been broken by DAF, the Düsseldorf band in whom Miller had invested much time and money – but who were in the process of leaving Mute for Virgin Records.

Also in the audience on the same night as Miller – and similarly impressed with Depeche Mode – was Steve Pearce, better known as Stevo. As well as managing Leeds-based electronic act Soft Cell, he had his own Thursday night residency at the Bridgehouse, and had already seen the band at Croc's after being tipped off by Rusty Egan. He was now in a position to offer them a deal, too, so he asked whether they'd like to contribute a track to an album he was compiling for his own label, Some Bizzare, with the backing of Phonogram.

Stevo was only 17. He came from Dagenham and had started out as DJ at the Chelsea Drugstore, where he played electronic music, before landing a residency at the Clarendon in Hammersmith. He played tunes by bands such as Chrome, Throbbing Gristle, Kraftwerk, and Yellow Magic Orchestra. He also famously compiled a 'Futurist' chart for the weekly music paper *Sounds* featuring demo tapes and independent singles – all of them by electronic musicians.

Miller and Stevo knew each other well. Fad Gadget, whose real name was Frank Tovey, knew Soft Cell's Marc Almond from their time together at college in Leeds. Stevo had always been supportive of Mute acts and had had DAF, Fad Gadget, and Boyd Rice at his 'Electronic Parties' at the Clarendon. He was chasing acts such as Throbbing Gristle and Cabaret Voltaire – the godfathers of the UK electronic scene – as well as newer bands such as Classix Nouveaux and Clock DVA, and wanted Miller to contribute a track, too.

Both men saw an important distinction between New Romantic bands – basically guitar bands with a synth player – and the all-electronic Futurist bands they both championed. But with both Spandau Ballet and Visage charting, the major labels saw little distinction; they were all keen to get their hands on their own New Romantic act, be it Liverpool's OMD, Sheffield's The Human League, or Basildon's Depeche Mode. B-Movie, another of Stevo's bands, were being tipped as the next Visage. There was a new scene bubbling under, and the majors each wanted a piece.

Suddenly, Depeche Mode were hot property, and Stevo and Miller faced competition. But the band remained level-headed; with no contracts signed, they agreed for Miller to produce 'Photographic' for Stevo's *Some Bizzare* compilation. Miller cut the track in November at a London studio of Stevo's choosing, Tape One. He also produced Soft Cell's contribution to the compilation, 'Memorabilia'.

In November the band played a one-off show at Southend Tech, where they debuted 'Just Can't Get Enough' – a song Vince had written, according to Deb Danahay, "about a girl he fancied in a pub". They also reintroduced Gore's 'Tora! Tora! Tora!' to the setlist. After the Southend Tech show they returned to their regular gigging pattern of Saturdays at Croc's and Wednesdays at the Bridgehouse.

The first press report of Depeche Mode appeared in the *Basildon Evening Echo* on December 1 1980, in a 'Rock' column by Mick Walsh. Leading with news about the future plans of local Canvey Island boy done good, Dr Feelgood guitarist Wilko Johnson (who was apparently not now planning to join The Blockheads, despite guesting on Ian Dury's latest album), Walsh went on to plug DM's forthcoming gig at the Bridgehouse:

> *Electro-pop band Depeche Mode, from Basildon, headline at the Bridgehouse, Canning Town, tonight. And the gig is more than just a chance to pay off the HP instalments on their battery of synthesizers. The young foursome will be watched by a cluster of record companies after catching their eye when they supported the highly-acclaimed Fad Gadget there last week. The line-up is*

*Vincent Martin, Andrew Fletcher, Martin Gore and David Garn [sic] – all from Basildon. Said Vincent: "Some people travelled from Southend to see us with Fad Gadget and we're hoping some fans will make the journey tonight. It's probably our most important [gig] yet." The band are a regular attraction at the Saturday electronic rock nights at Croc's, Rayleigh.*

Another *Evening Echo* article from later that same month, entitled 'Posh Clobber Could Clinch It For The Mode', concluded: "They could go a long way if someone pointed them in the direction of a decent tailor." The quote later appeared, infamously, on the cover of the band's 1985 greatest hits collection, *The Singles 81–85*. It was this article, featuring a photo of the band, that prompted Clarke to change his surname: he didn't want the Inland Revenue to find out he was earning money from the band while still collecting dole money. He later said he was inspired to choose the name Clarke by another Basildon face, Paul Valentine, who had a thing for US DJ and *American Bandstand* host Dick Clark.

The buzz around the band continued to build. Stevo was an ace publicist and both he and Miller were known to be at the cutting edge of electronic music. The *Some Bizzare* album was creating major interest even as it was being compiled. RCA, Island, Phonogram, Virgin, CBS, Polydor, and London Records all showed interest in the group. The band had an agreement in principle to record their debut single for Miller and Mute, but the figures being bandied about elsewhere – as much as £200,000 in one case – couldn't help but turn the heads of a penniless band.

However, Mute was more than just a one-man operation. Miller had a powerful and persuasive ally in former pop journalist Rod Buckle. Buckle, a bearded bear of a man in his late thirties, had been in the thick of the music business since the 60s and was the co-owner of Sonet, a record distribution company based in Sweden. With Sonet, Buckle had released a string of late 60s/70s hits in Sweden and distributed a swathe of labels in Scandinavia, including Sun, Chess, Epic, Roulette, Elektra, Island, Virgin, Chrysalis, and Stiff.

"Any band or label that started to get success, I went and banged on the door and signed them up for Scandinavia," Buckle recalled. "That's how I got Stiff, and then I pushed them in the direction of our guys in Italy, Spain ... the good labels out there." Rod also developed the UK end of Sonet with a series of what he described as "appalling but massive" 70s pop hits such as 'Mississippi' by Pussycat, 'Y Viva Espana' by Sylvia, and 'Seaside Shuffle' by Terry Dactyl & The Dinosaurs. (Later, in the 80s, Sonet was behind 'Agadoo' by Black Lace and 'The Birdie Song' by The Tweets.)

Miller had turned to Buckle and Sonet for promotional advice and international representation when Mute was in the process of releasing its first record by The Silicon Teens. The Sonet offices on Ledbury Road in London's Notting Hill Gate were close to those of Rough Trade, Mute's distributors. Buckle raised around £25,000 from various international labels for the Silicon Teens project – cash that kept Mute alive.

Miller had taken Buckle to see Depeche Mode at the Bridgehouse and Buckle's "commercial pop ears" were very quick to spot the chart potential of a string of Vince Clarke songs. He wanted Mute to get the band. "I had no idea that the band would go on to establish themselves as one of the most credible and great live performance acts of all time," Buckle told me. "I felt that they looked like a black-and-white version of The Bay City Rollers and might make a string of pop hits but not much more."

With the major labels also showing interest, Buckle stepped into the negotiations on behalf of Miller and Mute. "The band, although very enthusiastic about Daniel Miller's credibility, were also being wooed by Stevo's Some Bizzare label (with money from Phonogram) and by Richard Branson's Virgin label," he recalled. "Daniel was keen but the other labels were offering much-needed money."

The crunch came at a meeting in Buckle's Sonet office on Ledbury Road. He recalled the band being unwillingly herded in by Deb Danahay, Vince's girlfriend, who was a huge fan of Mute acts Fad Gadget, The Normal, and The Silicon Teens. They listened as Rod set out his sales pitch – a pitch that would ultimately create the most important building block in the career of the band.

"You guys are very, very lucky," he began. "You have the chance to record with Daniel and you have offers from others. Daniel understands you, your music, what you want to do; he's honest and you will make great records that you want to make with the minimum of interferences in your music and style. He's got pretty good distribution with the very credible Rough Trade."

After some fairly aggressive questions from Andy Fletcher, Rod replied: "No, Daniel cannot pay you anything like the £10,000 apparently on offer from Stevo, or the money on offer from Virgin."

"But we really need the money," Fletch said.

"That money is important," Buckle replied, "but actually it's peanuts. I could go out and get you way more from half a dozen UK companies, and I could charge you a share of that money for doing so. At first sight – good for you and great for me."

At this point Daniel Miller looked shocked; he later admitted to Buckle that he thought Buckle had "changed sides". But Rod carried on, and slowly Vince and the boys got the message. It was one that would define their career.

"Firstly you have to understand one thing: 99 per cent of your earnings will come from outside the UK," he continued. "You need credible hits here to wake up the world but the record sales and real concert money will all come from the rest of the world.

"I happen to like Virgin," he said. "And I represent them in Scandinavia, where we do a good job, and they are OK in Italy and a few other places, but in Germany there is no way they will work properly on a synth band without a drummer. The same with EMI – great in Cologne, terrible in Paris."

Buckle also urged the band to consider the US market. "Right now Depeche are worth jack-shit in the US," he told them, bluntly. "But with a few UK hits you'll be worth a million dollars or more to a label which may just get their attention and get them paying for some decent radio promotion out there. As it happens, in the US, Seymour Stein is building his new Sire label. I worked on product with his labels Blue Horizon and Passport, and Seymour is a friend of mine and he is in love with Daniel Miller's music.

"So my advice is: rather than be inflicted on one unwilling, non-working, non-understanding, unsympathetic multinational label, wait and let Daniel choose the right labels country by country as you become more well known and can get more attention paid to your releases."

The band were sold on Buckle's sales pitch, which was essentially that they should sign to Mute in the UK and then get other licensees interested on a country-by-country basis around the world.

Fletch butted in again: "But we really do need some money."

In the end, Rod advanced the band several thousand pounds against them signing publishing contracts with his Sonet company. He also advanced money to Mute and advised the band on setting up a unique 50/50 profit sharing deal with the label.

Miller quickly arranged to take the band into his favoured studio, Blackwing in South-east London, to record their debut single, 'Dreaming Of Me'. He'd already cut the track plus the B-side, 'Ice Machine', in Tape One during the 'Photographic' sessions. In Blackwing with his trusted engineer, Eric Radcliffe, Miller introduced Vince and the band to sequencers – new machines that DAF were already running with, and which made for machine-like perfection, with no further need to play rhythm parts by hand.

Vince's flatmate, Peter Hobbs, watched on as the band entered this period of development. "I remember Vince going to an evening with Warner Bros," he told me. "They were trying to sign him up. He was being invited to all these things, where they were trying to get him to sign on the dotted line to say: you're ours. But he wasn't having any of it. I was like: you're mad, they've offered you all this money and you won't do it.

"I'd been to the dentist one day and I came back and crashed out for 20 hours or something. I remember waking up and all of them were there: Daniel Miller – first and last time I've seen him – they were all having a Depeche meeting. It wasn't long after that Vince got his own flat in Vange Hill Drive.

"When he lived with me, to write his songs, Vince used to have a little mono cassette player and he used to go into the bathroom and lock himself in," Hobbs continued. "He'd come back out about an hour later and you'd think: what's he doing? But he had it all in his head: you'd hear him, he'd get what he wanted to get out, and he'd put it all on this little tape recorder, do sounds like 'phttt, phttt', beats and sounds, humming. He knew what he wanted and he'd put it all on this thing and play from that. He had it all in his head and that's how he'd express it."

Martin and Vince's pal Mark Crick took the band's first official photos and was asked to supply the artwork for the cover of the 'Dreaming Of Me' single. "They didn't have a manager," he told me. "They obviously had a relationship with Daniel. But I always thought of Vince as being quite a canny guy – in the early days I thought of him as the player-manager really. He was the one who was organising me to take photographs, organising gigs, organising everything. We did that first official photograph in a church on Clay Hill Road, a church hall, using a collection of angle-poise lamps, fairly basic stuff. I processed it, developed it, and printed it in Vince's mum's garage. I saw Vince as the driver, or harnesser, of the band, although Dave had a lot of drive and ambition as well.

"It was Vince who approached me to do the painting for the first single. Early on it would have been Vince doing all the practical things. I did the painting specifically for it. I think I'd been in an art gallery and the inspiration was people just looking at pictures. I'd probably been looking at some M.C. Escher engravings at the time – that idea of it repeating in the reflection was reflected in that. 'Dreaming Of Me' sounded like such a narcissistic title, I was perhaps thinking of trying to represent it in a less narcissistic way.

"Martin was certainly listening to DAF and Fad Gadget and was a fan of Mute Records," Crick continued. "I remember one day he had to leave the bank early to go to a gig and the bank manager said to him: you need to think very carefully about this, this band thing you're in. It could adversely affect your career."

□-□-□

Depeche Mode played their final show of 1980 on December 28 at the Bridgehouse. They were in high spirits, with much to look forward to in 1981: the *Some Bizzare* album would soon be coming out, with a tour to support it, followed by the release of their debut single.

What is clear as they prepared to make that leap into the unknown is that they had the support of a very tight-knit group of Basildon friends, and that many of those people remain friends: people like Mark Crick, Steve Burton, Rob Marlow, Paul Valentine, and Daryl Bamonte.

The younger brother of Perry Bamonte, who played in The Spurts and The Plan, Daryl first started humping gear for Depeche Mode when they were still called Composition Of Sound. He was younger than the others, just about to leave St Nicholas Comprehensive, and grabbed at the chance to be the band's roadie. Brian Denny was Daryl's best mate and lived in the same Lee Chapel North area as the band (and the Bamontes).

"I used to go to the Bridgehouse gigs and he used to hump the stuff around," Denny told me. "All of them Bridgehouse gigs, it was just: get it done and get away. There was no pissing it up. In those early days Andy Fletcher was very anti-drink and pornography. He appeared in some magazine campaigning against pornography. He was very upstanding. He still had that Christian thing."

In the coming year, as Depeche Mode found their fame, almost every major media story on the band would feature Basildon as a central theme, often in a derogatory manner. London journalists would visit for an hour or two and quickly dismiss the place. To his eternal credit, Daniel Miller called it "a pretty heavy place."

I asked Brian Denny to remind us just exactly where it was Depeche Mode were coming from as they hit the scene running – what Basildon was. It was a town every bit as interesting as Manchester or Glasgow, cooler even, a made-up place that mixed modernism with communism, the working classes with conservatism, all underpinned with a sense of brutality. It was a place ripped asunder by Thatcher's Policy & Research guru, Keith Joseph. More than anything, this was England.

"It's revolutionary, the whole thing," Denny recalled. "Basildon was a very new culture and as such you had no deep roots. It was like year zero. As a kid in the woods you used to come across abandoned plot-landers' houses, shells of old cars, very Huckleberry Finn. Wilko Johnson talks about the area being like the Mississippi Delta, and it was like that.

"Most people worked on the industrial estates," he said. "But what was interesting was most of the workers and the managers lived in the same sort of housing. We took good housing for granted. Then when Thatcher came to power, it was Keith Joseph who looked at Basildon and said: the reason all these bloody people are socialist is because they live in all these houses for nothing, for a very small rent, and they don't aspire. So unless you smash it all up and sell it to them, they're not going to vote Tory.

"Joseph was right, of course, and that's what happened. He did the same thing to Harlow. It was definitely the Basildon effect that had to be dealt with. Joseph said to Thatcher: your big problem is getting them to sell off their houses, or else they'll just sit there forever voting socialist. I think he came with a map to Margaret Thatcher and said: look, these blocks are red and the reason they're red is that they've all got good housing. It was deeply political. There was a block on building council housing from the early 80s. If you look at that whole 'Moscow on the Thames' thing, I think there were individual conversations going on in Basildon, of people changing their views. Before that, everyone voted Labour. Then it became really stark. If you disagreed with the selling-off of housing stock, you were a Bolshevik. The debate was that stark; there were no nuances. It was a working class area, there were no subtleties, and there were certainly no discussions about the nature of post-modernism."

This is Depeche Mode, then: their background and their future. "In Bas there were the beer boys and the weirdoes," Denny continued. "If you were culturally interesting you kind of kept clear of the beer boys." This was their culture. "There was a skinhead movement. There was a British movement. In my class there was a skinhead who had Holocaust-denial material in his house, because that was compulsory, but it never really seeped into anything. Culturally, it was unacceptable. My old man was in the Communist Party and I used to get beaten up at school about it. But it wasn't because they were fascists. There were very few black people, but the black people who did live there were very assimilated. You had the same accents, you went to the same clubs, listened to the same music.

"Soul boys were massive. Earth Wind & Fire were massive, and that led to an explosion of interest in soul music. That led to the explosion in the mod movement. Everyone used to go down to the Goldmine and Raquel's and other clubs like the Zero 6 [in Southend]. Gahan-y was at the centre of all that business. When *The Man-Machine* came out everyone in Basildon listened to Kraftwerk. You put that with the disco music at the Goldmine and you get Depeche. It was something familiar presented in a new way."

142

This was the band's milieu. "The thuggery – there was a lot of it about," Denny said. "It wasn't the result of a well-organised skinhead movement. It was the result of what was euphemistically called 'beer boys'. I got beaten up regularly, but never by skinheads.

"The Arts Centre was fantastic. You had everything: bands could practise; you had access to the theatre; groundbreaking stuff. Billy Bragg's first gig was in the Towngate. The influence of The Jam in Basildon was huge. All of a sudden there were a lot of mods around. Daryl was a punk but I thought it was a bit middle-class, walking round Basildon with chains going: I'm pretty vacant – it didn't really fit in. Weller comes from a New Town area as well. 'That's Entertainment', when we heard it, was like: yeah that's the town we grew up in – a mixture of boredom and aspiration.

"That's why the New Romantic thing was a bit naff because it was very pretentious and it was difficult to walk around Lee Chapel North pretending you're in Berlin. Dave had a stud in his nose but they weren't that showy. They wouldn't walk round with leather trousers. You had this whole London thing like Spandau Ballet and I remember being a bit intimidated by it. But you can't go to Basildon and be all: oh, look at me. It wasn't like a small town mentality, but people would take the piss out you all the time. People from Basildon still take the piss all the time. It's part of the culture.

"Raquel's was blood on the walls: rowdy, insane. The Highway pub was just incredibly violent. The lads in the band used to drink up there. It was bohemian in the sense that people would be selling each other drugs, but in no other way. Violence was always in the air.

"The Sherwood bar in the Bullseye was incredible. It had a ball and mace on the wall, and a guy walked in one day and pulled it off the wall to attack someone. Crazy. Just fucking crazy. There was a lot of violence. It was driven by alcohol. The Depeche boys always drank there; there was no question of them not going in. They'd go down the Arts Centre occasionally to get away from it but they'd always end up in the Bullseye and the Highway."

In the coming years, Depeche Mode would get called 'wimpy' and 'plinky-plonky'; those who were there at the time know better. The band emerged from this environment as a perfect product placement: brutal, modernist, commercial; all electronic and grime free. They hadn't named their band after a J.G. Ballard book – they hadn't even read a J.G. Ballard book. They were the real deal. This was certainly not like anything British music had ever produced before, and there was no art-school affectation, either. Presciently, a town with no precedents had produced a band with no precedents.

"They took something of the culture of Basildon into what they were doing as a way of expressing not only what they wanted to do but what they thought was popular, what people would want," Denny continued. "That's what people listened to in Basildon: soul music and Kraftwerk."

Brian Denny had one other thing he wanted to impart: something about the train line between Basildon and London. "The Fenchurch Street line was known for its old rolling stock," he said, "hence we had the good fortune to travel on 50s slam-door train units right up to the late 80s – beautiful material, pure heaven." Depeche Mode were travelling in style.

# CHAPTER 7

# NOT SO NORMAL

In the end it was 20-year-old Vince Clarke who had the final say in deciding whether to work with Daniel Miller and Mute. It was the best decision Depeche Mode ever made. There had been much soul-searching over the other major-label offers but what swung it was Rod Buckle's plain speaking and the small publishing advance he offered – plus the fact that Mute and Miller were seen as credible and had promised Vince a major say in all artistic decisions. The band had agreed, on a handshake, to a deal that would see them earn a 50/50 split of profits in the UK and 70/30 in their favour for the rest of the world.

Buckle, as we'll see, was crucial in running the band's international affairs, but Miller was the kingpin in the development of Depeche Mode musically. In the end, all you're left with is the music, and Miller's 1978 seven-inch single 'Warm Leatherette' / 'T.V.O.D.', released under the nom de guerre The Normal, remains a benchmark of British electronic music. (The year Miller met Depeche Mode, Grace Jones had recorded a cover of 'Warm Leatherette' for an album of the same name.)

Miller gave Depeche Mode a hard and heavy yet distinctly clean sound that can also be heard in other Mute acts such as The Silicon Teens and Fad Gadget. It seems odd that a man who appreciated such avant-garde noise as Boyd Rice's NON could also be responsible for such seemingly lightweight pop music.

Daniel Miller was born on February 14 1951 and raised in Hampstead Garden Suburb, a bohemian enclave of North London. Both of his parents were actors and liberals. He'd gone to the progressive, independent King

Alfred School on the edge of Hampstead Heath and then on to art school in Guildford to study filmmaking. His musical tastes were disciplined. He got interested in electronic music for intellectual and aesthetic reasons – he felt it was a genuine European music. He had a philosophical point: this music had come about without relation to American rock'n'roll. Miller also enjoyed free jazz and experimental music, but it was primarily electronic music – and in particular early-70s German acts such as Can, Faust, Amon Düül, Neu!, and Kraftwerk – that interested him. In the mid 70s he'd worked as a "ski-bum" DJ in a Swiss alpine resort. He had also worked as a taxi driver in somewhere like Budapest. Back in the UK he worked as an assistant film editor for ATV before becoming inspired by the DIY ethic of punk and the earliest UK electronic experimental acts, Cabaret Voltaire and Throbbing Gristle.

Miller bought a cheap synthesizer and a four-track tape recorder. He was still living at home and recorded his debut single there. He took test pressings to Rough Trade, which agreed to distribute 'Warm Leatherette' through its independent network. It was an instant underground hit, dubbed "single of the century", no less, by *Sounds*. Rough Trade was incredibly supportive of Miller and the single clocked up over 30,000 sales.

As The Normal, Miller played live with Throbbing Gristle and Cabaret Voltaire as well as another Industrial Records act, Robert Rental. He'd done a Rough Trade tour with Rental in support of Stiff Little Fingers, and had played at Southend Tech along the way.

Miller had put his address on the sleeve of 'Warm Leatherette', and people soon started to send him tapes. That's how he found Frank Tovey, aka Fad Gadget. Mute Records' second release, Fad's 'Back To Nature' (1979), was another underground hit. Next, Miller recorded an astonishing album of old rock'n'roll standards rendered in an all-electronic style. Tovey helped out on vocals and Miller concocted an imaginary band to front the material, The Silicon Teens, whom he dubbed "the world's first all-electronic teenage pop group". The singles 'Memphis Tennessee', 'Judy In Disguise', and 'Just Like Eddie' and the album *Music For Parties* were the sort of novelty releases that might encourage mainstream crossover attention – and that might encourage Rod Buckle to invest in the label.

Subsequent Fad Gadget releases such as 'Ricky's Hand' and *Fireside*

*Favourites* (both 1980) received much acclaim from the music press for their use of synthesizers and 'found sounds' such as drills but were too weird for the mainstream. But Fad was pop when compared with the two other acts Miller was working with prior to Depeche Mode. One of them was Boyd Rice, an American prankster with extreme tastes who recorded and performed as NON. His experimental debut album was made up of insane, noisy, primitive samples, closed loops, and locked grooves; he used homemade devices and made music that was just a fraction short of being unlistenable. Another way to look at him, perhaps, would be to say that his use of turntables as instruments and found sounds put him in the vanguard of musical experimentation, bordering on genius.

"I came to London in May 1978 and went to Rough Trade," Rice told me. "I had my first album, the *Black Album*, and sold them some copies of that. While I was there, the girl behind the counter was playing me anything she thought might interest me – anything with electronics. I think I got 'United' by Throbbing Gristle and 'Warm Leatherette' by The Normal. A few minutes later, Daniel walks into Rough Trade and the girl says: hey, Daniel, this guy just bought your record – he makes weird music too. We started talking about music and stuff; he was telling me about his synthesizer. He said while you're in town you should come over and we should record some stuff together.

"At the time he was living at his mother's house in Golders Green. We recorded several things there." One of these things was 'Cleanliness & Order', as featured on the *Dark Scratcher* compilation LP. (Rice added the vocal sample after returning to the USA.)

Rice hung out with Miller as 'Warm Leatherette' was starting to break. "Every week Daniel looked at Stevo's 'Futurist' chart in *Sounds* and 'Warm Leatherette' kept going higher and higher and higher," he recalled. "So he had these posters printed for this thing, and we drove around record stores in London taping them up. We'd drive around London and he'd tell me how much he liked J.G. Ballard, and then he started saying stuff like: oh, you see this intersection right here, I got in a great car crash once …

"I called Daniel at Victoria Station, when I was leaving the country, and he said: if this record continues doing well, I'm thinking of starting my own record label; how would you like me to release your *Black Album* over here?

I said yeah, great. The next thing I know I was back in the States and they're playing 'Warm Leatherette' and 'T.V.O.D.' every place.

"Have you heard the story about how he chose the two songs he put out for the Normal single?" Rice continued. "He had four songs, or six songs, and one of the songs was called 'Oh No The Brakes Have Gone Out' – he said it was a bit more punk sounding – but the reason he chose those two songs he did was because he was making the cover with Letraset and they have these generic images, and there was the one of the man helping the women out of the car, and then there the was one of the guy watching TV. He liked those images and he used those songs because those were the songs that went with those images.

"I felt it was a real shame he didn't make more music. There was a Silicon Teens B-side called 'Sun Flight' which is really beautiful – it's about taking a rocket ship up to the sun. What he communicated to me was he had a lot of different facets to his personality: there's one facet that just adores pop music, another adores abstract avant-garde stuff, and he said being the owner of a record label meant he could vicariously satisfy all these aspects of his personality. He can put out a band like Depeche Mode; he can put out noisy stuff by me; he can have a full palette.

"That was a real twist of fate, meeting Daniel. If I'd left the Rough Trade shop five minutes earlier, or if I'd come a bit later, I never would have met him. We took a liking to each other, had a lot of interests in common. I still think meeting Daniel Miller was the luckiest day of my life."

Miller would stick by Rice throughout his career, despite the increasing controversy surrounding him. "Daniel is a bit older than me but we both had the same pop cultural influences," he told me. "At the time I put out the *Black Album* it just sounded absolutely crazy to most people, but Daniel could see I was doing something that nobody else was doing, and so did the people at Rough Trade – they were playing it in the back when I was trying to sell it to them. Jon Savage was back there, the guys who owned Rough Trade were back there, and some other influential people, and they were all saying: wow, this is like music people will be making ten years from now. I think Jon Savage said: this will be what Kraftwerk will be doing ten years or twenty years from now." Rice also met Genesis P-Orridge of Throbbing Gristle on that first trip to London. They'd been in touch already, via the 70s phenomenon of 'mail art', sending each other small artworks through the post. He was in correspondence with Richard H. Kirk of Cabaret Voltaire, too.

"It was very strange that he and Genesis and all these people I'd been in touch with for so long would turn out to be involved in this weird genre of music," Rice recalled. "We were all supportive of one another: the Cabs, TG, Daniel. What was happening in the mainstream music was punk rock, so we were way on the outside of that. We all felt we had a lot more in common than any differences we might have. We were way over here in leftfield. Back in the day, there were riots at these shows. I had a beer glass smashed on my face. People would show up expecting some rock'n'roll show and they would get me doing noise, and there'd be one drunk in the crowd who would want to beat the hell out of me."

Rice became a regular visitor to the UK, and was asked by Miller to be the opening act on Fad Gadget's first European tour. Leading post-punk outfit Wire were another band Miller had close connections with; drummer Robert Gotobed was part of Fad's band. "I think Fad Gadget's first album [*Fireside Favourites*] may be one of the ultimate electronic rock albums," Rice continued. "It's kind of like what 'Warm Leatherette' was: the high-water mark of that genre. Frank was a lot of fun to be with. Daniel came along on the tour and did the sound – he got me a loud sound that I'd never got at that point: he blew the speakers out at some places."

Rice used a device he had invented to manipulate tapes and noises in a live situation. This primitive 'sampler' greatly interested Throbbing Gristle, Miller, and Fad Gadget. "Essentially, I've been doing sample based music ever since I started," he told me. "Everything on the *Black Album* was sampled. There weren't samplers, but I had means of sampling."

In 1981, Boyd Rice and Frank Tovey recorded an album together for Mute: *Easy Listening For The Hard Of Hearing*. They didn't sample from obscure vinyl, as Rice sometimes did, but used entirely found sounds, mainly from industrial sources. The concept pre-dated Depeche Mode and a host of metal-bashing bands doing the same things by a good few years.

"It came out three years after we recorded it," Rice said. "By the time it came out, there were all these bands like Einstürzende Neubauten and SPK doing something along those lines. But the album I did with Frank still – to me – doesn't sound like anything anybody else has ever done. I've never heard another record that sounds like it."

Boyd was in London when Miller came across Depeche Mode. "When Daniel first told me about Depeche Mode, he said: Boyd, I've found the real life Silicon Teens," he recalled. "He called me up one night and said: I've seen this fantastic band and I think I'm going to sign them to the label. He said: they're playing tomorrow in a pub in Basildon; you'll have to come along and see them. Me and the other people affiliated with Mute showed up at this tiny little club in Basildon, and that was the night he signed them.

"He was backstage telling them all this stuff about publishing and royalties and their eyes were just getting bigger and bigger. They just thought they were going to be super-rich pop stars instantaneously. I felt sort of sad for them. I thought oh, Daniel, give these poor guys a break, it's like you're building them up for a huge fall. Obviously he saw their potential. I saw their potential that night but I didn't quite think what would happen to them was going to happen and as quickly as it did.

"I remember that night Vince looked like Lucille Ball – drawn on eyebrows, way too much make-up – and they were very glammy for the time," Rice continued. "Most of the electronic bands around then weren't that glammy. And Dave just stood still like a scarecrow on stage; he didn't move at all. Later on, when they became popular, I think they hired someone to teach him some dance moves or something. There was the immediacy to their sound. I loved the poppiness of Depeche Mode, and every song was catchy, but they were just teenage boys wearing lipstick and make-up. But Daniel's thought was: if Vince is writing songs this good now, this young, he's got another ten, twenty years in him, he's just going to age like a fine wine. Daniel saw the hit potential."

Depeche Mode – especially Andy Fletcher – were left bewildered by Boyd Rice's avant-garde approach to music. It was all too much, Fletch thought, but fair play to Miller for having the balls to back it. In a way, it gave Fletch confidence that Mute would back anything they did.

"When we went on tour with Fad Gadget, it was right after Daniel had recorded the first Depeche Mode single," Rice recalled. "And Daniel was just playing that thing to death. He would play it over and over and over again. Those two songs were etched onto everybody's psyche by the end of that tour. It was a very short while later and we were driving around and we would hear the song on the radio. It happened really quickly. Probably nobody will admit to this but in the early days they insisted on being called *Depeche-ay* Mode. Everybody would call them Depeche Mode and they'd say: no, it's *Depeche-ay* Mode. I guess at some point they dropped that."

Boyd could see how the 29-year-old Miller was influencing the sound of the young Depeche Mode. "The way most people write electronic music, it sounds tinny and thin and it has no balls," he said. "Even some of the tinniest Depeche Mode stuff – the earliest stuff, the real Tinkertoy sound – Daniel was able to really beef it up, so even though it's electronic music it sounds like it has substance, it has a life to it. He would multi-track some of these things. I went into the studio once and saw where he had marked all the things on the mixing board, and every sound you hear it's got about five or six tracks that it's on. I think Joe Meek is a good simile. Daniel was very into Joe Meek. He was a member of the Joe Meek Appreciation Society. They had meetings at a pub on the Holloway Road."

As well as being a key player in the English underground electronic scene, Miller also opened up Depeche Mode to a whole new range of European influences, particularly the thriving German new-wave scene. "Daniel was totally hooked up with all the Neue Deutsche Welle scene," Rice told me. "I think because of the influence of 'Warm Leatherette' and especially when he started a label, he knew weird electronic musicians in every country. When I first met Daniel he gave me a list of people like: when you're in Berlin, Boyd, you have to see Kurt Dahlke [of DAF and Der Plan]. Daniel was a magnet for a lot of those types of people."

Boyd Rice played shows in Berlin at the influential SO36 club with Throbbing Gristle and at the XS club with Der Plan. "I met all those German people the first time when I was supposed to do a tour in England – they wouldn't let me in because I didn't have a work permit," he said. "So Daniel flew me to Düsseldorf and I stayed with Der Plan, and through them I met all the other German New Wave people, like DAF and Mania D and Fehlfarben. When I saw DAF in Berlin it seemed very aggressive, very aggro – it had a real hard edge to it. DAF was the first time I'd seen a band play to a reel-to-reel tape recorder and have a drummer. They were very goofy, like a surreal children's show. They had these weird painted backdrops that were really bright and they'd dress up in costumes."

Moritz Reichelt of Der Plan, who provided the artwork for the Depeche Mode singles 'See You' and 'The Meaning Of Love', remembered Daniel Miller visiting Düsseldorf in 1979, around the time of the release of the first DAF album. "He was interested in the product," he told me. "Later he would 'park' Boyd Rice at our house until he received an immigration permit to the UK. Boyd had been rejected at the London airport by the British authorities. So we have to thank Daniel for meeting Boyd Rice as well."

▭▬▭

Daniel Miller, Boyd Rice, Fad Gadget, Der Plan, and DAF were popular with a clique of hip music journalists like Chris Bohn at the *NME*, all of whom would also lend their support to the early work of Depeche Mode. DAF – Deutsche Amerikanische Freundschaft – were the band that had broken Miller's heart just before he discovered Depeche Mode. Formed in 1978, they were heralded as the pioneers of the sequencer sound. Their music and that of fellow Düsseldorf band Der Plan would have a major influence on Miller and Depeche Mode.

Before moving to London and signing to Mute, DAF had released an underground cassette album on the Ata Tak label. On Mute they began to develop a sound quite unlike anything that had come before it. While British electronic pop pioneers tended to be either morbidly alienated or camply futuristic, DAF combined disco and electronics into a heavy, relentless beat appropriated from the groundbreaking New York gay clubs of the time, from which the band also copped their look.

"Depeche Mode liked us a lot," DAF drummer Robert Görl recalled. "We met them a few times in London. We came over to London before they were formed, and then when they formed, right in the very beginning, we met them a few times in the Mute office."

DAF were influenced by the atmosphere and attitude of punk but not the sound. From the outset, they felt they should not sound like anything that already existed, and like many of the German new-wave bands of the time they were heavily tied in to the art scene.

152

"When we were in Düsseldorf in the very early days there was a famous art academy, which had this quite famous art professor, Joseph Beuys," Görl told me. "Beuys came to the Ratinger Hof [the famous Düsseldorf punk club where both Wire and Pere Ubu played]. He was not hanging out there every day but he came round sometimes to have a look. He felt something going in this music scene and in this youth scene."

Beuys's students came to be known as Die Jungen Wilden and embraced DAF. In the fluid Düsseldorf scene, Görl was also a founding member of Der Plan, involved in the band's debut release, *Das Fleisch*, a set of eleven songs, ten of them untitled, recorded cheaply on cassette tape.

"Between Der Plan and DAF we were all interchanging and at some points playing in different bands," he said. "We did our own record label with the first DAF album, the Ata Tak label. We decided to come to England after I visited a major record company in Cologne. DAF wanted to find a record label and get support to make a proper record. I was with [singer] Gabi [Delgado-Lopez]; I went in and I played them our cassette – our first kind of demos, which we thought were really good. They listened to it and just looked in a very funny way to us and they asked us if we think this is music? They really asked that – do you think this is music? – and at the same time they showed us the door."

Görl thought that DAF might have a better chance in Britain. The five-piece group arrived in London with no place to sleep and headed straight for the Rough Trade shop on Portobello Road. From there they found places to stay, which in Görl's case meant a squat in Camden Town. Miller heard about the band and was interested in signing them to Mute. They cut a single, 'Kebabträume', at Cargo Studios in Rochdale, near Manchester. (They had been taken to the North by another early champion, Bob Giddons, who lived in Germany but was originally from that area.)

"Daniel did not help develop the DAF sound," Görl told me. "We had our own ideas. It was very strange because we were very certain about what we wanted, especially Gabi and me. We had always in mind what kind of people we were searching for to work with, what kind of room we want to work in, and when you meet people you find out direct, no or yes. For example, when we recorded 'Kebabträume', Daniel Miller wanted to interfere in the studio a little bit but we did not allow this. In the end he

153

let it go. We said the only thing we liked for people to lay a hand on us is to give us a good sound, a good quality, but do not interfere with our musical ideas. We never allowed this."

Miller got the cash together for DAF to record their debut Mute album at the studio in Cologne run by Krautrock pioneer Conny Plank. Görl also played drums on Robert Rental's Mute single 'Double Heart', and for a while the band stayed at Miller's mum's house in London while Miller helped them get gigs in the UK, including a gig at one of Stevo's Futurist parties at the Clarendon. "We didn't feel part of any movement, though," Görl said. "We wanted to be nowhere at home."

When Kurt Dahlke left the group to join Der Plan, Görl brought in Chrislo Haas, who would later become a key influence on Depeche Mode as part of Liaisons Dangereuses. "Chris Haas was more of an extreme type of guy," Görl recalled. "When Kurt Dahlke was with us, the very early style was more like: if we would have gone in that direction it was almost like a normal band with keyboards, almost this pop-rock thing. And then we changed. We wanted to make it much harder – it was very heavy, electronic."

The single-minded DAF and Mute were a perfect fit. "We felt Mute was the right record label, for a while," Görl said. "But it didn't last too long. We did one album with Mute, *Die Kleinen Und Die Bösen* [*The Small One And The Evil One*]." The album was half live and half studio recordings produced by Conny Plank. "In a certain way we were happy with that album," Görl continued. "It was a development after at least a year of struggling and changing members." It was also popular with the British music press. "They really loved us. We were in almost every issue of the *NME*; they wrote about us all the time."

According to Görl, however, DAF were still in transition. "We were still not really there," he said. Shortly afterward, the band left Mute and signed to Virgin Records prior to recording their seminal album *Alles Ist Gut* with Plank. "This is exactly what we wanted," Görl said. "We always wanted to be perfect to listen to and we wanted bigger concerts. It was for this reason we went from Daniel Miller of Mute to Richard Branson."

Miller was not best pleased. "Daniel was really pissed when we left him," Görl continued. "Some other people say we were like a sell-out, but we had nothing against Daniel – we just didn't want to stay at the same point … you must realise Daniel still did not have the Depeche Mode success at that time, so he had very little money. He had helped us and this was great but we were always running further and further." The band eventually reached the point where they couldn't pay the rent on their basement flat.

"We wanted to end the struggling. We thought we'd get much bigger opportunities with Richard Branson and Virgin. It really was true. The moment we moved, everything changed. We got our own flat for the first time. That's what we wanted, too: we wanted to live, we wanted to buy an airplane ticket to go to Germany and back to London. From that moment on we saw that it was not possible with Daniel Miller."

DAF left Mute with a final single, 'Tanz Mit Mir' / 'Der Räuber Und Der Prinz'. Released in 1980, it proved to be a profoundly influential record, with Miller appropriating the sound of the B-side – more considered and melodic than the throbbing, sequenced music for which DAF were known – in his work with Depeche Mode.

"Before DAF split up [in 1982], we never looked to what other people were doing, we just did our own thing," Görl told me. "There was no time to analyse other bands. I was happy that Daniel Miller was very successful with Depeche. When we left him and went on to have huge success with Richard Branson, I thought nature gave him back a very big success with Depeche Mode. When I heard Depeche Mode was using this or that thing from our sound, I was used to that. Believe me, once we got this big success with *Alles Ist Gut*, I was always in the clubs, and then suddenly, six months later, I heard tracks which sounded like us everywhere. Major companies suddenly promoted bands – even found bands – who were in this line of hard electronic, sequence music. Suddenly there were many bands. In this first moment I thought: shit, fuck, how can they just copy us? How is this possible? But later this whole music scene went into this hard, electronic, sequence music – just what we did. So you get used to it."

Görl would later return to Mute for his 1983 solo single 'Mit Dir' and the following year's *Night Full Of Tension*. "When I came back to Daniel to make a solo album those hard feelings from years back were gone," he recalled. "Daniel was very busy then. He was happy and successful. Depeche told me they really liked what we did by smiling at me and treating me well. Daniel said those guys in Depeche Mode were really DAF fans. Then of course when they are such DAF fans they of course do something in their songs of it, but I did not care any more at that time. I realised those sounds were everywhere."

◻◻◻

Miller may have seen Depeche Mode as his real-life Silicon Teens but he also saw them as a means of filling the gap in his life after DAF signed to Virgin. At the time, Miller was still running Mute from his mum's house in Decoy Avenue with help from Hilde Swendgaard, the girlfriend of Tony James from Generation X. She worked for Mute for the first three years of its life, using a spare bedroom in her flat as an office while Daniel was in the studio doing his thing.

"We'd meet up every week at Mike's Cafe in Notting Hill to talk about what was happening and what needed doing for the forthcoming week – booking gigs, managing gigs, press releases, manufacturing, lots of stuff," she told me. "DAF lived in my flat for a while, as did Scott Piering of Rough Trade."

Simone Grant did all the artwork for the early Mute records. She had known Miller since they were teenagers and worked as an architectural and editorial photographer. "I'd done some design work and he was just starting up," she recalled. "He had recorded The Normal and he just asked me to do the Letraset stuff for the single sleeve. I wasn't at the same school as Daniel but we all lived in the same area. He was at a school with a load of my friends and we all just knocked around together in Hampstead Garden Suburb.

"The Letraset was Daniel's idea," Grant continued. "Typesetting was too expensive and nobody had computers, so Letraset was the thing to use. I'd been at Goldsmiths and done layouts so I knew how to lay down Letraset, which isn't difficult – you just have to have a good eye, really. I used it for all the lettering on the Normal single. I followed a design that Daniel had sketched. I misspelt 'courtesy' when crediting the crash photo – no spellcheck, big rush. I did the layout, the type for the poster; the budget was still zilch so it was also printed on lowest-grade paper. I hand-coloured a load as spot colour wasn't an option.

"The Mute logo is an architectural symbol from Letraset. When architects are designing buildings they want to see people from above, and that's what the Mute man was. Daniel always liked that simple design – and also because there wasn't any copyright on the symbol."

Grant had a better sense than most of the background of the mysterious Miller. "He went to Guildford with the guy I married," she recalled. "They both went there to do a film course. My husband was a film cameraman and he'd dropped out and just went off and did film work instead. But Daniel stayed on for the full course and made some amazing films. There was one – I can't remember what it was called, but I think it was based on 'T.V.O.D.', actually. It was very dark – very Joe Orton darkness.

"We kept in touch over the years. Daniel was my husband's best man in 1978. Then he went to Switzerland. He was – and is – a fantastic skier and he was a DJ in Switzerland. I don't think he likes talking about himself. He's private in that way, just a tremendously nice bloke. The nicest guy in the business: honourable, straightforward, talented, and honest. What more can you want? And he was very funny. He was running the company from his mother's house when he came back from Switzerland. It was 16 Decoy Avenue, the address on the record sleeves. He had a big back room; nobody knew it was going to take off so much.

"His mum, Hanne, was just a lovely lady. She was an actress originally, then she worked for the BBC. She was very easy going. She always had people staying. Don't forget, nobody had any money then. It was not an affluent background. The area has all swanked up now but back then it was more bohemian. Both his parents were actors. Not hard-up or anything but certainly not posh or swanky and very liberal, very intellectual – not caring about appearances. His father died in 1969."

Miller had asked Grant to photograph him for an *NME* feature on The Normal. "He wanted modern industrial landscape, which was obviously a bit tricky to find in North London," she recalled. "Brent Cross at that time had just been built and it's actually amazingly ugly. But it was also quite graphic. It would be quite a nice graphic picture in black-and-white – he didn't want any close ups or anything. So he was tiny in the lens. I just don't think he was interested in any personal publicity. Not his thing. On a damp Sunday morning, Daniel and I went to Brent Cross car park, the least glamorous and bleak of locations, which is what Daniel wanted."

Grant also went to watch Miller's early gigs. "The ones Daniel did with Robert Rental in West London – in a church hall near the Westway – were amazing. It was just Daniel and Robert and two synths. The gigs were absolutely rammed. It wasn't a punky crowd, more the sort of people you'd see hanging around at Rough Trade and people who were in the know."

According to Grant, Miller may have been inspired to make his first record by a band called Desperate Bicycles. "They were just a little bit earlier than The Normal," she said. "They came from the same area as us. They did the first DIY single, only produced about 300 copies."

Grant was also heavily involved with the Silicon Teens project. "It was just funny," she said. "There were a whole load of things, like in the *Evening Standard*: The Silicon Teens, who are they? Are they dead? It was all silly and quite good fun. When he put out the single, 'Sun Flight' / 'Just Like Eddie', we were having dinner – my husband, Daniel, and I – listening to John Peel, and Peel played it twice, which was just amazing, so that was a bit of a celebration. The Silicon Teens was fun. The Normal was something he wanted to do, something he was passionate about.

"The video for The Silicon Teens single 'Memphis Tennessee' was shot at the Charing Cross Hotel. That was quite a big shoot actually. Frank Tovey was in it. It was, again, quite cheesy but quite funny. I don't think it was a big budget. When people are writing about Silicon Teens or Daniel they often use a picture of Frank by mistake. Those are the ones I took, at the Science Museum, where they all had sunglasses on. Basically it was taking the mick – ripping up the music press."

Grant also did the drawing for the Silicon Teens album cover. "It was imagining what they'd do if they existed," she said. "The logos for Fad Gadget and Silicon Teens were hand done. I love the Fad Gadget one, actually. I was very proud of that. Now I'd use a computer but then it was all done with pen and ink. I just wanted something different and edgy. The 'Ricky's Hand' single sleeve – the drawings on there are all my drawings. It is a bit sick I suppose. I did the NON [Boyd Rice] lettering as well.

"I liked the cover of the DAF album Mute did – quite surprising and interesting. They used images of the Russian Olympics, which was very unusual." Her favourite, however, was Boyd Rice's *Black Album*. "No camera-ready artwork there, but a lovely idea."

Before she left Mute, Grant worked on the early Depeche Mode singles. "I did all the beginning stuff, which mostly was just doing preparation of camera-ready artwork from their designs. I just did the layout and the lettering and all the posters. With the Basildon stuff, they were really young lads from Essex and really quite shy. I thought the naive look from Moritz Reichelt was quite good. But it was funny getting the Sellotape in the post – they sent Sellotape with hearts and flowers on it for the borders. It was all really basic, a sketch of how it should be."

This is the team Depeche Mode were joining: Rod Buckle, Simone Grant, Hilde Swendgaard, and a roster of just NON/Boyd Rice and Fad Gadget. There was one other person in the equation: a guy who would be crucial in helping break Depeche Mode – and, like Rod Buckle, another odd fit for the Mute image.

Radio and TV promotions whiz Neil Ferris had been working with Mute since The Silicon Teens. He was one of the best – and most expensive – pluggers in the business. His style was so far removed from the Rough Trade crowd Miller was associated with that Buckle had problems persuading Miller to take him on.

Ferris had been around the block a few times and was working as a PR for CBS in London when he started his own company, the Ferret Plugging Company, in early 1980. Success came quickly. One of his first clients was UB40; soon he was looking after the Virgin Records roster, representing acts such as Japan and Human League. He'd also pick up Spandau Ballet, ABC, and Heaven 17 – all of whom were associated with the New Romantic movement that was about to explode in 1981.

Buckle saw Ferris's "magic formula" as simple: he was personable, trusted by the BBC to deliver acts on time, always had enough hits going for him to be able to be in daily contact with the important radio and TV producers of the day, and could occasionally trade favours by delivering a major band to a new or lower-level show. His hard work and credibility would prove to be another of the key building blocks in the success of Depeche Mode.

From the beginning, Ferris had a different kind of relationship with Daniel Miller. They became close friends (and remain so), and their tight, unique relationship would continue right until Neil became Managing

Director of EMI in 1997. Daniel looked to Ferris for advice on his fledgling record label – not just in the areas of plugging and promotion but also in the wider terms of the industry as a whole.

"In the very beginning it was a very small, close team," Ferris told me. He was appreciative of electronic music but didn't share Daniel's passion for the more extreme acts of the era, such as Throbbing Gristle and Cabaret Voltaire, or DAF and Fad Gadget, for whom he would struggle to get any sort of airplay. But he did form a close relationship with Depeche Mode: "the only band I really loved". Insightful as ever, he soon fingered them as a 'rock' band "even though they played synths and didn't have drums or guitars". Even so, they did prove to be a difficult sell. "They were the most difficult of all the bands I represented to get played on Radio 1," he told me. "Even though they were a pop band and the songs had great melodies, there was always something a little bit odd about Depeche Mode."

Compared with the fractured state of the media today, in the early 80s outlets for new music were limited. It was all about getting repeated daytime plays on BBC Radio 1. To do this, Buckle persuaded Miller, you needed a seriously well-connected radio promotions guy to get the message over to the executives and DJs at the BBC in a sensible and credible way. That was Ferris. He had a fantastic reputation – even though producers at Radio 1 were unsure about Depeche Mode in the early days, Ferris insisted that the band had commercial potential.

"The key to successful plugging is enthusiasm and being able to transmit that enthusiasm to producers and DJs," he told me. Getting Depeche Mode on the radio would become almost a personal mission for him. He started with "the more risk-taking DJs" of the era: John Peel, Janice Long, Peter Powell, and Simon Bates. "Once those key DJs were on board," he said, "the more mainstream element of Radio 1 fell in line."

Ferris and his business partner Nigel Spanner were the most highly paid in the business. So how did tiny Mute manage to pay them? Buckle wanted Mute's records to become a priority for Ferris so persuaded Miller to pay Ferris a royalty on all sales, as well as an initial fee (advanced by Sonet). The idea worked and Depeche Mode (and later Yazoo and Erasure) remained a priority for the Ferret Plugging Company for many years.

Later on, Buckle remembered being criticised by the band for agreeing to pay such large amounts of money to Ferris as the hits rolled in. But Buckle's original agreement was another crucial and decisive move.

"We were very expensive as a company," Ferris said, "but I had a very different relationship with Daniel. Basically, we got paid on kind of an artist's royalty. Daniel wasn't paying my company unless we were all selling a lot of records. That is probably the easiest way to put it. So I took a big chance when I met Daniel. There was no guarantee. If I make this work then I will make money for myself, and my company, whereas if I don't succeed I will make nothing. Daniel was driven. We were all driven. All the people around Depeche Mode were absolutely passionate about the band."

In his early dealings with the band, Ferris recalled Andy Fletcher as the band's spokesman. "I always remember we had a meeting round at my office with Roger Ames, who was at Polygram in those days, and who wanted to sign the band," he recalled. "Obviously, Daniel didn't have a deal with the band – it was a handshake. So Daniel said: can we have the meeting at your office?

"The band came to my office, with my wife and myself and Daniel and Roger Ames. Roger Ames stood there and said: you guys should leave Daniel and sign with me at Polygram, I can do this that and the other ... Fletch sort of said: well, you know, I've got to think about it. And then Dave said: if we get on *Top Of The Pops* do you think we can get a cheap-day return from Basildon?

"There was that sort of banter going on. I think Fletch was staking the role quite early on as kind of manager, because they didn't have one. In the early days they were just boys from Basildon, but there was something unusual about them. They were definitely an unusual bunch of guys. I don't mean that in a horrible way. To me they were really interesting."

# CHAPTER 8
# POP

Depeche Mode played four gigs in early January 1981: at Croc's, the Bridgehouse, a club in Southend called Rascals, and at the London pub the Hope & Anchor. The last of these gigs had been arranged by Stevo, according to Neil Arthur of the electronic duo Blancmange, who appeared with Depeche Mode on the bill and on the *Some Bizzare* compilation album.

"We did a few dates that Stevo had arranged around London and its environs," Arthur told me. "One particular gig I remember was at the Hope & Anchor in Islington. Depeche Mode supported us. We got on very well with all of them, but in particular Vince. We became mates. I used to see Fletch a lot, too. We both still had our day jobs. He used to work down near London Bridge and I worked as a graphic designer right next to Southwark Cathedral."

The tour transport for these early Depeche Mode gigs was often Daniel Miller's battered old Saab. The band debuted two new songs written by Vince, 'Boys Say Go!' and 'Puppets', both of which were destined for their debut album. (According to Deb Danahay, the latter song "sounded like a love song but was written about drugs".) They also did their first ever music press interview with Betty Page at *Sounds*, to promote the *Some Bizzare* album, which ran in the January 31 issue of the music paper.

Page would become a long-term ally of the band. She had started writing for *Sounds* in 1979 at the age of 22, and had been friends with Stevo since he approached *Sounds* to ask if the paper would run his Futurist chart. "He used to bring in this piece of paper with his chart scrawled on it," she told me. "It was difficult to read because Stevo didn't really know how to write properly. He was fairly famously not very well educated but he had a very different way of seeing the world. He was a teenager when I first met him. People used to take the piss out of him because of the way he dressed. He was just like a brickie with New Romantic clothes on – he was a bit laughable to look at. But you could tell, if you took the time to talk to him, that he did have a vision. And his vision was all about what he called Futurist music and Depeche were part of that. He was calling it that in '78, '79. So he may well have coined that term for that sort of music."

Page herself was credited with inventing the term New Romantic. "The provenance of a lot of those terms is hazy now," she laughed. "I'm sure I saw it somewhere else before I used it in *Sounds*. Gary Kemp of Spandau Ballet still insists it was me, so if he wants to say that, that's fine. But with Stevo it was all about how he hated rock'n'roll. He wanted it all to be about synthesizers."

Page's favourite tracks on the *Some Bizzare* album were Depeche Mode's 'Photographic' and the Soft Cell track, 'The Girl With The Patent Leather Face'. "Those two stood out for me," she said. Stevo had originally wanted Page to interview every act featured on the album for a piece in *Sounds*. He had planned to get a representative from all the bands to go to the *Sounds* offices, but Depeche Mode and Soft Cell didn't turn up. "All I got was Stephen Luscombe from Blancmange; The Loved One, who were a couple of weirdoes from Nottingham; someone from Naked Lunch; and someone else – someone from B-Movie who didn't say anything – so it was a bit laughable, really," Page recalled.

Stevo then encouraged Page to interview Depeche Mode for a standalone feature because he thought it would help sell the album. He got Daniel Miller to bring Vince into the *Sounds* offices to meet Page. "That was my first contact with them," Page said. "Nobody really knew anything about Daniel – he'd just put this record out that was amazing. That was the first time I'd met him and the fact he'd got this band and it had his seal of approval – that counted for a lot. But neither Vince nor Daniel were particularly good at selling themselves. Vince just looked like this little football hooligan. He looked like quite a tough nut but he wasn't like that at all. He hardly said a word. It was just Daniel doing the talking really.

Daniel was older, so he was the father figure. I think the band always saw him not as a Svengali but more as the guiding hand."

Page enjoyed hearing an advance copy of 'Dreaming Of Me', due for release on February 20, and agreed to interview the band. "The interview took place in the stock room at Rough Trade in late 1980," she said. "It was very awkward. They were very young and very inexperienced and bands didn't know how to deal with the press. I wasn't much more experienced than they were, so there were lots of awkward silences. They weren't very good at communication. They were quite young blokes and not very sophisticated, frankly – not very worldly. The only time they lit up was when I asked them if they wanted to go on *Top Of The Pops*, because that was the Holy Grail at the time: every band wanted to be on *Top Of The Pops* no matter what kind of band they were.

"They did have this schoolboy charm about them," Page continued. "There was a naivety they had which you could hear in the music but was part of their charm. They'd come along just at that point when synthesizers were becoming more affordable to boys like them. That was really an important part of the whole story: that in the early 80s you were getting all this new technology coming out that was becoming affordable. Just a few years before that you would have needed a lot money to buy a synthesizer. It was really exciting to me that you could buy a synthesizer and start writing songs in your bedroom. That's why I loved those bands. That, to me, was the spirit of punk. To me they were more punk rock than a lot of punk rock bands. Depeche Mode absolutely embraced that new technology. Computer games, too. They were the first generation to do that."

Even then, Depeche Mode were trying to distance themselves from the Futurist scene. "They learnt very quickly, actually," Page recalled. "There was probably more of a strategy than they were letting on. They were just observing what was going on with other bands around them at that time and they worked out pretty quickly that they didn't want to get attached to a particular scene. They were able to manoeuvre their way out it."

At the time, however, they were very much part of it, as evidenced by the number of gigs they played that had links to Stevo or New Romantic club kings Steve Strange and Rusty Egan, who had closed down Blitz following their chart success, as Visage, with 'Fade To Grey' and were now running a venture called Club For Heroes.

Some observers were left perplexed by the on/off nature of the Some Bizzare tour, which featured Soft Cell, Depeche, and Blancmange. "I think it was supposed to start in Manchester," Boyd Rice recalled. "It was going to be this big thing: the public's introduction to the New Romantic movement. One act on the bill, the first concert they gave, their idea was they were going to go on stage and slash their wrists. And they did. They went on stage and cut their wrists. That was the first and the last gig of the entire concert tour. The rest of the tour was cancelled.

"I remember saying to Daniel: how is this tour Depeche Mode are on? He said it got cancelled and told me that story. I've told it to people over the years. You would think a couple of guys who went on stage and sliced their wrists would be world famous but nobody remembers who they were."

Depeche did make it up to the North for a couple of dates with the Some Bizzare crew, in Leeds and Sheffield. They played at Strange and Egan's People's Palace night at the Rainbow in London, and at two other events promoted by Egan, at Flicks in Dartford and the Venue in New Cross, South London. They were also among the ten acts to appear at a Some Bizzare night at the Lyceum.

Elsewhere, Miller got the band three shows at West Hampstead's trendy Moonlight club, the venue famous as the one where Joy Division recorded the live tracks included on *Still*. On February 26, Depeche played a Mute night at the Lyceum with Furious Pigs! and Palais Schaumburg, another German new-wave band Miller was keen on. Fad Gadget headlined. They also gigged at the ultra-hip Soho club Cabaret Futura, run by former Doctors Of Madness singer Richard Strange.

Stevo's next live venture was more successful. The 2002 Review tour actually did make it around the country in March and April 1981, with Classix Nouveaux headlining and support from Theatre Of Hate, dance group Shock (who later became Tik & Tok), Nash The Slash, and Blancmange, but not Depeche Mode, who had turned down the opportunity.

Another band on the tour – and on the *Some Bizzare* album – was Naked Lunch. The band's drummer, Mark Irving, had grown up in Basildon in one of the town's few black families. They had come up against pockets of ingrained racism but were generally well known and well liked. Mark's brother Terry was the first black policeman on the beat in Basildon; another brother, Les, ran the Windmill, a legendary soul-boy hangout in nearby Hanningfield; the fourth brother, Ian, used to be on the door at Raquel's.

Irving had known Dave Gahan way back when, "as a beer boy, before he became weird". He'd played with Alison Moyet in The Vicars and drifted in and out of lots of other bands in London before joining Naked Lunch. Around the time of the *Some Bizzare* album he went around to Peter Hobbs's flat and found Vince "sat there strumming his guitar. There was no sense of competition".

According to Irving, the gigs in support of the *Some Bizzare* album were fairly loosely organised. "A couple of us would go do a gig, and then a couple of other bands would go do a gig," he recalled. "It never got into a structured tour." Naked Lunch were also due to appear at Steve Strange's People's Palace event. "Depeche were one of the main acts; it seemed they were really starting to make their mark. Naked Lunch were on the bill but dropped at the last minute. We'd been kitted up in these Cossack outfits – it was hideous, actually. There was something where one of the big stage curtains came down, a lighting rig maybe … someone was nearly killed."

'Dreaming Of Me' was the 13th Mute Records single, and with the support of Peter Powell and Richard Skinner at Radio 1 it peaked at Number 57 at the end of March. It was the label's highest chart position to date. The single had picked up good reviews, not just from Betty Page at *Sounds* but also in the *NME* and, in a sign of things to come, the more pop-oriented *Smash Hits*. They were picking up good press mainly because of the Miller/Stevo connection – their debut *NME* feature, for instance, was written by the supportive Chris Bohn. A month later, *NME* carried a much bigger feature on Miller himself. Depeche Mode were in with the in crowd.

In April, Depeche Mode returned to Croc's for a Saturday night Glamour Club show, where they played a widely bootlegged set consisting of 'Television Set', 'Dreaming Of Me', 'Big Muff', 'New Life', 'Boys Say Go!', 'Tora! Tora! Tora!', 'The Price Of Love', and 'Just Can't Get Enough'.

Then, after a couple more Some Bizarre forays to Leeds and Birmingham, they returned to Basildon for a gig at Sweeney's nightclub on April 28.

"It was a bit rough," Peter Hobbs recalled of the newly opened club. "But the night Depeche played it wasn't so bad. It was full of teenagers who'd made their own fashions and dressed up and had their hair all over the place. I went and I felt so out of place. I had my jeans and sweatshirt on with my long straight hair. I must have stood out like a sore thumb."

Also in the audience that night, after jetting in from the USA to see the band, was the highly influential boss of Sire Records, Seymour Stein. Stein's label had a rich history and an impressive stable: The Ramones, Talking Heads, The Dead Boys, Richard Hell & The Voidoids, The Rezillos, The Saints, The Undertones, The Beat, Madness, Echo & The Bunnymen, Jonathan Richman, The Pretenders, The Cure, and Kid Creole & The Coconuts. Warner Bros had bought out 50 per cent of the previously independent Sire in 1978 and had just acquired the remaining half. Stein kept a percentage of the revenue on any new act he brought to the label – a prescient move, it transpired, as he snapped up Depeche Mode and then Madonna in quick succession.

"I had met Daniel Miller about 18 months before I came to sign the group," Stein told me. "It looked to me like he was just hanging out at the Rough Trade distribution centre. We started talking; I told him who I was and he told me that he had started Mute Records and he had put out his first record by The Normal. He played it for me and I liked it very, very much. I asked who the group was and he said: oh, it's actually me. So I licensed it and we put it out in America on Sire. It actually did fairly well.

"Several months later I heard about The Silicon Teens, which was also basically Daniel Miller. By that time I'd really gotten to know Daniel and I thought he was brilliant. I was also very close with Rod [Buckle]. He ran the UK office of Sonet Records, the leading independent label in Sweden, and they had affiliations with companies in Norway, Denmark, and even in Finland. We put out The Silicon Teens in America on Sire as well. It did OK. Not great. It didn't spark the interest that The Normal did. Rod was looking after Daniel and sorting out European licensing, and I think he even had some behind-the-scenes role in terms of the United States as well. He was always very helpful to me.

"Several months later I'm up early in New York and I read – I think it was in the *NME* – that Daniel Miller signed Depeche Mode, and they're playing their first gig," Stein continued. "I look and – oh, shit, it's tonight. I said: my god – I just have a hunch about this – Daniel Miller is brilliant, he wouldn't sign anything unless they were great, too. So I call up British Airways and get a seat on Concorde. In those days I wasn't flying Concorde and I had to pay a very exorbitant price because it was last minute. Most people would have thought I was crazy to do this. I hadn't heard a note. But I booked it.

"I saw the band and they were brilliant. What I liked most about them, aside from their material, was the fact that even though they were young and really not that experienced they put on a good show. Most of the bands that were coming out of that genre, no matter how good the records were, they weren't exciting live. That's where Depeche Mode had the big difference, plus the material. It was fabulous. I said: Daniel, I want to sign this band. Rod Buckle was there. We did a deal right there. I was very excited. I knew I had signed a band that would become very important. I just felt it in my gut. I remember feeling so good about it."

Stein signed the band to a long-term, five-album deal. "I don't remember what the royalties were or anything like that," he said. "Usually, because I didn't have much money, I tried to make the advances as low as possible, so to compensate I tried to make the royalties as high as possible. The contract had one of those very standard clauses with regards to leaving members: that if anyone left we'd have an option on them and what they were doing, so that's how we were able to continue our relationship with Vince when he left.

"The deal with Sire was signed by the band. In fact, I think we had a stronger deal than Daniel had with them, because Daniel and the band had a handshake. Daniel was like the fifth Depeche Mode. In reality, he was a member of the band. The band loved him. They still love him. Daniel is one of the most talented people that I ever met in the music business on either side of the Atlantic. And he is the nicest person that I have met in the UK: the fairest, the most genuine. I can only imagine Depeche Mode saw those same qualities in him plus his talent as well – that's what kept the relationship going. Paper is important but, with the lawyers we have in our business, any contract can be broken. But the bond between Daniel and Depeche Mode was unbreakable, and it exists to this day."

According to Rod Buckle, the Sire deal was not agreed at quite the pace described by Stein. Buckle told me that when the first Depeche Mode record was released, Mute wasn't even a formal limited company, nor was it registered with copyright societies or other trade organisations required for chart recognition. Some months earlier, the band and Miller had shaken hands on a Rough Trade-style profit-sharing agreement, but behind the scenes Buckle had a lot of fixing to do. He eventually forced the band and Miller to sign a one-page letter setting out what was agreed between the band and Mute in principal; how to share costs and what they would include (studios, pressing, printing, promotion); and how the profits would be divided. Fletch and Vince "embraced" the idea of the letter, according to Buckle, although the rumour that the band and Miller continued to operate on a 'handshake agreement' was allowed to persist. The letter also stated that the band could leave Mute at any time.

"When I forced them to sign the letter," Buckle recalled, "the example I gave them was Tony Wilson, an artistic visionary but an unmitigated crook. It was Tony Wilson who deducted from New Order's royalty statements 35 trips to the States – 'I have to go and talk to the label and I'm gonna be a month in New York and my girlfriend's coming and we've got an apartment in Manhattan.' It was examples like that that I gave to Depeche when I said you've got to sign a contract with Daniel."

The all-important letter was signed "some time before" the release of the band's debut album. In this hectic period, before the Sire deal was inked, Buckle also took Miller to various international licensees to try to set up local releases of Depeche Mode product in the major European territories. They revisited France, Scandinavia, and Holland, where they'd been the previous year with The Silicon Teens project. Some of these companies would be prepared to offer much-needed advances. With guarantees from Sonet, Buckle chalked up deals for Depeche Mode in Holland, France (with Vogue France), and Scandinavia.

Miller was busy in the studio with the band; once the letter was signed it was agreed that for a share of international income Sonet would handle all international deals directly and pay Mute a percentage. According to

Buckle, the band weren't keen on the idea to begin with. Sonet already had the publishing rights, and Martin Gore worried that the "terrible pop hits" Sonet put out could ruin the band's credibility. "This was soon to pass as they discovered the impressive roster of labels Sonet actually represented," Buckle added. Sonet quickly chalked up deals for Depeche Mode in Belgium, Denmark, Spain, and Italy.

This network of international licensees was something Buckle had spent many years putting together. It was helped by the success he'd had with an act called Secret Service, who had sold millions of albums and had Top Ten singles in 11 European countries despite being virtually unknown in the UK. The territory where Buckle struggled the most – ironically, given that it would later provide as much as 50 per cent of Depeche Mode's income – was Germany. Six major labels turned him down before he managed to sign a deal with Intercord, a small label based in Stuttgart. The advance was tiny – around £10,000 – which did not please the band. In fact, it took much skill from Buckle to turn this deal to the band's advantage.

In total, the European companies Buckle had signed deals with guaranteed Mute around £100,000. It was a time-consuming and complicated business, with some deals lasting three years and the guarantees rising, but they all offered good royalties.

Miller came to rely on Buckle for organising Mute's business affairs; in the UK, he agreed to use a new distributor, Spartan, alongside Rough Trade. In terms of the USA, Buckle said several major labels had turned him down, including CBS, Capitol, and A&M. He knew Seymour Stein was keen and recognised him as a "creative and artistic genius" but had heard rumours that Stein had over-stretched himself financially at Sire. When news broke of the Warner Bros buyout of the label, however, Buckle was happy to give Stein what he wanted, and Depeche Mode signed with Sire. (In a third version of these events, Miller would later recall that the US deal happened just as Vince announced he was leaving the band.)

□-□-□

What Depeche Mode needed now was a Top 20 hit: something to get the attention of the busy distributors in the lucrative markets around the world. Before that, however, the band played at Raquel's in Basildon in

May. Rik Wheatley was in the audience. "I came home from Jersey to see my mum," he recalled. "I got home at 9 or 10 o'clock at night and on the way I met someone at Basildon station and said: what's going on at Raquel's, why's there's a big queue? And they said Depeche were playing. I blagged my way in and I was knocked out. The place was packed to the rafters and they were really making it.

"It was strange seeing them in *Smash Hits* sitting on the fountain [the Mother & Child statue in the town square]. We thought blimey, this is getting Basildon famous. With the synth-pop thing it was Depeche who really nailed it at the right time in the right way. But I don't think they'd have been at that point without everything else that happened prior in Basildon. So without The Vandals, and without Alison being quite famous locally, and without these other people like Rob being mates with Vince, all these strands came together and they just hit something at the right time."

The second Depeche Mode single, 'New Life', was once again produced by Miller and the band at Blackwing Studios in South-east London. The title came from a phrase from the spiritual teachings of Meher Baba, who had been brought to mainstream attention in the 70s by Pete Townshend of The Who. It was released on June 13 1981 and packaged in a sleeve designed by Vince's brother, Rodney. The band recorded a live session for Radio 1 DJ Richard Skinner's evening show, which aired in the week of the single's release. 'New Life' was also backed by a substantial feature in *The Face*, which made mention of the band still catching the last train home to Basildon after gigs, and their first ever cover story, written by Betty Page for *Sounds*.

"I interviewed them at Blackwing," she recalled. "They were a lot more confident and a lot more relaxed than the first interview, and they let their guard down a bit more. In those days you used to see people whenever you went out – everybody went clubbing, and if you went out in London you just got to know them. They didn't hang out with Spandau Ballet or anything like that but I do remember seeing them from time to time at clubs. There was this thing Steve Strange organised called the People's Palace; Daniel marched in with Depeche all very well scrubbed up.

"[Soft Cell singer] Marc Almond was there and he just thought the whole thing was preposterous. He used to take the piss out of Depeche –

he thought they were a bunch of choirboys. They weren't evangelical about their roots in Christianity but I was kind of aware of that, and that's why this choirboy thing stuck on them a bit because they had this Christian thing going on. I think it was something they went through that was quite personal. They probably realised it wasn't a great idea to talk to a rock journalist about it anyway. Nonetheless, certain assumptions were made about the band.

"Depeche were quite happy to be seen as a pop group in the early days," Page continued. "That was something they embraced. It was a time of great change in the music press. A lot of bands that would subsequently only be seen in *Smash Hits* were still being written about in *Sounds* because that whole colour pop magazine thing didn't really kick off until the early 80s. So you would still get *Sounds* writing about pop groups, and then *Smash Hits* started to really take off in 1981. I think Adam Ant was the first big pop star they championed and they rode on the back of that. That's when pop music and rock music split off a bit. The music papers didn't really write about pop music.

"Andy talked a lot during the interview and I was surprised by that. He was a bit of a worrier, Andy, but he was very thoughtful; he used to think a lot about how they projected themselves, and how they came across in interviews. If the others were starting to mess around a bit too much he'd say: c'mon, we've got to answer this question. He was quite often the one trying to get to grips with the question. I really liked Andy. He was the one people didn't notice as much but I think he played a very important part.

"Vince was very serious – the intense one. He was a man of extremely few words but all of his expression came out through the songwriting and the music he made. Martin was pretty quiet to start with but then he started coming out of his shell. Dave was always expected to be the spokesman to begin with, and he was the one who spoke more than the others. But that opened up a bit and by the time I did that second interview they were all a lot more confident about themselves and what they were trying to do."

Another breakthrough came with the filming of an episode of the London Weekend Television show *20th Century Box* focusing on the Essex scene and narrated by Danny Baker. Filmed around Basildon (and at

Croc's), it gave the band their first national TV exposure. The dressed-down band – jeans, leather jackets, sweatshirts – are shown rehearsing at Blackwing Studios, with Vince teaching Dave the words to 'Let's Get Together' – an old Christian song Vince kept up his sleeve and which the other band-members disliked. Later, Hilde Swendgaard arrives and tells the band they've been invited on to *Top Of The Pops* for 'New Life'.

After a stop-off at the Basildon bowling alley, the band (plus girlfriends Jo and Anne) were filmed at Dave's mum's house before being interviewed in the grounds of a deconsecrated church, with a statue of Christ prominent in the background. They are also shown indulging their passion for Space Invaders. This was the golden age of arcade games, and the sounds of Space Invaders, Galaxian, Pac-Man, Frogger, Defender, Donkey Kong, and Phoenix, with its haunting, melodic accompaniment, fed into the national consciousness. While Depeche Mode never used the sounds directly in a song (as Yellow Magic Orchestra did on 'Computer Game'), the bleeps, swoops, and pings were all-pervasive in their early music.

Gary Turner was also featured in the show. "I left Croc's pretty soon after that and went on to work at the Goldmine," he told me. "I DJed there for a couple of years, a regular night. It was a mix of the Croc's thing – I brought a lot of the crowd with me – but then we got into a lot more funk and stuff that was a little bit leftfield. I had bands like Pride – the Sade band, Blue Rondo A La Turk, Blancmange, Talk Talk – quite a mixed bag played down there. We used to do a lot of funk stuff, Kid Creole & The Coconuts, lots of ZE Records stuff, Material, Was Not Was. Also at that time we started going to a lot of clubs up in town. There was a lot of hard funk being played. Then you got things like Pigbag, Haircut 100, My Favourite Shirt, Funkapolitan. You got that funky thing that was going on in the very early 80s."

The look of this new Essex scene would have a trickle-down effect on Depeche Mode, who would soon be seen dressed in pastel suits and ties. For their *Top Of The Pops* debut, however, they were clearly lacking finesse. Martin had chosen a see-through top with bondage belts X'd across his chest; Vince was wearing a black leather jacket; Dave, still struggling with his hair, was in a foppish pink shirt and leather pegs; and Fletch was looking and feeling "like a plum" in his peaked leather cap. Nonetheless, the *Top Of The Pops* appearance helped 'New Life' to a chart peak of Number 12. The single stayed on the charts for 15 weeks, chalking up sales of around half a million copies.

Just as Rod Buckle had predicted, the UK success of 'New Life' sparked a frenzy of action in Europe, which as he recalled was where "the real earnings came from – both record royalties and concert receipts". Each territory began to demand advance samples of future product, manufacturing parts, special mixes, and time-consuming promo visits from the band. What started as a trickle with an appearance on a French TV show soon become a deluge as requests poured in for the band to mime on slightly suspect variety shows in Holland, France, and Germany, often requiring a 4am start in Basildon to get to Heathrow Airport.

The Depeche Mode girls – Anne Swindell, Deb Danahay, and Jo Fox – had started a fan club, the Depeche Mode Information Service, and were about to get very busy. These were exciting times – private jets were being chartered – but the band-members' lives remained rooted in Basildon.

"I met Rod Buckle quite a few times," Swindell said. "All the business decisions were difficult because they were all so young and suddenly they were being exposed to these people. There'd be times when these people would be spurting off all this stuff and you'd be thinking: God, have they really got their best interests at heart? Is this the right thing for them to be doing? I found it really difficult, because you never knew.

"There were times you'd feel they were being pushed into something they'd not necessarily chosen to do themselves. Not serious things, but occasionally you'd think: oh, that's a bit of a weird decision – I don't think that's theirs. Rod had a Mercedes sports car that I really envied. I always felt slightly unsure about him. I was always a bit on my guard really and on my guard for them, for Martin and Vince.

"We were really young and we could quite easily be taken for a ride," Anne continued. "They all had their feet firmly on the ground but they didn't know the business and they had to have an element of trust and go on their gut feelings, but personally I felt a bit uncomfortable around Rod. He used to call us the 'Mode-ettes' if me or Jo or Debbie were around.

"Vince wouldn't let Deb go anywhere. He didn't like Jo and I being there at all. He really didn't like it. Martin and Dave, it was one thing they did stand up to him about. They decided we were going to go with them and that was it – Vince wasn't going to stop them."

Anne also got to meet the other new people Depeche Mode were coming into contact with. "Working with Seymour Stein was quite a big thing for Martin," she recalled. "Sire had all these acts Martin adored: Jonathan Richman, The Ramones, Talking Heads. I remember the first time we went to New York to Seymour's office; the excitement of it. We all went out for dinner and everybody had lobster. For Martin it was important to be with someone like Daniel. The whole thing with Seymour Stein was important too. But to be with someone like Daniel, rather than some huge label, definitely suited them more. To be with an indie label allowed them to keep that slight edge in a way."

Anne's brother, Philip, designed the first Depeche Mode T-shirts, which featured a stave of music overlaid with the colours of the rainbow and the band's name. "I remember going up and buying the T-shirts from the warehouse up in London and him screen-printing them in the garage," Anne recalled. "The Depeche Mode Information Service did tick along, and then it suddenly took off. It was like: oh my God, this is like a proper fan club. There were all these letters coming in. It was bit overwhelming. We used to answer everybody's letters personally and individually, and sometimes it was quite hard to do that."

With demands now being placed on the band across Europe, it was time for Dave to leave college and for Martin and Fletch to give up their jobs. "Martin and Fletcher were much more cautious," Anne recalled. "I remember when they had to make the decisions as to whether they were going to leave the bank – and it was quite a big decision for them to leave and go for it."

"I thought they were mad to leave," Fletch's oldest pal, Steve Burton, recalled. "I was now going steady with my girl and thinking: you've got to put a little money aside. I remember thinking: oh, what a decision. But they had to do it because they were obviously becoming successful – it was an opportunity they had to grasp. But by the same token it's like: you're going to give it all up. It made me feel a bit nervous for them."

Amid the ongoing promotion for 'New Life', Depeche Mode played UK dates everywhere from Edinburgh to Brighton – where they were supported by Palais Schaumburg – and at Manchester Rafters, Leeds Warehouse, and at the Rock Week at the ICA in London. Between these gigs and the demands for European promotion, there was also the continuing pressure of recording their debut album. When he was not playing Space Invaders, most of the recording duties fell on Vince's shoulders.

There was much media interest in the band following the success of 'New Life'. They made the cover of *Smash Hits*, for which they were interviewed in the Highway in Basildon ("a tacky, plastic-lined pub above the concrete shopping mall"). It was interesting to see how journalists coped with Basildon. *Smash Hits* described it as standing "in some people's eyes as a cliché for soulless suburban development around a boring – the word is 'alienating' – centre where the entertainment is hard to find. The very stuff, you might be forgiven for thinking, of classic Urban Synthesiser Gloom. Well, here's the surprise: not that Depeche Mode come from somewhere like Basildon, but the fact that they play frothy, adolescent pop – with a tinge of moodiness, sure, but nothing that would qualify them for the Throbbing Gristle award for making the listener feel more suicidal than ever before".

By now, as well as distancing themselves from the Futurist/New Romantic scene, Depeche Mode – or at least Vince – also saw themselves as quite separate from bands such as Throbbing Gristle, Cabaret Voltaire, and Human League, and went to great lengths to point this out. Vince described these acts as "bleak and industrial"; Depeche Mode, in his eyes, were "ultra-pop".

This pronouncement would be Vince's last word on the band. On July 13 1981, Depeche Mode featured in the tabloid newspaper the *Daily Star* – a breaking point for Vince, who would subsequently refuse to take part in any other interviews. The article was titled 'Looking Good' and went on to claim that "Depeche Mode are one of the best-looking bands around" and that "they reckon that gives them an edge over the competition". The bit that really got to "Vince Clarke, 21," was a quote attributed to him that read: "Ugly bands really don't get anywhere in this business. But let's face it: being good-looking gives you a real advantage in life. It opens a lot of doors."

In response to the article, Vince went into a strop and wrote a song called 'What's Your Name?' for the band's debut album. The other band-members would later cite the song, with its chorus line of "Hey, you're such a pretty boy", as the worst they ever recorded. In fact, it is one of their finest: a camp classic on a par with the magnificent early work of The Four Seasons.

"'What's Your Name?' was Vince's albatross for a long time in many respects," his pal Rob Marlow recalled. "I remember going round to his flat in Vange Hill Drive and he was in a foul mood. I asked what the matter was, and of course it takes you an hour or so to get the story out. Vince never rated himself as a good-looking person but some tosser from the *Star* had written that Vince Clarke thinks it's great to be good-looking, and of course misconstrued his comments. Vince had said obviously in life it's great to be good-looking. That's what that song is about, not 'hey I'm such a pretty boy'. That was a real big thing – that was in the mix over the split because the others didn't understand why he'd taken such umbrage to this. They didn't understand the dark and sensitive soul of an artist! The worse thing you could say to Vince was that you're self-aggrandising."

In August, when the band appeared on the cover of the *NME* for the first time, Vince was noticeably absent. Paul Morley took the trip to Basildon with photographer (and future Depeche Mode collaborator) Anton Corbijn, who shot the band by Gloucester Park boating lake. Morley recognised the band as an "obvious part of the evolution from Kraftwerk, Yellow Magic Orchestra, Cabaret Voltaire, The Human League, and DAF – musically and conceptually – [whose] observation and explanation of SURROUNDING is dislocated and oddly associated" and who sounded like "a fairy tale full of silent machines, robots, consumer imperatives, and mute children in love with the sky".

Depeche Mode's third single, 'Just Can't Get Enough', was pure ultra-pop. The demands on the band intensified. They shot a first video – for which they all dressed in the heavy leather-boy look – in part to satiate the increasing demand for promotional appearances in Europe. They were under huge pressure from Neil Ferris, who wanted them to play kid's TV shows such as *Saturday Morning Swap Shop* and *Razzmattazz* to enhance their daytime Radio 1 playlist credentials. They were also juggling TV offers from France, Italy, Spain, Holland, and Scandinavia.

The band mixed their over-the-top leather-boy look with a totally separate, Goldmine-influenced assemblage of nipple-high baggy trousers, jackets, and ties – an Essex soul-boy affectation that suited them much better. They could have been two different bands. Dave, however, had finally settled on his hairstyle: a flat top, which bar the odd colouring would rarely change from here on in.

'Just Can't Get Enough' rocketed to Number Eight in the UK charts. It was a Futurist bubble-gum classic, and also one that saw the band tagged "the electronic Bay City Rollers". They were all over *Record Mirror* and teen mags such as *My Guy* and *Oh Boy!*, and appeared again on *Top Of The Pops*, with Martin bare-chested and wearing a Trilby this time, just braces covering his nipples, and all of the band-members pretending to play toy trumpets to the memorable riff. The song broke into the Top 20 in Sweden and reached Number Four in Australia, while also making waves in Portugal – two further territories in which Rod Buckle had organised licensing deals.

Songwriting royalties were starting to roll in, and Vince went up to Sonet to see the company's publishing guy, Alan Whaley, and collect his first serious cheque. The band's schedule – with promo appearances across Europe, live dates, interviews, and increasing demands for new material – was immense and relentless. Booking agent Dan Silver, whose clients included The Skids, Joe Jackson, The Rezillos, The Human League, and Gang Of Four, had lined up a major UK tour to support the imminent debut album the band had rushed to completion. Before that, the band headed out for a few live dates in Hamburg, Amsterdam, Brussels, and Paris – and a plethora of interviews and promo appointments with eager sales teams across the continent.

The gig at the Amsterdam Paradiso in September was captured on film and can be found on YouTube. The footage shows the band at an early peak as they come across – in their soul/funk suits – like an Essex Joy Division in both look and feel. The punk alienation and weird synth sounds of epic tracks such as 'Ice Machine' and 'Television Set' would never be repeated.

All was not well, however. Vince wanted out and his mood was not exactly difficult to read. One track destined for the debut album – previewed as an exclusive flexi-disc cover-mount on *Flexipop!* magazine – was recorded virtually as a solo project. It was called 'I Sometimes Wish I Was Dead'.

"I was probably the first person who knew," Deb Danahay told me. "The band were playing a mini European tour and I was allowed to go over to the Paris gig. We stayed a couple of days to look around the sights of Paris. I remember before Vince left for that tour he wanted to leave. He was very single-minded. I remember one day at one of the *Top Of The Pops* gigs, Dan Silver or Daniel [Miller] said something about some gig that they'd been invited to do. The other three said that's fantastic, that's great. Vince said no, we're not doing it. He wouldn't do it and they didn't do it. He had very strong opinions on what was the right direction for the band at that time.

"My impression was that he'd just got fed up with touring. The thing with Vince is he hates being in the limelight, but at the same time he doesn't like it when he's not. That's as blunt as I can put it. He did the same with Yazoo. That's how he is. He's a very, very private person, but at the same time he does crave the attention. That's how I remember him."

Rob Marlow was also aware that his friend Vince, the principal member of Depeche Mode, was planning to quit the band. "There were a couple of issues," he told me. "One was over petrol money – he got pissed off that they'd never chip in. Nobody drove, and he'd been driving for quite a while – he'd have to drive up the studio, Blackwing, and back again, and nobody chipped in – and they were working, Fletch and Martin. Vince got the ache about that.

"The other thing was they weren't particularly interested in the technology and where the band could go. They were more like: let's do another *Speak & Spell*. Vince is a complete catalogue-head and wanted to see what was out there and buy more equipment. The others were all young and they just wanted to enjoy the profits. Vince is a workaday guy. He's a grafter. He would say: let's buy this, let's see what it does, let's look around. Plus Vince is sensitive, and at that point it was quite easy to get on his wrong side. Them grumbling about some new song Vince played them seems to ring a bell as well. If you're sensitive about it, and that's your baby ... if that happened, maybe it would have pissed him off."

According to Marlow, Vince has "never really explained" his reasons for leaving Depeche Mode. "We laugh about how they never gave him no petrol money but it obviously wasn't just that," he said. "He wanted to fly, expand his wings, and see what else was out there. He's never liked feeling trapped. He gets restless. I have to admire Vince. I'm not sure I could have done that at age 21 – walk away from a band with three hit singles and an album about to come out and say: no, bollocks, I'm gonna do something else, I'm better than this – which is essentially what he must have thought.

"There was also the control-freak thing. He had his pals and brother doing the artwork and he'd been organising all the gigs – now there were people doing all that. You're young, you're brash, you've got opinions, and he wanted to have control – the other three didn't, and were happy to hand it over to Daniel and Mute."

# CHAPTER 9

# SWAN SONGS

C o-produced by Daniel Miller and the band, Depeche Mode's debut album, *Speak & Spell*, remains one of the greatest British albums of all time – a flawless synth masterpiece and a benchmark of the era. It stands head and shoulders above the other acclaimed New Romantic pieces of 1981 – The Human League's *Dare*, Heaven 17's *Penthouse And Pavement*, Japan's *Tin Drum*, and OMD's *Architecture & Morality* – in terms of attack, sound, melody, songs, tone, and sheer exuberance – and, as it happens, longevity. Even the cover – a photograph of a stuffed swan draped in plastic on a bed of silver twigs – has a quirky appeal.

The band had come a long way in a remarkably short period – the progression from first demo as Composition Of Sound to now was staggering. Much of that progress must be credited to Miller. "He'd spend hours on his own after they'd put their stuff down and marched off wherever they were going," said Brian Griffin, who took the distinctive cover photograph. "He stayed, twiddling and playing. He gave me the impression that his input was immense. Immense. Daniel was a real boffin and he was determined to hone, to ensure they progressed and that everything happened for the best for them."

Prior to the album's release, Mute Records had moved out of Miller's mum's house and into its first proper office on Seymour Place, just off the Marylebone Road, in North-west London. Miller rented the ground-floor space from Griffin's agent, David Burnham.

Griffin was a young, ambitious photographer who had already shot a number of great album covers for clients such as Joe Jackson, Elvis

Costello, Echo & The Bunnymen, Iggy Pop, and Devo. He was also closely associated with one of the era's leading graphic designers, Barney Bubbles. This and his bold and unusual portraiture work for *Management Today* magazine had emboldened him to enter the world of advertising.

"David Burnham had a shop with upstairs floors in Seymour Place," Griffin told me. "He said: there's a guy downstairs who's just started a new little record company, he'd be interested in you doing an album cover. So I went down and there was Daniel and one or two other people – just desks in a small shop really.

"Daniel looked at my portfolio. Joe Jackson's *Look Sharp* was massive in the world of album covers. It still is. So it did have a major effect on my position within the industry: oh, let's get Brian Griffin, he's really mega. There was a bit of that going on for them to dish out that dosh at the time."

Griffin and Miller bonded over a shared loved of Krautrock. "That's how we hit it off," Griffin said. "He obviously liked my work. I'd done a book with Barney Bubbles at the time called *Copyright 1978*. Barney was obviously very highly respected. Of course, when I did *Speak & Spell*, I got Barney to do the design." (Bubbles came up with the distinctive crown featured on the back cover.)

Griffin had risen to an influential position in the music industry. He even had his own section in the Hipgnosis books of album covers that came out every couple of years. "I was an expensive photographer at the time," he recalled. "They joke about it, don't they? I think I charged about a grand, £1,500 or something. They complain about it, and they've got a right to complain about it, really, because it's an awful cover."

Vince was flabbergasted – not by the actual photograph, but by the amount Griffin charged. To this day, Griffin himself is at a loss to explain the thinking behind the photograph. "I can't believe what was going through my head," he told me. "I'd begun to use this foil that you get to put behind radiators, against your wall, so the wall doesn't absorb the heat given off from the radiator. It produces all this glossiness and gave this metallic feel to the whole shot. And I got this stuffed swan. I can't remember why … I've no idea. I shot it in my studio – 121–123 Rotherhithe Street.

"I didn't have much discussion with the band before I did it," Griffin adds. "I don't think they knew what I was going to do or anything, really. It seems like I was off my head but I wasn't. It's a real departure for me at that time, almost schizophrenic – it's out there on a limb, isn't it? I never returned there again. I did use another shot from the session on a back cover of *Y*, a book Barney Bubbles did about a nuclear attack on London. The swan was the last remaining creature on earth after the nuclear holocaust. It's a crazy thought – very hippie – but it was good because Barney then used it to form the shape of infinity on the back of *Y*. The swan is a powerful image – it's the king of birds, owned by the queen – and obviously the crown is there from Barney.

"I took my work extremely seriously and I still do. I'm sure I approached this photograph with vigour and seriousness. I would not have occupied my day or days doing it unless I really believed in what I was doing. I was very keen to produce the best album covers the world had ever seen – not saying I ever did, but that's what I was trying to do. God, what made me get that swan? It's just crazy, because it doesn't apply itself in any way to anything. The band found the cover abhorrent. Why they commissioned me again after that is almost a miracle."

Griffin didn't much care for the music on that album. "I thought they were just little boys from Basildon," he said. "I wasn't fond of what they were doing at all. I much preferred something that was more like Can or Neu! or Kraftwerk. They were a bit plinky-plonky, so I didn't have a lot of time for them. They were very shy, down-to-earth boys. Daniel was very sensitive toward them but he was also like the headmaster as well. He respected them and had a lot time for them and thought they had a great future. So I don't know what he felt when he saw the cover!"

▭▬▭

Within a week of its late October release, *Speak & Spell* was in the UK Top Ten on the strength of advance orders of 80,000. It would remain on the charts for a remarkable 32 weeks. Reviews across the board were positive, with *Melody Maker*, *Record Mirror*, *Sounds*, and *NME* all offering high praise. In the *NME*, Paul Morley reviewed *Speak & Spell* alongside OMD's *Architecture & Morality* and came out heavily in favour of Depeche Mode.

Mute had belatedly issued Boyd Rice's *Black Album*, and *The Face* reviewed it with *Speak & Spell*. This disturbing, bewildering clash of sounds would come to define Mute's output – a mix of pop and noise – in the years to come.

The band showed up on a handful of kids' TV shows in support of the album. They were a parent's nightmare, whether they were dressed in incongruous black leather or like another band entirely in their 40s suits, pink peg trousers, and bowties, performing weird, disturbing album tracks such as 'Puppets' or 'Photographic'.

Vince had already told the others that he was leaving the band before they set off for their first proper UK tour, but he agreed to play this run of dates crammed into a two-week period without a day off. (It was Vince, in fact, who had chosen the tour support, his close pals Blancmange.) With 'Just Can't Get Enough' still on heavy rotation on Radio 1 and the band splashed across both the teen and rock press, the tour quickly sold out and the fans went wild.

"We shared a coach with them," Blancmange's Neil Arthur told me. "Girls were just banging on the windows on the side of the bus – it was mental. They really went for them. They weren't a pop band but they became the perfect pop band at that point. The fans went crazy for them. I watched them many times and I often thought it was like an electronic version of The Beatles or something. It was Depechemania. When Dave did his wiggle the crowd went wild. Even their names were perfect – their names were just absolutely right. I always remember lots of cuddly toys on the tour bus. I think they must have been given them by the fans. I was there with my Zoot suit on and my *Eraserhead* haircut … it took me a while to figure out what was going on with the teddy bears.

"I used to play chess with Fletch on the coach," he continued. "I don't think I won many matches. We had a magnetic chessboard, quite easily turned into draughts if you wanted to. Books were being read. But we used to have a bloody good laugh. We were in hysterics a lot the time. I do like a bit of a joke and they're definitely partial to a joke. Martin was very quiet but extremely loud in laughter. It all comes out at once. I can remember spending many hours playing Space Invaders. There was this game on tour called Tron: you could sit in it; I got obsessed by it. I'm sure they did, too."

Arthur was aware that Vince was going to leave the band but considered it a private matter between Vince and the others. "Nobody went into those things," he said. "We used to talk about electronics – how did you get that sound? – that sort of thing." He remembered Daniel Miller being very hands-on during the tour. "He and [tour manager] Don Botting were at the mixing desk doing the sound. Daniel was right in the thick of it. He was giving up smoking and he took a photograph every time he wanted a cigarette. So he must have a lot of imagery. On the first tour Daniel was there all the time."

"Vince told us he was leaving before he told them," Arthur's band-mate, Stephen Luscombe, added. "It was a bit of a shock. I don't think the band were ever happy about Vince leaving. They'd be going out and doing all the work and he was taking all the publishing money. I wouldn't be very happy either. But that's life – he felt he couldn't go any further with what he was doing and had to stop.

"The tour was crazy," Luscombe continued. "It was the first time I'd seen this Beatlemania for a synthesizer group. I remember very vividly getting into a coach after Portsmouth Guildhall and these girls started rocking the coach. I thought we were all going to die – they were going to kill us. It was a very strange feeling. It was that level of hysteria from these kids. They were all pretty good-looking lads, the girls were screaming, lovely tunes – they were like a pop group. After the show finished they'd go to tables all set up and do loads and loads of autographs.

"You'd got your Kraftwerks and Brian Enos and your more esoteric sort of things and then out of the blue this little pop group comes along with their synths and causes mass hysteria on the streets. I don't recall any other band like that. I think Daniel was like an older brother to them. They were very young. All this was very new to them – being pop stars, teen idols."

The band played sold-out shows at venues that held up to 2,500 people. Raquel's in Basildon was full to its capacity of 850, with hundreds locked outside. Martin's sisters Karen, 13, and Jacqui, 14, attended the show, chaperoned by his fiancée, Anne Swindell. The band's close-knit family touring party included Daryl Bamonte, Swindell, and Dave's fiancée, Jo Fox. Apart from Vince, all of the band-members were still living at home.

"I suppose the touring was kind of mature in a way, considering they were all so young," Anne recalled. She and Jo would sell merchandise at the gigs. "It was like being family. They'd known each other for a long time – not so much Dave, but they were all good friends. I suppose with Jo and myself being there it did change the way it was. That was their choice. I think they wanted a bit more stability, and that says something about the people they were – they didn't want to get suddenly caught up in all that stuff. They wanted a bit more solid ground, really. Ultimately both Martin and Vince were more interested in the music. They weren't hankering for fame and fortune. They wanted to make music."

Depeche Mode may have wanted stability, but there was no getting away from their fans. "It was a real mix because the more serious music press was writing about them and they had all these teenage girls fans," Anne continued. "I remember getting to the dressing room at one venue and the windows were just completely covered with faces – they were just all piled on top of each other trying to get a look in the window. It was mental. And when we went out, they were just pulling at the band, trying to get bits of them. There were lots of girls who had been sold those good-looking, teenybopper types. They did two nights at the Lyceum in London to close the tour, and looking out and seeing all these people screaming at them, it was just like: my God, this is like The Beatles, this is happening – they were getting bigger and bigger and bigger. You could feel something was going to happen."

With the UK tour over and *Speak & Spell* riding high in the UK charts and breaking around Europe (particularly Sweden), Mute announced to the press Vince Clarke was leaving Depeche Mode. Already, Martin, Dave, and Fletch were thinking: what next? All eyes fell on Martin, who had written two tracks on *Speak & Spell* and was the only other songwriter in the band. "There was quite a bit of bad feeling after Vince quit," Anne recalled. "It was difficult. It was a bit like someone had pulled the rug out from under their feet. They had to completely change the way they were going to do things. Daniel was quite important in the shift to get Martin taking control of the songwriting. Fletch would have been really important as well in that transitional phase after Vince left. Martin really needed to be … it's hard to go back to that, knowing how much more confident Martin is now, but I think it was quite a big thing for him to take over the reins – to know he could produce enough work that was going to sell, enough to go on tour, and to just being confident he could do it.

"I think if you're writing songs, you're putting yourself out there. It's much more exposing. Songs are very much part of who the writer is. It was quite a difficult thing for Martin to do – suddenly he had to take on a whole album. It was a bit daunting, really. I think when Martin says the songs are open for interpretation and never says specifically what they're about, I think that's a part of keeping him a little more screened from view. It's like: they mean something to me but they might not mean that to everybody. They're there, and you can have them as you want them."

Vince had two further obligations to fulfil following the announcement of his departure: a live recording for the *Off The Record* TV show and a mimed performance of 'Just Can't Get Enough' for the Christmas 1981 edition of *Top Of The Pops*. Clips of Vince's final live performance – the original band's final gig, playing to a packed Chichester Festival Theatre for the *Off The Record* show – can be seen on YouTube. For their Christmas *Top Of The Pops* date, the band abandoned both the leather boy look and the 40s suits for what would become recognisable as their third look: Fletch and Martin in nicely patterned jumpers; Dave looking like a Basildon barrow boy on payday. And with that, Vince was gone.

"Martin's a genius," Vince told *Smash Hits*, "he just doesn't know it yet." Two geniuses in the same band would be a rare thing. What Vince didn't reveal – what he has never revealed – were the two things that had bugged him most during his time in Depeche Mode. Firstly, he thought that songwriting should be his domain alone and didn't appreciate any interference. Secondly, and more importantly, he couldn't bear Dave Gahan as a singer. It was as simple as that. For Vince, Dave's voice didn't have a wide enough range.

Vince stayed in his Basildon flat for a while, messing with new equipment and seeing pals like Neil Arthur. The revenue stream from publishing royalties and his share of record sales meant he was in a healthy financial position. He'd formed a strong bond with Blackwing engineer Eric Radcliffe, with whom he continued to work, and was still being advised by Rod Buckle. He would soon resurface with a new band, Yazoo, and a singer he found more to his taste: Alison Moyet.

Meanwhile, the three remaining members of Depeche Mode knew they needed to bring in someone else for their upcoming live dates. UK-based booking agent Dan Silver – who unusually also represented the band worldwide – had arranged a major European tour for February 1982. More pressingly, they were committed to dates in the USA at the end of January. They briefly considered Leah Aiken, a keyboard-playing friend of Andy Fletcher's new girlfriend (and future wife), Grainne Mullan, but in the end they chose a musician who had answered an ad placed in the *NME*, auditioned for Miller, and been accepted by the band after a try-out during a hastily arranged and frenzied show at Croc's.

His name was Alan Wilder. He was 22, middle-class, and came from Acton in West London. He was a bit of a hippie but he was good-looking and a professional musician. He wasn't too keen on Depeche Mode's music but he needed the money after playing in a succession of bands – including The Dragons, Reel To Reel, Daphne & The Tenderspots, and The Hitmen – who all failed to take off. He could play Vince's parts with ease, sang good backing vocals, looked OK, and kept his thoughts on those awful jumpers the rest of the band were wearing to himself. For £100 a week, he was in.

As well as a new keyboardist, Depeche Mode also needed new material to keep the machine going. Martin offered up an old song, 'See You' – one he'd written almost four years earlier and performed with Norman & The Worms. Miller beefed up the bottom end at Blackwing, and 'See You' appeared as the band's next single.

In the USA, 'Just Can't Get Enough' was climbing up the *Billboard* Dance charts, while *Speak & Spell* was "doing reasonable business", according to Sire Records boss Seymour Stein, who was now busy pushing Madonna. Depeche Mode were due to play two dates in New York City in late January at Jerry Brandt's ultra-fashionable new club, the Ritz. Success in America was firmly on the agenda, with Depeche being sold as part of a new British Invasion of new-wave acts such as ABC, Heaven 17, Culture Club, The Associates, Simple Minds, and Ultravox.

Prior to leaving for America, the three-piece Depeche Mode appeared on the cover of *The Face*, looking strangely normal in jumpers and shirts, as the hip magazine's band of 1981. Another of the bands featured heavily inside was Soft Cell. Guided by Stevo, they too had enjoyed a phenomenal year – one that had brought them even more success than Depeche Mode. 'Tainted Love' had been a massive worldwide hit, even breaking into the US Top Ten. The group's debut album, *Non-Stop Erotic Cabaret*, was also doing good business in America, and, like Depeche Mode, they were with Seymour Stein and Sire, while current single 'Say Hello, Wave Goodbye' was in the UK Top Five around the turn of the year.

"When Soft Cell got their big hit in America with 'Tainted Love' the spotlight just really came on those early electronic bands," journalist Betty Page recalled. "The Human League were successful in America as well. A lot of the black acts listened to a lot of that music and what then became hip-hop was hugely influenced by electro. Depeche got flak in 1982, after Vince left, from the media. They made the decision that they were going to break America and everybody was laughing at them: you can't do that!

"Bands were put in a box by music journalists from day one and they weren't allowed to get out of that box," she continued. "I think a lot of journalists probably had them down as a fairly inconsequential synth-pop group not really capable of anything particularly meaningful. They were a little bit written-off. Bands who started out in the early 80s who were originally lumped in with that New Romantic/Futurist scene suffered because they weren't taken seriously. They were just seen as pop groups. It wasn't just Depeche that suffered from that. Duran Duran particularly couldn't understand why no one would take them seriously."

In New York, the band's two shows at the Ritz were a sold-out triumph. U2 had made their American debut at the same club just one month earlier; later in the year, MTV would hold its opening-night party there. For now, however, Depeche Mode struggled to make an impact on the US mainstream. Even with a club hit and a buzz about them in New York, gaining nationwide visibility would take work. But they were serious about cracking the States, and a second US tour was scheduled for May, with another gig at the Ritz to be followed by further dates in Philadelphia, Toronto, Chicago, Vancouver, San Francisco, Pasadena, and Los Angeles.

Alan Wilder got his first taste of Depechemania on the See You UK tour, which took up most of February. The first gig of the tour was taped for a BBC *In Concert* special at the famous Paris Studios situated on Regent Street in central London.

Blancmange were once again chosen as the support act for the tour. "It was a similar sort of thing but without Vince," Stephen Luscombe told me. "We did miss him a lot because that's how we'd all come together." The outpouring of fan devotion was identical to how it had been on the first tour, however, and the setlist was virtually the same, too, with just 'See You', the B-side 'Now, This Is Fun', and one new song ('The Meaning Of Love') added to a show still dominated by Vince's songs.

The 'See You' single had received mixed reviews but fan power had propelled it to Number Six in the charts – the band's highest entry to date. Julien Temple shot a video for the song, which featured new boy Alan and a cutesy narrative starring Martin's fiancée, Anne Swindell, as the shop girl Dave was desperate to see.

The band featured on the cover of a new magazine, *Record Mirror*, and appeared in the *NME* and *Smash Hits* – dressed, for some reason, in full cricket gear. There were more awful kids' TV shows, including one seriously schlocky performance in a mock barn, another visit to the *Top Of The Pops* studios, and more demand from Europe as the single made impressions in Germany and Holland.

After the sold-out UK leg, the See You tour continued across Europe. The band did their first dates in Spain; went back to Sweden, Holland, France, and Belgium; and then performed several shows in Germany as Rod Buckle sought to unite the relatively small Intercord sales-force across this vast territory. Germany was proving to be a difficult market to crack, so Buckle made the risky decision to hire independent promotion people in each major city. If anything, the media and TV appearances the band made in Europe were even cheesier than the ones they had endured in the UK, as exemplified by features in teen mags such as Germany's *Bravo*.

Between the end of the European tour and start of their second US tour, Depeche Mode released a new single, again penned by Gore: 'The Meaning Of Love' backed by the elegiac instrumental 'Oberkorn (It's A Small Town)'. It's no wonder Kraftwerk had gone to ground after their 1981 album *Computer World* – Gore and Miller's instrumentals set a new electronic benchmark. There was another video: a fantastic piece of work, again shot by Julien Temple, that perfectly complemented – and in fact enhanced – the song. The clip sets identically suited futurists against a cheesy cabaret backdrop and also reveals the band's sense of humour as they appear dressed in lab coats, literally trying to discover the meaning of love.

TV and radio plugger Neil Ferris was keen to keep Depeche Mode on the daytime Radio 1 playlist and argued that producers and DJs would be more likely to believe in a hit if the band appeared on kids' TV. The band, by now, were reluctant; although they could generally be persuaded, they always looked ill at ease – like Sparks but without the irony. It was an awkward time: a battle between credibility and popularity.

Ferris had mixed feelings about his handling of the band's early promotion. "There weren't that many outlets for music and most of it was kids' TV like *Tiswas*, *Multi-Coloured Swap Shop*, and *RunAround*," he told me. "Having the band on those sorts of shows was necessary and it wasn't a bad thing if they came across as slightly awkward." He tried to get more serious shows like the *Old Grey Whistle Test* interested in the band, but remembered one particular TV director who filmed the group in France for a slot on the show refusing to come to a gig later that evening. "He was just not interested."

"Playing live was absolutely fundamental to building their fan base," Ferris continued. "You've got to be hard-working, you've got to tour, you've got to be hungry to succeed. If you want to succeed, you've really got to be absolutely starving, and to do that you've got to work all hours and you've got to keep playing. It's all about playing live, building up a fan base, and, as I've said, back in those days there wasn't that much media, so you were very reliant on Radio 1, *NME* probably, and a few TV shows – and then playing live."

'The Meaning Of Love' reached Number 12 in the UK. Lyrically, it seemed odd by comparison to 'See You', with both "scars" and "God" mentioned; musically, it was upbeat but a little skewed. It went down well in Sweden and Hungary, but the band were disappointed by the UK chart position – especially in light of the incredible success of Vince Clarke's new band, Yazoo.

Vince hadn't wasted much time: Yazoo were sitting pretty at Number Two with their debut single, 'Only You'. Vince claimed to have offered the song to Depeche Mode but said they'd refused it. Yazoo remained on Mute but there was clearly bad blood between the two groups.

"There was obviously some tenderness there," Alison Moyet told me. "Vince didn't talk about it a lot but he obviously loved them. They were his mates, and it's very hard when one falls away and you're slightly ostracised. It was a like a marriage, how significant that relationship was for all of them. They would have felt betrayed by him and he would have felt excluded by them. You could see both sides. Depeche had a bit of a fallow time and Yazoo hit the ground running. His headspace was proving Depeche wrong and he was always happy to be out of the limelight. He was a very angry young man.

"In one of the other Depeche Mode books Fletcher remembers me as being the best fighter in school," Moyet continued. "I had one fight in school. It was because I threatened to nut him one time that he remembers me as a fighter. After I joined Yazoo, Vince and I went up to Mute and Fletcher was part of a group of about seven or eight people standing in a corner. There was just me – the new person – and Vince, standing on our own. Fletcher was being a bit lairy and sniggering, and it's intimidating when there's fewer of you and they're a crowd. I just said to Fletcher: you're going to stop laughing or I'm going to kick you in the nuts – and he did."

Yazoo remained on both Mute and Sire, with Rod Buckle guiding the band's international affairs. 'Only You' was quickly followed by 'Don't Go', another Top Five smash; debut album *Upstairs At Eric's* went to Number Two. Vince's new band easily outsold Depeche Mode in Germany and the USA as well. Second album *You And Me Both* went to Number One in the UK and 'Nobody's Diary' was another huge hit. Then, after 18 months together and one tour, Vince split up the band.

"As people it was strange, we were very different," Moyet recalled. "I couldn't warm him up – couldn't get inside him. I think he was horrified by my volatility. But he wasn't controlling at all during that period in Yazoo. Maybe he was fighting that because he'd been accused of it in Depeche. When he was working with me he was determined to show a really free hand. He was a really generous collaborator. He'd ask me if I had any songs; he'd sing me a song and I'd learn it and change the melody so it suited me, or I would bring something to the table. His staying power in the studio was incredible. Everything was done quickly; songs were written and taken to completion in three days. It was like he was speeding all the time."

After the split, Moyet signed a six-figure deal with CBS – a decision she came to regret, and which really cut up Daniel Miller. "Everything in Yazoo was done through Vince's contacts," Moyet recalled. "Daniel wasn't the most gregarious person, and I was really shy. Vince introduced me to Dan Silver, and when Vince and I split up and I was still with Mute, Silver was going to become my manager. He took me straight to meet a lawyer and accountant who did a job on me, telling me I had to leave Mute. I was 21. They talked me into it. I regretted it for many years."

Despite the disappointment of losing Moyet to CBS, Daniel Miller had two hit bands on his hands – Yazoo and Depeche – and was clearly enjoying himself. Mute released 'Fred Vom Jupiter' by Die Doraus Und Die Marinas, a must-have piece of bubble-gum pop kitsch from Der Plan's most influential label, Ata Tak, said to be Miller's favourite track of the period.

Moritz Reichelt of Der Plan supplied the colourful, distinctive artwork that graced the cover of both 'See You' and 'The Meaning Of Love'. "At the time I had been painting in an illustrative, narrative way with influences of cubism and comic art," he told me. "I also had this idea of 'German psychedelic', which the 'See You' cover is a true example of. I made it while on vacation in the Austrian Alps. The single cover of 'The Meaning Of Love' was a failure in psychedelics, because I had been on acid while painting it. That does not work!"

Mute also released ex-DAF member Chrislo Haas's huge German hit 'Los Ninos Del Parque' with his new band Liaisons Dangereuses, which Haas had formed with Beate Bartel of Einstürzende Neubauten. Produced by Conny Plank, the single was a massive underground hit and would later be cited as a key influence by many prominent Chicago house and Detroit techno DJs.

Miller released a second NON/Boyd Rice album and continued to persevere with Fad Gadget, even though Neil Ferris was having getting him on the radio or TV. He was also eyeing up a couple of new acts he liked the look of: The Birthday Party and Wire. These more leftfield bands and niche records helped keep Mute safe from ridicule and scorn at a time when much of it was being aimed at Depeche Mode.

By now the music papers had turned away from a group that had, in the course of two singles, suddenly gone from cool to cuddly. They were now perceived more as slightly naff teen-pop stars than as electronic pioneers. Only *Record Mirror* – where Betty Page was now working – remained loyal throughout this period. The band even found themselves lampooned by the political performance artist Attila The Stockbroker in his infamous poem 'Nigel Wants To Go And See Depeche Mode'.

What wasn't reported was how quickly Attila changed his opinion of the band. Rik Wheatley, the former Vermin singer now back in Basildon organising clubs under the Party Freaks banner and events such as a 'ranters' weekend attended by Attila and a young Phill Jupitus, recalled being told by Attila, a few months later, that he had completely reassessed his opinion of the band. "When he found out what their album covers were all about, he thought there was a lot of communism hidden in the lyrics," Wheatley recalled. "He was very left wing. From then on he wouldn't hear a word against them."

The press backlash continued, however, and it hit the group hard, particularly when they found themselves bracketed alongside acts like Kim Wilde, Altered Images, and Kajagoogoo. This was far from the image they wanted to present. At the suggestion of Neil Ferris, Mute hired an independent PR man, Chris Carr, in an attempt to claw back some credibility for the group.

Carr would end up working with the band for the next ten years. He ran a company called ARK PR with Claudine Martinet-Riley; both had previously worked for famed rock press agent Keith Altham, while Carr had also been responsible for introducing The Cure to the Altham roster. "With Neil Ferris it was a mutual appreciation," Carr told me. "He recommended us to Daniel and we recommend him to UB40 – it was a kind of plugger/PR alliance. We got involved just as the first Depeche album was coming out."

ARK's impressive roster of clients included Siouxsie & The Banshees, The Associates, The Birthday Party, Bauhaus, Southern Death Cult, 4AD Records, Beggars Banquet Records, and more. Carr also had close contact with The Cure and the Australian band The Saints, and would prove instrumental in bringing The Birthday Party to Mute.

"At that time The Birthday Party were still on 4AD," he recalled. "Daniel had been a fan of The Birthday Party from way back and had wanted to sign them, but it was at the time that he had spent a lot of money on DAF. Because he couldn't take them on he handed them to Ivo Watts-Russell at 4AD. Then, when Ivo was having to pay all the royalties to their Australian label and the money wasn't being transferred back, I went in to 4AD with Mick Harvey on behalf of the band and said: we can't exist. I had various members of the band sleeping in my flat. I approached Daniel and he said as long as Ivo isn't upset, Mute will sign the band. I said he's in no place to be upset – this is about survival."

For Carr, working with Depeche Mode felt a little odd at first. "Neither Claudine nor I were that comfortable with it, partly because members of our roster were slightly derisory about 'plinky-plonky pop bands', as they were described at the time," he recalled. "I found Depeche in the beginning to be somewhere between precious and naive."

The ARK offices were in Kilburn but Carr was often doing the rounds of the music-paper offices and would always call into Mute. He was a shrewd judge, having worked closely with labels such as 4AD and Beggars Banquet, and quickly noted how Rod Buckle was "a major, major part" of the organisation. "At that time everybody was so mistrustful of business," Carr recalled. "But without people like Rod Buckle, especially in Mute's case, Mute wouldn't have been able to make it to the next stage. For a long time I regarded him as the devil's spawn because of the business chicanery and all of that. But Rod had facilitated connections in Europe and the States – and with it, I guess, cash injections – to keep the whole thing afloat."

Carr put much of the early press euphoria surrounding Depeche Mode down to respect for Daniel Miller and Mute. "That's what got us off to the start," he said. "Now the press had turned and the band were really sensitive to the situation. They hadn't got to understand criticism yet. We then had to wait it out and develop various ... I wouldn't call it strategies, but maybe play it more instinctively. Daniel and I looked at the long term, and the band, to a great extent, were kept busy in Europe and the States and did their growing up. The one thing they were was voracious in wanting to experience new stuff and move onto a bigger playing field."

To begin with, Carr and ARK controlled all of the band's European press. "America was very much Sire – we had very little to do with it," Carr said. "There was some interest, but in America, by and large, it was still the case that *Rolling Stone* ruled the roost."

Carr often found himself diametrically opposed to Neil Ferris, who continued to push for the band to appear on more mainstream TV shows. "In the end, Daniel had to stand between Neil and I and side occasionally with one of us," he recalled. "On the PR side it was much more to do with credibility and wanting to be seen as credible, and Neil seemed to be undermining it. From the band's point of view it became less and less important to do those kinds of shows. Their attitude became: just go out there and get the radio play; you've got your Porsche, they're gonna play our records anyway. It does sound like dissing Neil, and it was to some extent. It was just a weird separation. For a large portion of the band's contemporaries, Radio 1 didn't matter that much, whereas the *NME* and *The Face* did.

"There was a whole different mind-set between press and radio," Carr continued. "With the press, taking someone out for a meal or taking them on the road was as far as it went. With radio it was: what are you into, man? Do you need tickets for the Tottenham game? There would be all these calls going on whenever there was a Wimbledon final. Radio was just seen as a much more corrupt environment, and to a certain extent pluggers – apart from people like Scott Piering at Rough Trade – were seen to facilitate that."

Depeche Mode started recording their second album over the summer of 1982. They had just returned from their short tour of the USA and Canada, during which Martin's relationship with his fiancée, Anne, had hit the rocks after a series of rows. The band made the decision to record the album without Alan Wilder, who was still considered to be nothing more than a hired hand.

*A Broken Frame* was recorded at Blackwing, with Daniel Miller again overseeing the production. It would prove to be an odd album – probably my favourite of all the albums this book covers. The standout track was another phenomenal Gore instrumental, 'Nothing To Fear'. On this album, his oddball influences were allowed to breathe, be they The Durutti Column, Jonathan Richman, or Der Plan. In terms of songwriting, Gore brought to the table far more romance and painted with much deeper colours than had Clarke. This was a ferocious talent's first full showing. It would sound unlike anything else out there. Miller was not a man afraid to experiment; together with engineers Eric Radcliffe and John Fryer, he and Gore began to fashion a new Depeche Mode.

The first track to be released from the album sessions was 'Leave In Silence'. Released in August 1982, it was a classic example of how a Martin Gore song could be interpreted in many different ways. Some people saw it as a comment on Vince's defection, others wondered if it was about the recent Falklands War (after all, Fad Gadget had weighed in on the subject with his single 'For Whom The Bell Tolls'). More than likely, however, it was about his break-up with Anne.

'Leave In Silence' was a long way from the perky pop Depeche had been associated with. It found fans among the more alternative spectrum of Radio 1 – John Peel, Peter Powell, Janice Long – but the daytime DJs hated it, telling Neil Ferris it was too doomy. The single peaked at Number 18 in the UK, didn't fare any better in Europe, and was never even released in the USA. Ironically, the song would end up bringing many new fans on board, but not the instant credibility the band craved. PR man Chris Carr realised that gaining the credibility of a narrow-minded press pack was going to be a long game, so he sought to send out signals that this was a band with more to offer than pop. "Artwork was the first sign," he said.

The 'Leave In Silence' single cover was designed by a newcomer to Mute: the young, energetic Martyn Atkins. Atkins was an associate of celebrated Factory Records sleeve designer Peter Saville: the pair had bonded over a shared appreciation of Jan Tschichold and worked together in London at Dindisc Records, the indie label associated with Virgin Records, where Saville was art director. Dindisc was home to Martha & The Muffins, The Rezillos, The Monochrome Set, and OMD, and had an office just down the road from Rough Trade. Prior to joining Dindisc, Atkins had produced a couple of single covers for Factory bands. Tony Wilson later described one of them, for 'Tunnel Vision' by Watching The Hydroplanes, as Factory's most beautiful cover design. "He probably said that to wind Peter up," Atkins laughed, "and to get a bit of competition going, hoping that Peter might get stuff done quicker!" Atkins had also designed a new Factory label, a musical 'f' in a circle that the label decided to use for Fractured Music, Joy Division's music publishing company. He and Saville also co-designed the famous Joy Division *Closer* album cover.

Atkins had recently hooked up with Bill Drummond and started doing the covers for Drummond's Zoo Records and the label's major act, Echo & The Bunnymen. He was exactly the kind of guy who would confer cool by association on Depeche Mode. "Depeche were not in the same league as the other acts I was working with at that time," he told me. "They had a few hit singles but they were not great songs. I think Anton [Corbijn] called them 'wimps with synths'."

It was not an appreciation of Depeche Mode that attracted Atkins to the band. It was Daniel Miller. "I was a big fan of Mute Records," he said. "Daniel and Mute were at the forefront of electronic music at that time. I went round to the Mute office on Seymour Place, near the gates to the back of the Marylebone court. It was like a little shop with a shop window. Right opposite were the back doors to Marylebone court, so you'd see the prison buses coming in and out all day. Daniel's assistant, Sue, seemed to really like my portfolio; she brought Daniel in and Daniel and I got on really well. He was The Normal – how tasty was that? We were into all the same stuff: Kraftwerk, La Düsseldorf, Harmonia, a lot of the Krautrock stuff. Even going back to stuff like Stockhausen. They were all reference points for us. Daniel was similar to Bill Drummond. Everything Daniel or Bill ever did was because they believed in it. It never seemed like any decision was ever made for financial reasons. They totally believed in whatever decision they made."

Miller and Atkins also shared a similar aesthetic that would come to bear on the Depeche Mode covers and the band's ads. "Even though Daniel is Jewish, we were both enamoured with the visual look of what went on in Nazi Germany and what was and is still going on in Germany – Audi, BMW, and so on," Atkins said. "They always had a strong ethic for trademarks and logo styles and colour schemes that somehow said strength and power. In the same way the Russian Communist iconology did as well: very similar, really, the images and the way it was presented.

"Daniel lived and breathed Mute Records," Atkins continued. "I think a lot of the bands who were on Mute didn't have managers, so he was like a dad to all these bands. He was such a great fucking guy and he had such conviction and scruples. Everybody just listened to him."

Miller told Atkins that Depeche Mode were making a new album and were interested in having him design the cover. They specifically wanted to lose their reputation for wimpy teeny-bop. "Daniel said he really wanted to do something that makes them look a bit more like a serious band," Atkins recalled. "He said: we really want to develop the music; they want to write more serious songs and they want to be around for a long time.

"They were gonna bring out a single before the album and they wanted that to be something of a taster for what the album was going be, both musically and visually. So for 'Leave In Silence' I came up with this logo that was like a wheat sheaf and sickle, using this Russian/Soviet-looking stuff. And they loved it. We had nice big 12-inch singles to deal with then; printed on reverse side of the board … things like that."

After the single was done, Atkins, Miller, and the band started talking about the album cover. "They wanted Brian Griffin to shoot the album cover because he'd shot the first one," Atkins recalled. "Why they wanted him back I don't know – that first cover is appalling. A stuffed duck inside a plastic wrapper? He came out with some bullshit story about it being symbolic of something in the womb.

"We talked to Brian and showed him what I was doing for the single cover," Atkins continued. "He talked about how maybe we could use someone who looked like a peasant, so I said: let's do something that looks like we're on the steppes of Russia – we can tie in the whole wheat sheaf thing, find a cornfield. Do something that feels like the worker … there was something romantic at that point, because it was post-punk, there was a romance again in the working class."

The inspiration for the cover for *A Broken Frame* – which remains one of the best album covers ever – was the 'Leave In Silence' single. Griffin loved the German romantic painter David Freidrich and intended to try to create a similar sense of light in the photo. Atkins found the location, a cornfield near Duxford, Cambridgeshire, just off the M11, with pylons in the background.

"I liked the idea of pylons because I liked the symbolism with their electronic music," he said. "Plus it was kind of a sense that technology was coming – if it hadn't had the pylons in, it would have almost looked like a period photograph. I thought the pylons were important because it gave it a thread to the modern age."

The band were blown away by the result. "I'd really passed the audition at that point," Atkins said. "It was great for me because it was obvious what an influence I had if you look at the first cover and then looked at the second cover." Atkins quickly got to know the Mute team. "Rod Buckle and Neil Ferris were a little bit old-school, very mainstream and kind of square," he said. He had more time for Chris Carr. "He did a lot of more respected bands, so he definitely wanted to steer them more in that direction. He was an interesting guy."

*A Broken Frame* was released at the end of September 1982. It was supported by a huge tour of the UK and Europe that would run for the rest of the year. Advance sales of half a million took the album to Number Eight in the UK. It also did good business in the Sonet stronghold of Sweden, and in Germany, where – thanks largely to Buckle's hiring of independent promo people – the band had begun to make inroads. The critics, however, were unsure how to react.

All the songs were written by Gore, whose tone was far warmer than Clarke's had been. Slow, aching, artful tracks such as 'My Secret Garden', 'Monument', and 'The Sun And The Rainfall' could be interpreted in many ways, but the whole album felt like a reflection on Martin's failing relationship with Anne Swindell. The words also pointed toward a more serious tone, with hints of social observation and even politics.

Making the album had been a struggle – note the inclusion of another old Norman & The Worms song, the slushy 'A Photograph Of You'. As a whole, however, and despite the band going on to virtually disown it, *A Broken Frame* was a superb piece of work, romantic and quirky, with upbeat tracks such as 'See You' and 'The Meaning Of Love' perfectly punctuating the more downbeat moments. The album signalled a real intent – a commitment from both Miller and the band to move forward. It was a challenging work, an exquisite mix of melody and melancholy. There was a sense of a real intelligence at work, with the band beginning to mark out a new territory for themselves beyond the boundaries of Basildon synth pop.

The packaging similarly spelt out how serious the band wanted to be taken. The impact of the artwork, which showed a peasant woman wielding a sickle in a field of wheat below a brooding sky, was huge: it was voted one of the most extraordinary photographs of the decade by *Life* magazine, which reproduced the shot on its cover in 1989. It was perhaps the greatest colour photograph ever taken. The man responsible was Brian Griffin. "I was most excited about the concept of this peasant," he said. "It was right up my street. It was a bull's-eye for me in terms of subject matter. It was everything I loved: Russia, social realism …

"I can tell you exactly what happened," he continued. "Jaqui Frye, who was my stylist at the time, designed the outfit, and we put this middle-aged dancer in it. It had been pouring with rain all day, all during the journey there, and it looked very dismal, actually, but we had the patience to wait for the rain to stop. Then I had a stroke of luck: the sun broke through those storm clouds and produced that wonderful light, combined with the lights I had on the subject. It produced a one-in-a-million effect. A feeling. We nearly shat ourselves when we saw the Polaroid. We could hardly speak. The Polaroids were as good as the cover. And we shot it quickly, of course.

"Then we brought it back to my studio. I had a working table at one end and there was a sofa and a coffee table and a little office at the other end. We laid them all out on the light box and Daniel came down. We were rubbing our hands in glee. As he walked in the studio he said: where are they? I said over there, go and have a look. When Daniel saw them … I don't know whether he wanted to have a heart attack, or what."

## CHAPTER 10
# BETTER RED THAN DEAD

**M**att Fretton was 18 and, for £60 a night, the support act for Depeche Mode's A Broken Frame tour of the UK and Europe at the end of 1982. "I thought *A Broken Frame* was beautiful," the outspoken Fretton told me. "That was Martin. He's a melancholy guy, very interior. I was very moved by his romantic feelings. The Vince Clarke stuff, I thought, was just trite rubbish." Fretton was on the verge of signing to Chysalis Records and about to find himself becoming the flavour of the month – and appearing on the cover of *Smash Hits* – with his debut single, 'It's So High'. His parents were old pals of Blancmange, who had recently been signed to London Records and were developing more of a pop sound wth Human League/Heaven 17 producer Martyn Ware.

The connection with Blancmange had allowed Fretton to step in when they couldn't make it for a date at the Hammersmith Odeon on the See You tour. He'd impressed Depeche Mode and was, in his own words, "an easy gig" – just one man and a backing tape. He was no novice, either, having already toured with The Boomtown Rats, Eurythmics, and Gang Of Four. "It was a funny stage for the band," he recalled of the 1982 tour. "They'd been successful with these pop songs and then they'd made quite a decisive and daring move with *A Broken Frame*. When you listen back to that music on that record it has an oddly unfinished quality to it – it sounds like somebody forgot to finish doing the overdubs. There's an awful lot of empty space in it – very sparse sequencers. It was a transitional period for them. Were they going to be able to make it without Vince? The mood changed quite profoundly when Martin started writing the songs."

Daniel Miller was once again very hands-on during the tour and Fretton observed the relationship between him and the band. "They would often take the piss out of him, and they used to laugh at the records he had made," he said. "They thought it was a bit funny, like finding out your dad had been in a band. I think they did like those records very much but they liked to poke fun at him as well because he was older. He was a huge influence on them – there's no way they could have done what they've done without his influence; certain instruments they would use, which were his, which he brought to the production, which they had no clue about before he came along. But I think they just liked to tease him a bit. His National Health glasses were held together with a bunch of Sellotape because he sat on them. He was always a bit overweight and scruffy and just so unlikely."

Fretton travelled on the tour bus with Depeche Mode and observed the inter-band dynamic. "They were obsessed with arcade games," he laughed. "Every time we'd stop at a motorway service station, they'd rush in to stick all their money into Space Invaders and stuff. They were all pretty excellent at those games, except for Alan." The new boy was still on the sidelines. "He always seemed like an odd man out to me. He certainly didn't fit. He was a musician among non-musicians; he was middle class among working-class guys; an older guy among younger guys, classically trained. It was a slightly odd thing but it worked."

Fretton was closest with Gore. "Martin was reading Brecht in German when we were touring," he said. "We would talk about music. I loved Sparks – the *No. 1 In Heaven* album was a big influence with all of us. Martin said they'd asked Sparks to tour with them as a support act but Sparks had been such arseholes about it, demanding so much money that it didn't happen."

Fretton remembered Dave and Martin's girlfriends, Jo and Anne, "sitting looking at catalogues" on the back of the bus. "They were like young working class girls who had rich boyfriends and they were going to buy everything in these catalogues," he recalled. "Some giant catalogue full of bad jewellery and horrible clothes – they'd sit and flick through these things and work out what they were going to order. I'm sounding like a terrible snob – which I suppose I am – but it was quite funny so see and so alien to me."

This was Anne's final tour with Depeche Mode. Shortly after the tour ended, she and Martin split up. "We broke up when it was just the very beginning of them having a bit more money," she said. "We'd bought a car, a second-hand car. Martin didn't drive so I was driving. I saw a Triumph Spitfire I wanted and he said I couldn't have it because I would drive too fast and we had to get Andy in the back. Andy was with us all the time. We had to have space in the car for Andy so we couldn't have a sports car."

I reminded Anne of what Martin had said about the breakup with "devout Christian" Anne in an interview with *Uncut* magazine in 2001: "She had me on reins, she was ridiculous, anything was perverted. If I was watching something on TV and there was a naked person, I was a pervert."

"I don't think it is an unfair observation," Anne told me. "My first reaction was I think I understood him more than he realised. When Martin subsequently adopted that S&M look – and some of the stories you'd hear – it was difficult. But it was something I always knew was there, so it wasn't unexpected. It wasn't something I was really shocked or surprised about but it being so out-there was hard to see.

"I could see the changes that were happening in him that just then escalated after we split up," she said. "The bigger they got, the more exposure, the more he travelled, the more he was away. I could feel him slipping away from me. I could see what was coming, really, with the changes that were going on. I didn't know how to handle that. I was too young, too inexperienced. Kind of what I did was to make it worse, really. I just panicked and clamped down and freaked out a lot of the time.

"My mum remembers it being a really traumatic time, constant phone calls from America in tears: Martin doesn't love me any more – how am I gonna get home? Then, by the evening: oh, it's OK – we're sorted now. Something would have happened and I would have gone into a panic. I was really insecure, desperately insecure. I felt like I was in a world I didn't belong in. I had no resources to draw on to try and know how to belong in it. It was very exciting and I wouldn't have missed it for the world, but it was very difficult as a young person with a very Christian background.

"Martin had much more freedom to explore because he didn't have the close affinity with religion," she continued. "It was much easier for him than it was for Andy, or Vince, or me, who had that very strong Christian background. When you're told you've got God watching everything you do, and he's going to have you up in front of the Pearly Gates questioning you about everything you've done – it's quite hard sometimes.

"Somebody showed me a photo of me and Martin at Greenbelt. Steve Burton took it – we look like two little hippie chicks, two eco-buddies – a beautiful photo, so unlike his later S&M look. It couldn't be more extreme to what he was like when we were together – that very earthy, slightly hippie feel and that harsh S&M look. But it was very much part of who he was, so although I found it kind of difficult to see, I also knew it was a part of him he needed to explore."

◻▪◻

The A Broken Frame tour proved the loyalty of the band's UK fan base with a run of successful gigs including two sold-out dates at the Hammersmith Odeon. In Europe the band focused on the German market, playing over half of their 15 continental dates there. In early 1983, prior to embarking on the US leg of the tour, they recorded some more material and released a new single, the first with Alan Wilder actively involved.

Recorded at Blackwing, 'Get The Balance Right' was the strangest Depeche Mode single yet – a further step to the left, lyrically and musically. Once again, Gore's words could be interpreted in several different ways. Maybe it was about struggling with pop fame; maybe it was about finding your own path in life; maybe it was the most beautiful love letter to Anne. The single peaked at Number 13 in the UK charts but picked up little action in Europe. A new director, Kevin Hewitt, shot the video, this time casting the band somewhat inexplicably as scientists and fairground carnies, although he did manage to get the Galaxian arcade game in there.

Alongside features in *Smash Hits* and *Record Mirror*, Depeche Mode were also back on the *NME* radar. The kids' TV shows continued, with the band playing weird tracks like 'Monument' on air. Plugger Neil Ferris also got them booked onto the hip new Channel 4 music show *The Tube*, while Martin's image was undergoing a subtle shift. The Marks & Spencer jumpers were out.

The band's six dates in America in March were not a success. They struggled to make any impression on the Top 40, and even their show at the Ritz in New York was deemed a failure. They could command a crowd in Los Angeles but elsewhere they were faltering, unable to cash in on the British Invasion taking MTV and the American charts by storm. It would be two years before Depeche Mode toured America again. The band's US label, Sire, was a small operation, albeit one backed by the major muscle of Warner Bros. Label boss Seymour Stein was having tremendous success with Madonna, The Ramones, and Talking Heads, and perhaps his enthusiasm could only be spread so far.

What the band didn't realise – what no one realised at the time – was how influential 'Get The Balance Right' had been on the black club scene. I spoke with John McCready, author of a famous 1989 article about the band for *The Face*, which asked: 'Did Depeche Mode Detonate House?' McCready took the band to the best club on the planet, Detroit's Music Institute, to meet pioneering house DJs Kevin Saunderson, Derrick May, and Frankie Knuckles, to whom Depeche Mode were a major influence – on par, these DJs said, with Kraftwerk and New Order. Each of these DJs talked about their admiration for the band's clean European sound – something that, at the time, was very much standing in the way of the band achieving mainstream success in the USA. Derrick May hijacked the interview; McCready had to pull him apart from a ready-to-fight Dave Gahan. May nonetheless acknowledged Depeche Mode as a key influence on house and techno music. The tracks he talked about most were 'Get The Balance Right' and 'Just Can't Get Enough'.

The A Broken Frame tour concluded with April dates in Japan, Hong Kong, and Thailand, where the band-members were besieged by fans and bemused by a full itinerary of press interviews and appearances on bizarre TV shows. Touring the Far East for the first time was an eye-opening experience and one that would filter back into the making of their new album. Keen to take the Depeche Mode sound further, the band and Miller started looking for a new studio to record in. They were particularly interested in the Garden, the studio run by former Ultravox singer John Foxx in Shoreditch, East London. Here they would begin a fruitful relationship with in-house engineer/producer Gareth Jones, who would play a pivotal role in the recording of the band's next three albums. Jones was living in a licensed squat in Brixton and would describe himself as an "acid-head hippie". He had a broad but elitist range of tastes from Talking Heads and Pink Floyd's *Dark Side Of The Moon* to classical music and contemporary experimental jazz, such as the Spontaneous Music Ensemble. He started making records at Pathway studios in Islington, North London, a "small and scummy" analogue studio, where he'd worked with acts such as Lene Lovich, Dire Straits, Madness, and "a whole load of punk" bands, including The Motors.

Jones's relationship with Foxx dated back to when the electronic music pioneer had used Pathway to record his first solo album, *Metamatic*, which Jones engineered. Foxx turned Jones on to The Normal and Conny Plank, who'd produced Ultravox's *Systems Of Romance* album, which opened up "the whole Neu! and Kraftwerk thing".

Jones had also been working with the Belgian independent label Les Disques Du Crépuscule, which had close links with Manchester's Factory Records. He produced an album for the label by new-wave group Tuxedomoon, *Desire*, which was sure to be on Daniel Miller's radar. He'd also produced *The Lost Jockey*, a systems-music record featuring young British minimalist composers Orlando Gough, Andrew Poppy, and John Wesley Barker.

Systems music was of particular interest to Jones. "There is a kind of repetitive, synthetic sequenced element in all that early Steve Reich stuff, at the time when he was doing like six pianos, drumming and clapping music, *Music For 18 Musicians* – it's really almost sequencer based," he told me. "Working with John, we were using an ARP sequencer [the same machine Depeche Mode used] and a drum machine, so they were starting to be a massive part of my life."

Foxx had built the Garden after self-funding the recording of *Metamatic* and selling the album to Virgin. The advance allowed him and a few others – a photographer and a sculptor among them – to buy a warehouse in the then derelict area of Shoreditch. Jones helped Foxx build the studio in the basement. "I was very interested in gear and nitty-gritty, and John was more interested in concepts," Jones said. "And that studio became a little bit known on the London scene because it was one of the first studios that an electronic musician had ever built – that's why Depeche and Daniel got interested."

"They thought: oh, that's cool, it's not your normal rock'n'roll studio. In those days, for the purist pop-electronic bands, 'guitar' was like a dirty word. No one wanted anything to do with guitars and drums kits – that was really 70s. John's studio was streamlined and a bit sleek and built from a minimalist aesthetic."

Depeche Mode went down to the Garden and did a test session over a couple of days. Foxx had wanted Jones to engineer the session but he'd refused. "It was like pop music, not my thing," Jones explained. Depeche Mode told Foxx they liked the studio but they didn't particularly like the engineer who worked with them on the test session. Foxx had a word with Jones. "He said: look, they like the studio, this is a good thing for you to get involved in, it's Daniel who made that record The Normal that we loved when we heard it in Pathway, and they're an interesting band – you should be doing it," Jones recalled. "So I kind of begrudgingly went to meet them. And we all hit it off, and it turned out to be a fantastic, creative relationship. But it was not something I went for – it was something that arrived in my life, and thanks to John's mentoring, really, I followed it up."

Jones became instrumental in the recording of the new album, *Construction Time Again*, and in changing the sound of the band. "I came to the project with an obsession with trying to make the band sound tougher," he said. "I had a real interest in acoustic spaces. Up until that time, the way the synthesizer was recorded seemed to be to plug it into the mixing desk. You had no sense of acoustic space around it. So one thing that seemed to be really obvious to me was to get the synthesizers and shove them through amplifiers, so they went into an acoustic space, and put a mic on the amplifier and a mic at the back of the room. And it changed everything. It gave the synthesizers a distorted edge. It was like the synthesizers were recorded in a real space rather than in a virtual electronic space."

Another outstanding feature of this album was the use of found sounds. Jones and the band used a high-quality tape recorder to record themselves in Shoreditch's desolate wastelands, banging metal with hammers, bashing anvils, creaking doors, smashing corrugated iron, old cars; on construction sites, in disused railway yards, piles of junk metal, empty workshops, smashing glass – and of, course, playing ping pong. They would then sample these sounds in the studio.

Jones and the band took to it all with real gusto. "We did that fabulous track 'Pipeline', which is all made up of sampled metal," Jones recalled. Gore even recorded the vocal for 'Pipeline' in a disused workshop out in the Shoreditch wasteland. Boyd Rice and Frank Tovey had of course done something similar, some years earlier, for Mute's *Easy Listening For The Hard Of Hearing* album, while Throbbing Gristle had recorded the sound of lathes, electric saws, and trains. And Kraftwerk had said, prosaically, "You will discover the car is a musical instrument." In fact, a major thrust of the original Italian Futurist movement was to value noise and to place artistic and expressive value on sounds that had previously not been considered even remotely musical. Francesco Balilla Pratella's *Technical Manifesto Of Futurist Music* (1911) sums up the group's credo: "To present the musical soul of the masses, of the great factories, of the railways, of the transatlantic liners, of the battleships, of the automobiles and airplanes. To add to the great central themes of the musical poem the domain of the machine and the victorious kingdom of Electricity."

What was new was the technology cascading toward Depeche Mode at a rapid rate. Whereas Throbbing Gristle and to an extent Fad Gadget and Boyd Rice used their industrial noise as just that – industrial noise – Miller, Jones, and Depeche Mode had a key new piece of machinery: the digital Synclavier sampler, which Miller owned, and which could reprocess the found sounds and allow them to be played in any rhythm or melody. The E-mu Emulator, which performed a similar task, became another key tool. "The manual's very thick," Gore deadpanned at the time. This marked a definite move from the sequencer to the sampler, from analogue synths to the world of digital technology.

Around the same time, Vince Clarke, having recently split Yazoo, was working on a new project called The Assembly, his plan being to use a conveyor belt of vocalists. He had acquired the most expensive sampler machine: the Fairlight. It cost £40,000, as opposed to the £5,000 Emulator. Gore's Basildon humour – and maybe a little rancour – surfaced when he'd used crude tape to spell out the name 'Fairlight' on the back of his much cheaper synth for the band's performance of 'Get The Balance Right' on *Top Of The Pops*.

There was major change at Mute during this period as the label moved out of Seymour Place to new offices at 49–53 Kensington Gardens Square in Bayswater, London W2. They were more functional than plush. Miller also began collaborating with his long-time friends from the angular post-punk band Wire, Graham Lewis and Bruce Gilbert. Together, they recorded a one-off album at Blackwing under the name Duet Emmo. Robert Görl of DAF had also re-joined the label, and his single 'Mit Dir' was pure class. This was all well and arty, but far more perplexing to Depeche Mode was Miller's announcement that he'd signed Australian wild boys The Birthday Party, a junkie rock'n'roll aberration.

Miller still found time to work on the new Depeche Mode album at the Garden. "We were all obsessed by sound," Jones recalled, "and luckily we had the time and budget to experiment. We all seemed to be very much on the same page really early; we were all trying to do something we'd never done before, to be darker and to be more edgy. We created all our samples ourselves; everything we did was new. We never used anything that we'd done before. The whole point was this constant voyage of discovery.

"It was fantastic working with Daniel," he added. "He was very challenging and inspiring and it was a great learning curve – for all of us, actually, looking back. Working with a songwriter of Martin's calibre was just a fantastic experience for me. I learnt so much about effective pop songwriting: partly from being able to dissect his songs, dissect his demos, and reassemble them as part of the team, and partly from all the work we did in the studio on changing structure and enhancing changes and choruses and middle-eights and so on."

▭▬▭▬▭

Depeche Mode spent three months making *Construction Time Again*, during which Alan Wilder began to play a more significant role in the recording process. "He was a total sound-nut as well," Jones recalled. "It was always me, Alan, and Daniel for those three albums – we were always there from the beginning of the session to the end of the session. Alan was a complete producer-head as well. Still is. Complete sonic-nut."

The new album was mixed at Hansa Studios in Berlin, a place that would have a radical influence on the band and their next two albums. It was Gareth Jones who had suggested working there. Prior to working with

Depeche Mode, Jones had mixed *Bi Nuu*, the third and final album by the German new-wave group Ideal, at Hansa. He then went on to mix an album by DOF, a "very melodic, middle-of-the-road pop" project founded by Ideal singer-songwriter Annette Humpe and her sister, Ingrid, but fronted by two Austrian comedians. (The single 'Codo' went on to be a massive German Number One hit.)

Hansa was a "big, big studio complex" in Potsdamer Platz, in the Kreuzberg district, which Jones described as being "like a bombsite". The studio was equipped with a Solid State Logic mixing board, the pinnacle of mixing technology at the time. "It was an incredible state-of-the-art mix room in the penthouse, overlooking the wall," Jones said. While he was mixing the DOF record, Miller was downstairs recording The Birthday Party in Studio 2. "I said to Daniel: hey man, come and look at the mix room – maybe we can mix *Construction Time Again* here?"

Miller was soon sold on the idea. "It just felt like totally the right thing to do," Jones recalled. "He was equally taken with it. And it was very cost-effective. The deutschmark was very weak against the pound and there were tax incentives on offer from the West German government to go and work in Berlin, because it was like an isolated city in the middle of East Germany with a wall around it – it all just seemed to make fantastic economic sense. Beyond that, we could feel the creative vibrancy was there as well."

This was the start of a three-year Berlin phase for Depeche Mode. The band loved Hansa, recognising the studio and the city as the inspiration for Bowie's *Low*, *"Heroes"*, and *Lodger* albums, and Berlin itself, where Bowie had lived with Iggy Pop, whose albums *The Idiot* and *Lust For Life* also bore the imprint of Hansa. (Gore would later name Bowie and Iggy as his two musical icons.)

As Jones said, Hansa overlooked the Berlin Wall, and the city itself had an edgy feel and reputation as the counter-culture capital of Europe. The vibe was dark, druggy, sexually free, alcoholic, avant-garde, with lots of black leather, all-night bars, and young, creative artists all interested in alternative lifestyles. It was a 24-hour city, an erotic city, adventurous, exciting. Martin, now single and fluent in German, was particularly captivated.

While mixing the album, Depeche Mode and their small contingent stayed at the InterContinental Hotel and were keen to taste the nightlife, particularly at Dschungel, a favoured hangout of Einstürzende Neubauten, the hippest and hardest of all the German new-wave German bands, and other Berlin hipsters. "Depeche were young, very young," Jones recalled. "Daniel and I were older – I was about 27, 28. The band were exploring and consuming the world. Germany was very important because we loved Kraftwerk, Neu!, and Can. We seemed to appreciate that music more than a lot of the Germans we met, who were kind of obsessed with English and American rock'n'roll. We were like: no, Kraftwerk, Can, Neu!, Cluster, Tangerine Dream – these are the great bands. It was very important for us to connect to Germany musically as well, and it was a huge territory, so a real big revenue-earner as well."

By now, Jones himself had decided to live full-time in Berlin in the midst of its burgeoning influential musical scene. Nick Cave and Mick Harvey had split up The Birthday Party and were sounding out Blixa Bargeld of Einstürzende Neubauten to form a new group. Harvey was also working on a new project called Crime & The City Solution. Both bands would continue to work with Mute. Daniel Miller also remained close to former DAF sequencer man Chrislo Haas. (Der Plan were also part of this radical and vibrant scene, but according to the band's Moritz Reichelt, Miller was no longer interested in working with them or the Ata Tak label's other main act, Pyrolator, despite the fact that Gore was a huge fan.)

Jones opened a small window into the band's dynamic of the period when I asked him whether Andy Fletcher, with his obsession over chart positions, was more concerned with keeping things 'pop'. "Didn't Andy famously teach Vince Clarke how to play his first three chords on the guitar or something?" Jones replied. "I don't know if that's an apocryphal tale or not, but Andy was really important as a member of the group dynamic. The thing about it was, although Alan wrote a bit of *Construction Time Again*, it was just Martin, really. Martin wrote the songs; Dave sang most of them and Martin sang some of them, and Martin sang backing vocals and Alan sang a bit of backing vocals. But everything was played by machines, so it was more about what atmosphere we teased out of the machines, and Andy was a really important part of that, because he was a really important part of the group dynamic. And he would also put his foot down sometimes and say: it's not weird enough, that sounds a bit too normal. I know what you're saying – Andy was very concerned that we should maximise the potential of Martin's songs, very concerned that that should be the case – but not necessarily in the most simple, 'pop' way. With that album they were determined to do something that would earn the respect of their peers. They were determined not to be dismissed as synth-pop. That was very important to Andy as well: that the band should reinvent themselves in some kind of successful but moody, dark, edgy kind of way.

"Andy was also very concerned – they were all very concerned, as far as I assess it – by the way the English media had fallen out of love with them and dismissed them as super-upbeat pop, to the point that we all had this joke about us being in the uncool corner in Dschungel when we were doing *Construction Time Again*."

□–□–□

In July, Depeche Mode released a new single with a strong melody and a memorable – if somewhat unsubtle – hook: 'Everything Counts'. It put the band back in the UK Top Ten and became their first German hit, while also performing well in Austria, Switzerland, and Sweden.

The single's release coincided with Labour being crushed by Margaret Thatcher's Conservative government in the 1983 UK general election. 'Everything Counts' was interpreted by many to be an anti-capitalist address and a condemnation of multinational businesses and/or Britain's industrial sell-off. It could also have been about the music – the handshake that sealed the band's contract with Mute and the grabbing hands of their distributors at the time. The subject matter didn't stop the band being splashed all over a new teen-pop magazine called *No 1*, or appearing on *Top Of The Pops*. They looked far from radical, with Dave, Fletch, and Alan dressed in clean-cut shirts and slacks, and only Martin in Berlin black.

Meanwhile, in Basildon, the Conservatives had strengthened their grip on the town following a reorganisation of constituency boundaries. Basildon had been a testing ground for the council-house sell-off, and a staggering 95 per cent of the New Town had voted Tory. Of the 25,000 dwellings built by the Corporation, 10,000 had been sold. The Conservatives were selling off huge chunks of Corporation land to private investors, and the building of public housing for rent was all over. After the Carreras Rothmans factory closed down, unemployment reached the critical level of 10,000. Andy Fletcher's dad was one of 1,500 Carreras employees to be laid off.

Released a month after 'Everything Counts', *Construction Time Again* was a timely album. Musically, it took Depeche Mode into innovative sonic territories; lyrically, tracks such as 'More Than A Party', 'Pipeline', 'Told You So', and 'Shame' could be seen as protest songs. There was much talk of the band maturing. The album matched the single in reaching Number Six in the UK. It sold over a million copies in Europe, breaking into the Top 10 in Germany (where it sold a quarter of a million copies – double what it sold in the UK) and the Top 20 in France and Sweden, while also shifting units in Italy, Holland, Spain, and Switzerland.

In Belgium the band performed on TV in front of 20-foot red flags on a set featuring hammer and sickle and heroic peasants. On other occasions they mimed on completely naff pop shows and faced countless banal press interviews. The experimentation angle was a little overplayed. *Construction Time Again* was more of a stepping-stone to what was to come. In terms of beats, there was still plenty of sequenced DAF in the mix but not so much of the heavy, metallic Neubauten influence. The album would certainly have benefited from a classic Gore instrumental, while the lyrics were unusually direct and largely anti-capitalist (something Gore would avoid in the future). The strong look of the artwork and its plundering of fascist and communist iconography seemed planned to emphasise the songs' socialist message and the celebration of the worker.

The album cover was a Brian Griffin photograph of an industrial worker in a leather apron with a sledgehammer on the Swiss Alps with the Matterhorn in view. "The reaction of Daniel and the band seemed quite positive," Griffin told me. "But to repeat *A Broken Frame* was like asking to do the *Mona Lisa* again. We couldn't reach that, but we reached pretty high. I thought we did pretty good."

"It wasn't just about the music, it was about the whole package," the album's designer, Martyn Atkins, recalled. "Dave seemed to be the main guy I'd speak to about the covers. Then later on it became Alan. I started to do their merchandising stuff, too – designing their T-shirts. Because they didn't have a manager, they delegated: Fletch was responsible for the merchandising stuff; Dave was responsible for the packaging, the graphics;

Martin had his hands full doing all the writing. It seemed like a good setup. They didn't seem to pull each other down if somebody had an idea that was different. They were very open to each other, very un-English in that sense. That's what's cool about guys who grew up together: they're all mates and they're all on a journey together. It's better than working in a factory, isn't it? There was a camaraderie there. They were all comrades. Dave was still a bit of a wide-boy. We were doing a photo session in the old Docklands and he turned up and he'd just bought a brand new XR3 Escort – a white one with spoilers on it and everything."

Atkins was unhappy with the album cover. "I didn't have much to do with the photograph for that cover," he said. "I guess Brian steamed in and told Daniel he'd got this idea for putting a guy with a hammer up the Matterhorn. Obviously he was trying to take the reins back from me. They approved the idea and he went and shot that, but I never liked the photograph because I thought it looked like he'd shot it in the studio. It just didn't have the realism of the *A Broken Frame* photo.

"We'd used graphics of men with hammers on the cover of 'Get The Balance Right' and 'Everything Counts', all with splashes or red: red hammers, red hands. It felt like it was good to celebrate the working classes in that period. You could have a job and still be glamorous. It just seemed like Depeche were growing as band. Their music was getting more mature and they were getting more respect from more serious magazines than *Smash Hits*."

Both the album and the 'Everything Counts' single had smashed open Europe – not just for the band, but also for Mute. "It got out of control because there was so many copies and different versions of stuff going out in all these territories," Atkins recalled. "Then we'd have all the posters and the ads. That was the beginning of the frenzy of creating different mixes for everything: doing limited edition 12-inches and then doing a limited-edition collectors' 12-inch. It was great because you got to do stuff that you wouldn't ordinarily do because it was a collector's item. They knew it was going to sell. You could kind of do anything and you wouldn't get anybody saying the name of the band's not big enough or you can't see Dave Gahan's crotch. Depeche Mode never wanted to be on the covers of their records."

Atkins was also busy with the growing new Mute roster. He did the

artwork for Vince Clarke's new project, The Assembly, as well as records by
Robert Görl and Nick Cave. "Cave was a fucking nightmare," he laughed.
"He came in to the studio and just sat there and said: I fucking hate
everything, all right, so just show me what you got."

*Construction Time Again* put Depeche Mode back on the cover of the
*NME*. Martin – not Dave – was up front, dressed all in black; inside, X
Moore of The Redskins wrote a heavily politicised piece that applauded the
brutal socialist message of the album. That same week Dave appeared alone
on the cover *of Record Mirror*, looking tanned and exceptionally pretty.

The *NME* cover was part of a concerted effort by the band's PR, Chris
Carr, to get the serious music press interested in what the band was doing.
"I slowly but surely got to appreciate them as individuals, and then
collectively I could see they were working toward something in a fairly
brave, artistic manner that demanded respect," he told me. "They were
growing up. There was also an expansion at Mute: Hansa, Berlin, Nick
Cave. Depeche were highly suspicious of Daniel's involvement with Nick,
something they didn't understand at the time but came to appreciate
because they were fairly open. But initially it was like: what the hell has he
done now?"

Carr also saw Depeche Mode develop as a band. "It was run very much
as a democracy once Vince had gone," he recalled. "Everybody was given
a role. There was this whole period with Alan Wilder, who seemed to be
perpetually on trial. When it came to interviews the idea was at times we'll
do two of you and then two of you, and then as they got more respect it
was individually. Initially, Alan thought: why the fuck should I bother? I
remember thinking: God, he's an obstinate bastard. Then, finally, Alan
became an official member of the band. That was the whole democratic
thing. It would take a while to get a decision. There's always been this
weird timing they have throughout their history. Either Dave or Martin will
lead the way, and Dave was at the time very much more the sophisticated
of the three of them, once Vince had gone. Dave used to look at them like
stupid young boys, but then, at a certain point, as Martin started to grow,
Dave became more domesticated. That continued through their career –
with either Dave or Martin stepping up. Martin was very gauche to begin
with but the confidence started and then the experimentation.

"Daniel was totally hands-on, but he had other acts to think about as Mute was growing," Carr said. "I remember he came round to mine in the early hours of the morning with the new Fad Gadget album and it wasn't the right thing to listen to in my front room with a missus and two young kids. So we went to sit in his Saab, which had a decent sound system, and he played me what Frank Tovey had handed in as the completed album. Daniel had an incredible soft spot for Frank, and at the end of it he goes: well, what do you think? We'd always been honest with one another, and I said: Daniel, it's not up to scratch. He said he knew and started to cry. What was I supposed to do? Put my arm around the old bloke and go: now, now? Frank developed a chip on his shoulder: everybody else had success, he was as wild as Nick Cave in a given way, he had commercial songs – he became resentful and he became desperate, then resigned to it, and then bitter again."

In September, with the band about to set off on another mammoth tour of the UK and Europe, 'Love In Itself' was released as a single. It was more a gesture than anything; it peaked at Number 21 in the UK and barely registered in Europe. As Andy Fletcher would later put it, it bombed. A few critics took note of the band's willingness to challenge preconceptions, but beyond the X Moore piece, the credibility that everyone at Mute was hoping for had failed to come.

The single was the only song on the album to deal with what would become familiar territory for Gore: love and relationships, the end of one thing and the start of something else. *Construction Time Again* had been set aflame – and largely carried – by one strong single, 'Everything Counts.' What was most noticeable about 'Love In Itself' was the video, which shows Gore starting to more openly flaunt his fascination with bondage, with belts X'd across his chest and wrapped around his groin, and handcuffs dangling from his belt.

The Construction Time Again Tour reached its UK climax with three nights at the Hammersmith Odeon. The European leg in December was focused almost entirely on Germany, with 13 of the 18 dates in German cities, including three in Hamburg, where the band were now playing to crowds of 10,000 people. They also played to massive audiences in Sweden, Denmark, Holland, and Belgium. The stage design saw the band on risers, surrounded by three wooden towers with light playing through slats – a first sign of spectacle.

Mark Fretton was once again chosen as the band's support act. "The Construction Time Again tour was really a big shift musically," he recalled. "There was also a noticeable expansion in scale. I remember doing a Velodrome in Paris with 20,000 people; I remember walking out on stage and thinking: oh, shit – it was huge, really massive. For them, that tour was definitely a move toward massiveness. There was a profound shift in their status. Oddly, they'd become rather unfashionable in the UK, but they were massive in Europe, particularly Germany."

Fretton had a tough time playing to partisan Depeche Mode fans across Europe, and recalled how, in a sign of derision, money was thrown at him in Italy. He wanted to quit but instead cut his set down to the bare minimum and got off quick. Depeche, meanwhile, were still playing songs like 'Photographic', 'New Life', 'Just Can't Get Enough', and 'Boys Say Go!' as well as 'Big Muff', 'See You', and 'The Meaning Of Love'.

With this tour a familiar pattern emerged that would be repeated over the next two years: release an album in the autumn, tour the UK and Europe in October and December, break to cut a new single, and then play more dates in March. On the A Broken Frame tour, the final set of dates had been in the USA; on the Construction Time Again tour, those final dates were in Spain and Italy. The USA was missed out entirely.

The band had asked Fretton to tour with them as a friend, at a time when buy-ons – when new acts paid to support an established act in the hope of developing a fan base – were commonplace. As before, he travelled with the group on their tour bus. "I was on the tour because they wanted me on the tour," he said. "Fletch used to regularly point out to me – slightly tersely and slightly humorously, because he did like to be provocative in a low-key way – that I ought to be paying to be on the tour. There was a little part of Fletch who thought: why are we giving this away when we could be selling it? But they liked me and I liked them. I was rather too earnest at the time and they used to take the piss out of me quite a lot. Fletch used to say he thought Dave Gahan was as good as Prince, and I'd get all wound up and say: don't be so fucking stupid, Prince is a genius. They'd just do it to get me going."

Dave was very much the front man but the music was all Martin and Alan. "To a significant extent, Alan Wilder did bring a musical sensibility to the band," Fretton said. "I'm never sure, because Alan always felt his contribution was perhaps underplayed, and he never quite felt one of the band. And yet I suspect Alan overplays his hand. I don't think Martin needed Alan, really. I think he was there mostly because they needed another keyboard player on stage to play live – whatever you call 'live'. They had an eight-track tape recorder playing in the background and Dave sang live and they sang backing vocals live and Alan and Martin played some keyboards, but they were heavily reliant on their backing tapes. I thought that was so boring, because it meant they had to do the same thing night after night: same tempo, no variation, nothing could change, switch a tape on and it would run – and they had two eight-track tape machines running in parallel in case one broke down. Nothing could stop the set – once it was off, it was off, which must have been so boring, night after night."

Fretton told the band they should get a drummer. "I suggested they got that guy from DAF, Robert Görl," he said. "I always felt the tape machines they used were a bit rubbish. I felt a drummer would bring a bit more power and dynamic to it. They were kind of interested but I think they were keen to avoid anything obviously rock'n'roll-ish at that point."

As before, Fretton spent most of his time on the tour with Gore. "I remember listening to Weather Report or something like that and talking to Martin and he said: I don't want to listen to sophisticated music, I want to keep my ear innocent," he recalled. "He wanted to retain a certain naivety; he didn't want to become technically competent musically, he didn't want to know what a scale was or what a mode was or what polyrhythms were. He wasn't interested. He wanted to allow the music to come to him as he felt it and not then feel the need to push it here or there because he was using a wrong note or something. So while in many ways he was sophisticated, strangely, in the area in which he excels, he wished to remain naive."

Fretton also recalled how Gore loved the Phil Spector Christmas album and had approached Spector to remix one of their tracks. "They'd sent the multi-tracks off and they didn't hear anything for ages," Fretton continued. "Then they'd occasionally get in touch with Spector's management and they'd say: no, nothing's ready yet. At some point all the tapes came back mysteriously with no remix and Martin said: where's the remix? They said: no, it's not possible, it's not going to happen, no fee will be charged. Martin said: well, did he do anything? And they said they couldn't discuss it. Martin said: look, I'd just like to know if he did something, I'd love to hear it to just hear that Phil Spector had remixed one of our tracks, we won't do anything with it, I just want to hear it – he's my hero, I want to hear what he'd do with one of my songs. Nothing was forthcoming. Typical Phil Spector mystery."

It was apparent to Fretton during this tour that the members of Depeche Mode were growing in different directions. They were all still living at home with their parents, in Basildon, but their aspirations were quite different. Gahan wanted to stay in Basildon and was looking to buy a house there and settle down with his fiancée, Jo. Gore and Fletcher couldn't wait to escape and were looking at property in London's Maida Vale. "They used to laugh at Dave, who seemed frightened of leaving Basildon," Fretton said.

Their behaviour on tour was also divergent. "Martin was certainly the one most up for having odd and wild times on tour," Fretton recalled. "Martin had broken up with Anne and started going out with these more sophisticated women. We'd go to some strange fetish-style club somewhere in the Netherlands and he'd do a striptease on the table, but I have to say it was mostly harmless fun of people being silly rather than anything heavy. I don't remember there being any drugs. They drank – everyone drank – but not to excess.

"Fletch was quite quiet: a steady guy, quite a homeboy. It really wasn't wild touring. None of the tours I did them were debauched. People would drink and occasionally we'd go to slightly risqué nightclubs after concerts, but it was hardly Led Zeppelin stuff. Other tours I did at the time, there was a lot of coke around. That was the awful drug of the 80s that made everyone behave like a wanker and made all the records sound terrible. With Depeche they just wanted good ordinary food to eat at regular hours, stay up a bit late, watch television on the bus, and play computer games.

"Dave used to carry around this medical case with him and Alan used to roll his eyes at it, thinking it was deeply psychosomatic. Dave was always thinking he was about to get ill and always taking endless prescription medication for mystery ailments. He would tend to be fairly careful with his voice. He hadn't had any training. It wasn't a weak voice but he didn't particularly know how to look after it.

"I think Martin took over quietly," Fretton continued. "In a way, obviously Fletch is as important to Depeche Mode as anybody else, even if it's difficult to know exactly what his role is, but it's Martin's band. You can't have that band – that sound, that image, that sensibility – without him. That comes from that quiet and rather elusive particular quality which is Martin's. I'm sure it was a bone of contention with Dave, which is why he got a bit more influence in recent years. I'm sure that was always the tension between Dave and Martin. It was clear to me even at that stage it was Martin's band, even if no one was saying so."

For Fretton, Gore was at the heart of everything that was changing about Depeche Mode during this period. "Martin's the key to all this," he said. "Berlin was a huge transition. That's where the funny hairstyles came in and it all got a bit darker. Something definitely happened in Berlin like it did with David Bowie and Iggy Pop. Martin's got a dark side, apart from this endless desire to get his clothes off at any given opportunity – although when he did he always had leather underpants or something on underneath it all. I think the enigma at the heart of it all is Martin."

# CHAPTER 11
# PEOPLE ARE PEOPLE

H ow to unravel the enigma that is Martin Gore? Lets start at Skin Two, the ultra-trendy underground fetish club he'd started to frequent in London. It was here that he indulged his penchant for bondage harnesses, leather, rubber, and handcuffs.

*Record Mirror* writer (and soon to be editor) Betty Page was one of the leading ladies at Skin Two; a rear-view image of her in a back-laced dress made by the scene's lead designer, Daniel James, became an iconic fetish image. "When Martin got quite heavily into the rubber and leather thing it was like: oh blimey, who'd have thought you'd have been doing this when I first met you," she recalled. "It wasn't something he suddenly did. It was a gradual development, but it was a lot to do with the prevailing mood."

Gore was into leather for the image – strong, magnetic, attractive, powerful – and the feel. He admitted his attraction to bondage gear and women's clothes, skirts and suspenders, stemmed in part from a desire to "disorientate" people. He'd always hated macho rock'n'roll; his new look was totally anti-macho.

"I got a feeling Martin was not just using the imagery but got into it on a deeper level," Page said. "I remember his leather skirt. A lot of other people were doing that kind of experimentation as well – it was all about exploring your sexuality and being a bit exhibitionist and being allowed to be like that without being condemned for it. Even though, at that time in the early 80s, if you were a musician it was not a great idea to say you were gay. Marc Almond didn't for years. Same with Boy George; he didn't really talk about it either. It was still quite a taboo thing. All that gender-bending stuff that started in the New Romantic era with Boy George and Marilyn, toying with your sexual identity, developed into clubs like Skin Two, where people were playing with their sexual relationships and identities and role-play. It was people just expressing something in a way that they'd not been able to before. It was fun.

"Martin was definitely opening up more," she continued. "You were really getting to the essence of him there. Martin and I used to joke about Skin Two and the fetish scene but I don't think we ever got too deep discussing it. It wasn't really the done thing to talk about what anybody was into on that level. It was more about what you could read into somebody by the way they dressed and keeping people guessing: will he, won't he; does she, doesn't she? It was that kind of playfulness. Who knows how far it went with him. I suspect he did get into it quite heavily, though."

Skin Two took place every Monday night at a club called Stallions, behind Tottenham Court Road tube station in Soho, and was typically attended by 100–150 people. It was opened in early 1983 by David Claridge, a puppeteer who'd worked with Gerry Anderson of *Thunderbirds* fame, and would run for about a year. Claridge had been a barman at the New Romantic Blitz club. He was interested in the Japanese techno-pop scene and released a sample album of Japanese artists such as Yellow Magic Orchestra. Before Skin Two, he ran a club called the Great Wall on Oxford Street and brought Japanese group Sandii & The Sunsetz over to play there. (Later, after Claridge left the club to pursue fame as the creator of the kids' TV character Roland Rat, he was hounded by the British tabloids for his involvement in Skin Two, which subsequently became known as Maitresse.)

Claridge was friendly with Betty Page and her boyfriend of the time, *Sounds* journalist Tony Mitchell, and asked them to help publicise the new club. Word spread after it was mentioned in the gossip columns of *Record Mirror*, *Sounds*, and the *Evening Standard*, and eventually Skin Two was on the cover of the London listings magazine *Time Out*.

"The whole point was to make it cool," said Mitchell, who is still involved in the fetish scene as editor of *Skin Two* magazine and thefetishistas.com. "Skin Two was the bastard child of the Blitz/New Romantic scene and the earlier punk scene. A lot of people had discovered pervery though punk imagery. There was a bit of crossover. There was a stringent dress code with the door policy we operated. In the same way as the early Blitz club did, you really had to dress the part, not necessarily at great expense but you had to make an effort."

Gore, like all the early patrons at Skin Two, had trouble finding the right gear; Mitchell, for instance, wore a black vinyl jacket bought from Top Shop. Gore was always looking for new things to wear but there still weren't many new designs in bondage stuff. He often shopped at Frisco in the Great Gear Market on the Kings Road.

"The thing that made Skin Two different to anything that had gone before was that it involved a bunch of people from the music industry, graphic designers, other youth-orientated areas of commerce and artistic activity," said Mitchell. "You had young, cool people at the heart of it. By not appearing to be a bunch of middle-aged perverts who were doing vaguely disgusting things behind closed doors and net curtains, it was about being out and proud, saying: yeah, rubber's great, I love it. It caught the zeitgeist.

"Pop stars were attracted to Skin Two right away. Adam Ant and Marco used to turn up. Part of the attraction for a lot of them was that they would be unmolested in a place like that, whereas going into a normal club they might be recognised and attract a lot of attention. In Skin Two, because there's a very strong etiquette of not getting closer to people than they want you to get, it was possible to go there and be fairly anonymous and be fairly sure your face wasn't going to appear on the front page of the tabloids the next day."

At the start, Dave Gahan had been the club kid in Depeche Mode, but now Gore was the one at the hip clubs. "Someone would say Martin was there tonight, and I would say: oh, was he?" Mitchell continued. "If I was there as a journalist looking for stories, I would have spent more time looking around for recognisable faces, but I wasn't. I was there to enjoy girls in latex, basically – they didn't need to be famous.

"Martin in his leather skirt, lace slip, bondage harness – a lot of people were flirting with that kind of imagery. When you're trying to make a name for yourself, trying to create an image for yourself, there's quite a lot of pressure to find something that will help make you distinctive. Basically, if you're in a reasonably successful band like that you can pretty much do what you want to in terms of dress. I don't think it was a great stretch of the imagination for a lot of people in the music business to wear that kind of stuff. Rock'n'roll has always had an association with leather – previously it was the Jim Morrison macho leather look. Depeche Mode always struck me as representing some kind of softer, alternative sexuality, regardless of which team they played for. It was something you could do at that time. There was a lot of that in the air."

Martin Gore certainly belonged to the more effeminate camp of leather-wearing than the Morrison/Marlon Brando motorbike/mirror-shades camp. But despite his new look (and some of the ultra-camp songs on the band's first album), Depeche Mode never picked up much more than a niche gay following. They appealed to men and women equally, but then men tended not to take Gore's dressy nature too seriously.

"If you actually liked that stuff, then being in a band and being able to wear it on stage in front of thousands of people is a fantastic way to enjoy your sexuality without any recriminations," Mitchell said. "A lot of people are into it on the dressing up level – they get a certain sexual buzz from wearing certain types of clothes and they may not be interested in any of the other stuff some people would do. You can dress up without being interested in bondage or flagellation or anything like that."

Even so, I did wonder what kind of things Gore would have got up to at Skin Two. "The fetish scene at Skin Two was less about sex and more about showing," Mitchell said. "It was very much a social thing – socialising and networking. There would always be some kind of performance, impromptu or otherwise; there would always be pro doms who would come with their slaves and do some kind of whipping or something like that. It was a tiny little club. It didn't have space for a play area and a performance area, as most fetish clubs today have. It was tiny.

"The standard sort of sexual interaction you'll most likely find in fetish clubs is doms leading men around on chains. Fetish clubs aren't sex clubs in the way swingers' clubs are. Loads of men who have submissive fantasies are looking for the perfect dominatrix. But it's not really about shagging. That's not the primary motivation. Maybe at a private event, after, things would get ruder. You might get people who are into whipping at fetish clubs, but generally speaking fetish people are about the most non-violent people you will meet: gentle, welcoming, and accepting."

Music-wise, the big tracks at Skin Two were Bowie's 'Fashion' and 'Let's Dance' and 'Venus In Furs' by The Velvet Underground – plus anything with a fetish reference by acts such as Grace Jones and Soft Cell. Gregorian chant was the favourite if anyone was going to do a 'performance' on the square of floor that passed for the dance floor. Music, however, wasn't the main reason people went to Skin Two. It was the people. Gore was drawn to the dark side of electronic music and at Skin Two became firm pals with the king of the hill: Throbbing Gristle legend Genesis P-Orridge.

"I think I got whipped by Genesis P-Orridge once at Skin Two," Betty Page laughed. "He scared me though. He's quite a scary character. There was a lot of dark stuff going on. He was a friend of Stevo's. All those bands Stevo was putting out on Some Bizzare – Scraping Foetus Off The Wheel and Einstürzende Neubauten – were very industrial, metal, electronic stuff. I think that had an impact as well on Martin. That was a bit too dark for me. I was interested in bands that covered dark subjects, but that was just a little bit too hard-core for me."

Genesis Breyer P-Orridge, to give him his full name, would have a profound effect on Gore's musical development. By the time he hooked up with Gore he had disbanded his pioneering band Throbbing Gristle and started up the equally provocative Psychic TV. (When he refers to himself as 'we' below, it is in tribute to his late partner in pan-gender experimentation, Lady Jane Breyer P-Orridge.)

"Martin and I were friends," he told me. "Dave Ball [of Soft Cell] was my other dear drinking-chappy friend at Skin Two. We'd be there every week propping up the bar and Martin would come in; we'd hang out and we might go and whip somebody's ass, and talk about music, sometimes even DJ. When it was my turn to DJ we'd DJ under the pseudonym of Brian Jones. It was early Skin Two, before it got written up in all the fashion mags. You know when you read about the 60s and it talks about how all the bands would go off to the Speakeasy and a couple of other clubs and just drink and hang out until the early morning, wind down from having done gigs? Well that's how it was at Skin Two on Monday nights: we were all winding down after a weekend of gigs, or being in the studio, or whatever. It was a safe place. The press couldn't come in. For a while, pretty much anything could be done – and would be done – and it was completely safe, so we let off steam there.

"We also played each other music we liked. Martin would come in and say: we've just done this new single, can I put it on and play it to you, see how it sounds on the speakers? That happened a lot. We listened to each other's test pressings. I do remember, as Depeche Mode got more and more famous, Martin was having to think about that band in a whole different light. It was turning into this monstrously huge phenomenon, that none of them expected. They handled it pretty well, overall.

"Vince was starting to work it out by finding different vocalists, and Depeche found a look that implied erotic, slightly sinister undertones – so it wasn't too squeaky clean," he continued. "The sound was so squeaky clean: beautiful done, all the sounds are perfect, sculpted, but technologically dry and precise. So it was important for Martin to get that look going, suggesting a sinister undertone to what had previously just been pop music. It had this other level now and a lot of people followed it. Daniel had an obsession with the perfection of the sound: it could still be a fuzzed-out piece of somebody screaming but it would be perfect. It might take him three days."

I put it to Genesis that Miller was similar in this regard to Joe Meek. "That's an interesting comparison," he said. "That obsession with sound, and then being a recluse too. Yeah, you're right, I think that's a really good parallel: Daniel Miller, the Joe Meek of industrial. Depeche Mode stood out at the time. There was lots of other stuff – Orchestral Manoeuvres, Human League – that to me just didn't have that same central passion for change. There was this sense with some of the groups, this second wave after Throbbing Gristle, that they tidy it up and they take away the weirdness and they're working in terms of a business plan, almost. And that's of course everybody's right and privilege to do things the way they want, but when it's only a business plan it doesn't have real longevity."

From the start, Genesis felt that he and Gore were kindred spirits. This may come as a surprise to those who have always considered Depeche

Mode to be lightweight synth-pop and Throbbing Gristle to be the godfathers of industrial, and never the twain shall meet. Except they did – and they were brothers.

"This is the thing that is really special about Depeche Mode, and my experience of Martin especially – they've never ever changed toward me, no matter how famous or infamous they've been, no matter how successful or how wrecked," Genesis continued. "When they did the last huge tour [in 2010], they sent me the super-duper-deluxe VIP box signed by all of them: to our friend Genesis, an influence on us all. They didn't have to bother to do that. Or they could have got someone else to do it – said to some secretary: go get a box and send it. They didn't. They thought of me and they did it themselves."

Genesis was – and still is – a true legend of British music, and his relationship with Gore added real depth and weight to the Depeche Mode songwriter's exploration of darker spaces. Daniel Miller and Stevo, the maverick boss of Some Bizzare, had retained a sense of mutual admiration ever since they worked together on Depeche Mode's 'Photographic'. After his huge success with Soft Cell and The The, Stevo had begun to develop relationships with bands and artists Miller admired, such as Cabaret Voltaire, Jim Thirwell, Test Department, and Einstürzende Neubauten. But it was Throbbing Gristle that really rocked everybody's boat – and indeed had built and launched the boat that Stevo and Miller sailed on. The seminal Gristle track 'United' (1977) had a gigantic influence and formed the root of the whole British electronic explosion. Much is said about the influence of bands such as Neubauten on Depeche Mode, but through his relationship with Genesis, Gore had gone to the very source for his inspiration. He was in awe.

"Although I played drums all my life, we didn't want a drummer," Genesis told me. "We wanted to do a new form of music, and what we thought really paralysed the evolution of pop and rock music was the drumming, the traditional drum set. It tends to lead you into these very straightforward blues and 4/4 rhythms, which in turn – because we've all been used to hearing that music for so long – makes the song structures almost always the same."

Stepping well away from rock music, Genesis and his cohorts turned to what he described as "the cutting edge of sound": synthesizers and electronic music. "We were very quick to spot part of the resolution of the problem, which was: how do you make music that is a reflection of the Western European post-industrial, post Second World War, post-annihilation with an atom bomb, all those things – how do you make that music so it's absolutely about your own environment?"

Throbbing Gristle started their own label, Industrial Records, under the slogan 'Industrial Music for Industrial People' and drew together a group of acts such as Boyd Rice and Cabaret Voltaire. Genesis knew Daniel Miller from when they'd both hang out at the Rough Trade shop on Saturdays in the late 70s. "We went to the London Film-Makers Co-op and booked it for a night and invited various people, including Daniel Miller. Daniel decided instantly that he wanted to work with Boyd – he was really excited about it." The show was recorded by Genesis and released in part by Mute on Boyd's live *Physical Evidence* album.

"All the connections happened very organically, very naturally," Genesis continued. "It was a tiny scene – it wasn't even a scene, we became the scene. And because of Boyd signing to Daniel, we heard about Depeche Mode. Daniel said that our single 'United' contributed to his conviction that there could be interesting … music made with electronics that could also be a chart record – be intelligent and be in the chart – and also have a sense of irony.

"Martin Gore told me that Depeche Mode were madly in love with 'United' and that it also inspired them to look at making electronic music that was even more potentially popular without in any way demeaning its content. All of us in that scene – Boyd, Monte Cazazza, TG, Cabaret Voltaire, Clock DVA, Daniel, and Depeche Mode, and so on – we were all different styles but we were all saying music is sterile, it's finished in terms of its current biological length of time that music lasts, it's time for change, it's time to do something about what the world has become."

Miller's Mute Records, Stevo's Some Bizzare, and Throbbing Gristle's Industrial Records were the three key British electronic labels. They were uniquely supportive of one another. "That's something exciting – no one was competing," Genesis continued. "If Daniel's record did well we saw all of that as vindication of everyone's attempts to do something more exciting." By mutual consent, Mute would end up taking over both the Industrial Records back catalogue as well as that of Cabaret Voltaire.

"When you go and mine that era, you see how quickly everyone found their space," Genesis said. "It's like a jigsaw. All those bands that we're talking about, they found and declared: here's our space in music, you're all welcome to come and join in, but it also fits perfectly anyway with what you're all doing, so in a sense we're all one great big cultural rock band. And each band within that is one of the musicians."

The influence of Genesis and Throbbing Gristle was not just a British phenomenon. The band's biggest market was Germany, and they were a key influence on the German new-wave scene – a scene Gore was now very much in the thick of. "It was Einstürzende Neubauten we became friends with in Berlin," Genesis explained. "And people like Klaus Maeck – a central figure in the Hamburg punk/industrial scene, and a close friend and collaborating manager of Neubauten."

Another notorious Berlin figure was Christiane F. She had been living as a junkie and prostitute in the city's notorious Bahnhof Zoo area; her story was serialised in a national newspaper and then printed as a paperback shock-horror book that was eventually turned into a feature film. She got clean and became "a real fan of intelligent, difficult, and experimental music, especially industrial," according to Genesis. "She was the girlfriend of Alex Hacke of Neubauten for quite a while."

A key event for Gore was the January 1984 Concerto For Voices And Machinery, performed by Einstürzende Neubauten at the Institute of Contemporary Art (ICA) in London. Appearing alongside Neubauten were Stevo, Frank Tovey (Fad Gadget), Genesis, and an array of concrete mixers, electric saws, acetylene torches, and generators. Something went wrong and a large piece of the stage was destroyed, leading the ICA staff to bring the concerto to a quick end.

"They said: what do you want to play tonight?" Genesis recalled. "We said: what you got? They said they had a cement mixer, a circular saw, a road drill ... that's when we all started to fantasise about drilling through the stage and into the floor and through the floor and into the tunnels, the subway system, the Tube, and then either causing the Tube to shut down when all this debris fell through or else finding a way to lead the entire audience out through there and suddenly appear in some Tube station. It never got deep enough, unfortunately. But that's how these things begin.

"All those musicians were from the school of 'what if': what if we did this, what if there wasn't a guitar in that, what if there wasn't any drums, what if it wasn't about being in love in the usual way, what if it's about S&M, what if we use computers? And so on and so on. Road drills – a moment of having no imaginary restrictions on the imagination – those are what Brion Gysin used to call hotspots."

These influences were brought to bear as Depeche Mode, Daniel Miller, and Gareth Jones gathered at Hansa to record a new single in early 1984. Gore was keen to reflect the immensity of the Neubauten ICA show by incorporating the ferociousness of bashing and crashing metal in a pop context. That single was 'People Are People'. This was the second key moment in the career of Depeche Mode, following the recording of 'Just Can't Get Enough'. The fetish scene had informed a developing look, the patronage of Genesis had further enhanced the band's underground credentials, and the wildness of Neubauten had opened up a whole new musical world. 'People Are People' nailed it. It was a high point for the 22-year-old Gore.

During this period, Gore began dating a Berliner, Christina Friedrichs, who along with best pal Nanni Froehlich led him into a new lifestyle away from Basildon. Together, they moved into a flat in Maida Vale, West London, while also sharing a flat in Berlin. Gore was drawn to Berlin because of the Bowie/Iggy connection. He was widely respected among the hippest musicians in town and was now a huge star there. He also felt the city would be good for his creativity. At the back of his mind was the worry that his talent would disappear or be exhausted. Berlin would provide a new injection of inspiration.

Essex boy Andy Goode had become part of the Depeche Mode organisation through his friendship with Brian Denny and Daryl Bamonte, who was now a key figure in the band setup. "Daryl started working for them right from the early days, when they were playing up Croc's," Goode recalled. "But he couldn't drive, so that's where I came in, about 1983. They kept it like that – people who worked for them were friends, people they knew. When they did TV, they wanted their own instruments, not hired out stuff. But they didn't want them flown over; they didn't want them to get damaged. Daryl and I used to drive to Berlin, Vienna, all across Europe with all their gear. We used to get to the studio and set up."

Goode was also part of Gore's new life. "Christina was lovely, gorgeous – a really funny, nice woman," he said. "She did have quite a bit of influence on his new look. I went out with Christina's pal, Nanni, who looked like Brooke Shields. Christina used to dress really nice – her own thing, but really quite modern. Nanni was quite possibly into fetish wear, but not that I noticed at the time. They weren't going round in rubber and leather. She wasn't leading me round on a dog chain," he laughed.

"I moved Christina and Martin to Maida Vale, from Basildon, from his parents' house to this little basement flat in Maida Vale, near Little Venice. We all jumped in the transit van and unloaded it ourselves. Then Martin went to live over in Berlin with Christina, because she lived there. It was mostly Martin in Berlin, not the band. Daryl and I were travelling out to Berlin quite a lot. Martin wanted keyboards taking out there, stuff taking back. At the time those Emulator keyboards were £8,000 apiece – a lot of money for those times, and you couldn't hire them out. Emulator 1 and then Emulator 2 – Martin had both. They wouldn't have them to hire out because they were so new. They used big old floppy discs – innovative for the time – and weighed a ton.

"Berlin was brilliant," Goode continued. "Even on a Sunday evening you didn't have to go out until round about 11, midnight, because all the places stayed open. We always went out late and came home in the early hours of the morning. At the time there was a real mystique about the East. When we drove in to Berlin there were only three roads you were allowed to go in – corridors – to West Berlin. We actually veered off the Autobahn once and went on this country lane and it was full of flat-roofed houses with no windows and all these Russian soldiers, pictures of Lenin, red stars, and we was a bit scared because we'd obviously come off the beaten track. Depeche was massive in Germany. I don't think people in this country really realised how massive they were. In Dortmund one time there were so many fans banging on the window that the glass was buckling. It was scary."

Back in Basildon, Dave Gahan, just 22, was happy to put his wild days behind him and was building a solid family unit with his fiancée, Jo Fox. He didn't feel any urge to move out of Basildon – he wanted to stay, in fact, and bought what he jokingly described as the biggest house in Basildon. The joke was that there weren't any rock-star mansions in Basildon – he'd be living in the same sort of house as a window cleaner.

Gahan's new house was in the most scenic part of town, Langdon Hills, from where on a clear day you could see St Paul's Cathedral and the Post Office Tower, 25 miles to the west. The area had been planned for heavy redevelopment but local protest had curtailed the level of housing there. Gahan lived on Berry Lane in a fairly standard home. He planned to trade in his boy-racer wheels for a Porsche but otherwise he was heavily into the quiet life. He'd had his teenage tattoos removed – he now thought they were a bit naff – and spent time fishing with his brother. It was said among the band that Dave was the most disorientated by fame – a feeling compounded by what many saw as his diminishing role in the direction of his band.

As much as Gore was beginning to take control of Depeche Mode, however, Gahan was still the focal point. Some have said that Gahan had little input in the band's sound and didn't spend long in the studio, that he simply learned the songs and sang them, and was beginning to feel insignificant to the process. In truth, his voice *was* the sound of the band. Although critics would call it dull, flat, and uninflected, it was always distinct and warm, always beckoning. On stage, too, he was a key figure.

"I know people say Dave's not got the greatest voice but it was three blokes stuck behind keyboards, which isn't very eye-catching, is it?" Andy Goode said. "Dave was a top frontman, going side to side on the stage – the physical stuff he used to do, jumping about, dancing, he was a really good frontman. He was excellent. He could really lift the crowd. After the early days of the camouflage gear and the sunglasses and all that, Dave would wear black leathers and a shirt and a vest under that – all the time, that's what he'd wear. Martin would come out with all the things he'd wear and Alan and Fletcher were just in jeans and leather jackets."

Gore may have been moving away from Basildon but it was still his hometown and he had not abandoned it. The band would famously organise a big party once a year for all their pals at a snooker hall in Basildon called the Q Ball. "We had a few of them," Goode recalled. "They invented this cabaret singer – Johnny Diamond they called him. It was me. We got a curly wig, sunglasses, frilly shirt like a cabaret singer; I wore leathers and all that. Martin did the backing music. I think there was an Elvis Presley one, a Mud one – about four songs. Martin and Fletcher all had T-shirts made up with the slogans 'Diamonds are a girl's best friend' and 'Diamonds are forever'. We did a little show for everyone at the Q Ball every year."

Gore and Fletcher would still go out locally, according to Goode, but Gahan had given up. "Everyone knew each other in Basildon," he said. "In the early days Fletcher and Martin would still go out to the all the parties, the same places the normal crowd would go. Dave wouldn't. He was up the Highway once and someone went: oh look, that's that geezer from Bucks Fizz – silly shit like that. And he just thought: bollocks to it."

"People were really unimpressed in Basildon with their success," Rob Marlow told me. "That's why, for many years, Depeche were quite centred and grounded – people wouldn't let them be pop stars or be snooty." At the Q Ball parties, which took place between Christmas and New Year, Gore and Fletcher would "put a couple of grand behind the bar. I remember that period with a great deal of affection. I worked with Jo during that period – we had Christmas jobs at the Body Shop in the newly opened Eastgate centre".

The Eastgate Shopping Centre – the most under-cover shopping precinct of its time, and the largest of its kind in Europe – opened in 1985 and brought with it 2,000 new jobs. It linked to, and was integrated with, the town's existing shopping facilities and bus station. The credit card company Access also moved in, bringing the chance, finally, of some white-collar jobs in the town.

"When they got associated with socialism during that *A Broken Frame, Construction Time Again* period, I don't think they were thrusting, reading Karl Marx, thinking this is the moment," Brian Denny, another Basildon friend of the band, recalled. Denny was part of the group's football team, the Mode 11. "It was very retrospective – ironic even. Saying that, Martin Gore was a big fan of Billy Bragg and liked the way he constructed his ideas of politics through music. But at that time it became *de rigueur* to wear black jeans and have pictures of Chairman Mao on the back of your green jacket. I think they were in on the ground floor of the irony thing. It was fed by Basildon. I think they understood that, the Soviet thing. Coming from a New Town, you can recognise that. And it was an easy look to understand and to communicate to people.

"I'm convinced that the Soviet thing – Communism, socialist realism – that Depeche adopted could all be traced back to Basildon. Socialist realism is very recognisable but you could transpose it onto Basildon as a kind of new society. You can even see all the reasons it went wrong. There is a parallel between the Soviet ideal and what happened in Basildon."

Denny would talk politics with the band. "Gahan-y might have been a Tory but Fletcher was very pro-Labour," he recalled. "But by the miners' strike [of 1984–85] they were all virtually millionaires. I distinctly remember in 1984, going to Ramsden Bellhouse [a village on the outskirts of Basildon] to play the local team with the Mode 11. We all went to the pub after and I had a big row with Andy Fletcher about the miners' strike. He was kind of less for it and I was all for it. I talked a lot with Daryl about it.

"I think the Mode understood the optimism of modernism, and that fed into *Construction Time Again*. Funnily enough, the Mode got darker and darker. From 'New Life' to *Black Celebration*, there's a mirror to Basildon there. How far that was deliberate or not I don't know, but it's uncanny."

Denny also had a run in with Gahan in Basildon during this period. "I had a 1962 Beetle," he recalled. "It was a beautiful car but it couldn't go above 60mph. I was driving around Basildon and this brash fucking silver Porsche comes right up my arse. And he was flashing his lights and beeping his horn at me so I slowed down and I was getting more and more angry. This was going on for a long while and I pulled up and jumped out to fucking say: come on then, let's have it! And it was fucking Gahan-y. He was very playful with it. He wasn't a boaster. Some people in Bas used to have a go at him about his wealth – especially the soul boys, they resented him. He got some grief for that. It couldn't have been easy, still living in Basildon. But their roots were always very important to them."

'People Are People' was released in March 1984, having been introduced to the band's live set a few weeks earlier during five final Construction

Time Again dates in Spain and Italy. The reaction was immediate. "When they went back and did some of the earlier stuff like 'New Life' as encores they sounded really wimpy by comparison," support act Matt Fretton recalled. "When 'People Are People' started, the sounds they got through the Drumulator were pretty heavy, big sounds, a lot more powerful. Certainly *A Broken Frame* sounded extremely delicate by comparison."

The opening seconds of the single heralded the coming of a new band: metallic, clanking, booming, tougher, and more powerful but, crucially, with a hook that was even more memorable than 'Everything Counts'. It was industrial music with mass appeal: metal pop. The lyrics – ostensibly about racism – played second fiddle to the music and the way Gore and Gahan shared vocals (a trick already used on 'Everything Counts' and soon to become something of a trademark for the band during this period).

'People Are People' went to Number Four in the UK and to Number One in Germany. It was Top Ten in Austria, Norway, and Switzerland and a hit in Italy and Australia. It was the band's biggest ever single. It was used as the theme to the German TV coverage of the 1984 Olympic Games; if there was any doubt about it before, now it was confirmed: Depeche Mode were German megastars. Gore was taken aback by the success of the single. It led to more awkward appearances on middle-of-the-road European TV shows, with Gahan often forced into explaining the meaning of songs – which he did manfully, fronting it out – sometimes brazenly and inadequately but always looking great.

The cover of the single featured a priest as a solider carrying a wreath – a Martyn Atkins idea. The guy playing the priest/soldier was a then-unknown actor by the name of Hugh Grant, who was paid £20, according to Atkins, "to dress up in a camouflage outfit and priest's collar". In the video for 'People Are People' and during promotion, Wilder and Gore took a very gung-ho approach to the metal-bashing, and this alongside Gore's increasingly kinky dress and bleached-blonde hair with shaved sides – a very Berlin haircut, apparently done by Christina – brought a strong new visual aspect to the band, whose uniform was predominantly black leather.

British critics remained undecided about the band, however. In February, they were filmed in all their glory for the BBC's *Oxford Road Show*. Narrated by John Peel, the documentary special was a huge deal – a whole show devoted to the band. It was an important moment in their history and one that cast them as a more mature proposition.

The band also continued to feature in *Melody Maker* and *Smash Hits*, while Martin appeared alone on the cover of *Record Mirror*. They expressed a preference to not do Saturday morning TV in the UK any more – it was too embarrassing – but they could still be swayed by Neil Ferris, which lead to to all sorts of incongruous moments. On *Top Of The Pops*, Gore toned down his look to a singlet and leather jerkins. There was another solid performance on *The Tube*.

'People Are People' also opened up a new avenue for the band when Adrian Sherwood from the underground On-U Sound label radically reshaped it for release as a 12-inch single. "I knew Daniel from when he was just putting out his first single as The Normal," Sherwood told me. "We met in the back of Rough Trade and talked about doing an electronic dub record together. Daniel was always driving around, selling records out of the boot of his car, just like I was doing back then. Obviously, the music he was doing was completely different to the world I occupied, but he was such a good lad I always really liked him. Dan, to his credit, liked things like NON – mental stuff – as well as the more commercial end."

Mute's new offices were in the same building as Cherry Red Records. Sherwood was doing business with Cherry Red and was working with Mark Stewart & The Maffia, whom Miller admired (and would later sign up for a Mute album in collaboration with Sherwood). Depeche Mode knew Sherwood and respected his work with Prince Far I, Creation Rebel, Head Charge, and a few other acts such as Judy Nylon.

"What you've got to bear in mind is that what they were into was not black music," Sherwood said. "Even Daniel Miller – he's not a big fan of black music. They all liked electronic stuff that's programmed. If you look through most of Mute's stuff, it's not played – most of it's programmed. With 'People Are People', I had some of his samples and I just made this nutty version on a four-track in my house by cutting up bits of tape I made. Dan really liked it and asked if he could release it. I said no problem. So it wasn't actually instigated, like: can you remix this for me? It was more like I had some of his samples and cut up the thing at home. For me, it was more Daniel than the band.

"Lots of people thought the remix was nuts but they liked it because it was so different," Sherwood continued. "It was one of the earliest remixes. There weren't loads of remixes being done at that time. For me it was just like the art of version. With Jamaican music, you've always had versions – a history of it. So I just saw my 'People Are People' remix as a 'blow up your speaker' kind of version, something like Mark Stewart would do. It was just like a collage of noise to me. I did it at the time for fun more than anything.

"I didn't see the point of doing a remix unless you made it completely different to the original. Then after that people started getting me in to do remixes because I think they'd heard 'People Are People'. It helped me quite a lot. I never got royalties on 'People Are People' so it wasn't the best deal in the world for me. But to be honest, that tune helped me on a little down payment on the first place I bought in East London. It wasn't a large amount of money but whatever it was it was good money for me at the time. I was very glad to do it – I was hired to do something mad on someone else's tune. I'm a disaster, business-wise, but I'm still making tunes, I still got respect, so what the fuck. It was a little house – you could buy a house in those days for £25,000 and maybe you put down a grand. I think that came from the lads."

Sherwood's remix of 'People Are People' was one of the most radical slices of electronic music of the era. By now, Depeche Mode were hugely influential on the black club scene in the USA, massive across Europe, and pushing the envelope at every opportunity in terms of sound and look. They had left their New Romantic/Futurist peers in the dust and stood alone among that group of acts in being able to sit alongside more traditional rock-orientated acts such as The Smiths, New Order, and The Cure. And still they remained purely, devotedly electronic: a class apart, an act ahead of their time; admired by the godfather of industrial music, no less.

One only had to look at Daniel Miller's track record and his devotion to the band to realise that this was music of significance. Yet still the British critics didn't respond. If anything, the band were ridiculed by all but the pop press – which didn't really treat anything too seriously. This would continue, in the main, for the next few years. It was Gore who, showing remarkably prescient insight, suggested the rock critics of the era were all too tied to trad-rock ideas to appreciate what his band were up to – and that Depeche Mode would have to wait until a new, more contemporary generation of writers emerged to finally get their dues.

Boyd Rice – Mute's most provocative, aggressive, noisy act – could see what was going on. "I was in Mute's offices sitting waiting to talk to Daniel one day and these two girls from Japan came in and said: we have come from Japan and we have come to see Depeche Mode," he told me. "And the girl in the office said: well, you know, the boys pop in the office every once in a while but it's not like they hang out at the record company office. And these girls said: can we just wait and stay out of your way and maybe one of the boys will come in? The girl said: do whatever you want. So they're sitting down there and five minutes later Martin Gore walked in with a newspaper full of fish and chips. And he just sits down and eats these chips and these girls are screaming, pointing at him, and just losing their minds. He was thinking this is mad, crazy.

"I was never sure if that change of sound for Depeche Mode around 'People Are People' was Daniel as much as it was Dave and the rest of the guys. All the critics were taking things like Einstürzende Neubauten really seriously: they were on every cover of *NME*, *Sounds*, all this stuff. I think the boys just wanted a harder sound. They wanted to keep that poppiness but wanted a harder edge to it."

Years later, Rice stumbled upon a pair of DVDs containing music videos by Devo and Depeche Mode. "I took them home and I expected Devo to be really good and serious and it seemed ridiculous, they were just so cartoonish and overstated – and then the Depeche videos, which I expected to be just light fluff, they really stood up," he recalled. "The music was still as good as the day it came out – it's quality music – and the videos are compelling and strange; some of their videos were more bizarre than the Devo videos. It was surprising. I was expecting one thing from one group and got exactly the opposite. I always felt Depeche Mode's music was well crafted, well produced. It's like Abba or something – people can be dismissive of it because it's so mainstream, but if you go into a studio and try to recreate that … good luck to you."

# CHAPTER 12

# BERLIN

I n the spring of 1984, following the huge success of 'People Are People', Depeche Mode regrouped to start recording a new album. Work began at the Music Works studio in Highbury, North London – close to Arsenal Stadium, the home of Gore's favourite football team – where Gore presented the band with demos that were more polished and confident than any he had ever made before.

In recognition of his growing influence, Gareth Jones was promoted from engineer to co-producer for the new album. "When we got to *Some Great Reward*, we were renting bigger rooms and massive PAs and just really trying to take another step," he told me. "The plan was not to repeat what we'd done before. By then I was having a great time working with Depeche. It was fantastic. We were mutually inspiring each other, I suppose. My concerns about making pop music with Depeche had been laid to rest because I felt we were making experimental pop music. This whole sense of experimentation and doing new stuff was a very important part of my creative life."

After completing the "first half" of *Some Great Reward* at Music Works, Depeche Mode returned to Hansa Studios to finish the record. Berlin was already a second home to Jones and Gore, but now the rest of the band were beginning to feel more comfortable there, too. "They were huge in Germany," Jones said. "It was a massively important territory and it just felt great to be working there, very creative and productive, everyone loved it.

"We used to work until very late," he continued. "We could work until two or three in the morning and still go out and have a beer and a snack if we wanted, even if it was just a little café. Everyone loved that European nightlife thing. At that time in London, everywhere shut at 11 o'clock, but we felt compelled, in our youthful enthusiasm, to work much later than 11."

After finishing work in the early hours, the band often took to the Berlin clubs, where they were no longer restricted to the 'uncool' corner. "We used to go to the Linientreu club, and later the Ex'n'Pop," Jones recalled. "Ex'n'Pop was a hardcore Neubauten bar, vodka and amphetamines big time. You were lucky to live through it. But I was pretty much a compulsive worker, I was basically a studio animal and I was in the studio a lot. When Martin moved to Berlin we didn't hang out that much. He had his own life and his own girlfriend. We might have seen each other occasionally but we had such an intense relationship when we were working, it was almost like when we're not making the album we have a bit of a break from one another. We had a little bit of social contact but not much."

Depeche Mode were now firmly influenced by the Berlin look. "I was wearing black nail varnish when I first met them," Jones recalled. "But I remember being very influenced by them as well, to the extent that I think we were all wearing black leather. That was the influence of the Liaisons Dangereuses/Neubauten scene as well. It was like a gang – we were like a big gang doing our thing." Palais Schaumburg, Chrislo Haas from Liaisons Dangereuses, and members of Einstürzende Neubauten would all drop by Hansa while work continued on the album. Depeche were no angels – a lot of dope was being smoked in the studio – but by comparison, Jones recalled, Neubauten seemed like "very hard-bitten amphetamine freaks to our rather naive English sensibilities".

By now, Jones was in real demand as a producer. He invited Gore to play "a middle-eight melody on a little Casio synth" on a record he was co-producing by Humpe Humpe, aka sisters Annette and Ingrid, formerly of DOF. He was also now working with Palais Schaumburg.

"They came to me because of Depeche Mode," Jones said. "They loved Depeche. They could hear the experimentation and the art in the project we were working on – the art in making the pop music. The cool British press lost interest in them because of the cheesy press and TV they were doing ... but they never did that in Germany. In Germany they were always thought to be interesting and dark."

Around the same time, Jones produced 'Collapsing New People', a Mute collaboration between Fad Gadget and Einstürzende Neubauten about the nihilistic youth of Berlin. He also produced Fad Gadget's album *Gag* at Hansa, while Mute put out the Neubauten compilation album *Strategies Against Architecture 80–83*. Neubauten had signed to Stevo's Some Bizzare label, rather than Mute, for future releases, but Jones would continue to produce them.

"In the same way as one was doing metal sampling with Depeche, I introduced the sampler to Neubauten when we made *Halber Mensch*, and the 'Yu-Gung' single," Jones recalled. "There was massive cross-fertilisation going on, both from being inspired by Neubauten, making rhythms and melodies from banging metal, to inspiring them to use samplers. I always felt like I was carrying the torch in both directions, really. There was a sense of everyone listening and everyone getting ideas from everyone else. There was a unity because of the edge, the creative energy, and the use of modern technology, sequencers, and electronics, which all those people were really super-interested in … Daniel Miller was the centre of this super cool label, being a bit of a sun that everyone was circling around."

Another visitor to Hansa Studios during the *Some Great Reward* sessions was Gudrun Gut. "That was wonderful for us," Jones recalled. "We had these really cool German girl musicians who would visit and hang out." Gut was an original member of Einstürzende Neubauten. She had come to Berlin to study visual communications in 1978 and fell in with the art-school punk scene. She formed relationships with Bettina Köster, Beate Bartel, and Blixa Bargeld, all of whom were very much at the centre of all that was hip in Berlin.

Gut and Köster opened a shop in Schöneberg called Eisengrau, where they would sell clothes, tapes, and fanzines. It was here than the Neue Deutsche Welle scene started to gel. The initial line-up of Neubauten featured Bargeld on guitar, Gut on synth, and Bartel on bass; Gut, Bartel, and Köster also formed their own band, Mania D.

"The late-70s Berlin scene was not so influenced by English bands," Gut told me, although she did recall seeing Throbbing Gristle playing at the SO36 club in the city. "We had a really strong German scene. In those days there was a lot of connection between the music scene, the arts scene, and the filmmakers. The German artist Martin Kippenberger ran the SO36 and he even had a band where he played. It was very much linked –

we played a lot in galleries, for example. We all wanted to do something new and we were doing events together. So that was a rare moment in history when these three were together very closely."

The two hip districts in Berlin were Schöneberg and Kreuzberg. "That was the West Berlin scene," Gut recalled. "Most of the artists lived in Schöneberg or Kreuzberg, and all the clubs were there. Charlottenburg [where Gore lived] was a good area, too. Now it's much posher but it wasn't in those days. Mick Harvey [of The Bad Seeds] lived in Charlottenburg, too, and I had a lot of friends there."

By the time Depeche Mode were recording at Hansa, Gut had disbanded Mania D and was playing in a noise band called Malaria! with Köster. She had formed a strong bond with The Birthday Party and had introduced Blixa Bargeld to Nick Cave. She'd also formed a synth-pop band, Matador, with Bartel and Köster.

"Of the bands I had, Matador was the one most influenced by Depeche Mode," she said. "When Depeche Mode started they were really young. I think the Berlin influence was good for them. That's what I like about Depeche Mode: still now, they are not only a pop band. There's a danger for a pop band: they pop up and they pop down, but because Depeche developed their artist-ship – I wouldn't say musicianship because they acted more like artists – they always made themselves interesting with every new album. They did a really good mix of pop and underground.

"Mute was the favourite label of everybody in Berlin. It was the label that did the most interesting music. With *Some Great Reward* there was an obvious link to Neubauten, but it was a nice one. They were informed. They knew what was going on. I know Martin is really interested in all kinds of music, what is going on in the music world. That's really important, I think. Not just wanting to be a rich pop star, it's more than that. They are going much deeper than that but they have this pop angle.

"There was definitely a cross-fertilisation of ideas between Depeche Mode and Neubauten," she continued. "It's not all in one direction. For us it was cool to see a band like Depeche Mode recording at Hansa and making such a great production out of having a total different approach to music, and making something really pop out of it. That was nice to see because suddenly: ah, you can do it like this too."

Of the other musicians on the scene during the recording of *Some Great Reward*, Gut described Chrislo Haas as a "super talent". "He was a very important part of DAF," she said. "He was the sequencer man. Without Chrislo, DAF wouldn't have existed. Beate Bartel was more connected with Depeche Mode [via Liasons Dangereuses]. When they played Berlin, Beate had 20 tickets for Depeche Mode, and in the end we had so many that I sold them outside the hall. That's changed now. I saw them very often. I think I saw them every year when they played and we mostly went out afterward and did something."

I told Gut what Gareth Jones had said about Depeche Mode's first visit to Berlin: how they'd felt as if they were in the "uncool corner" at Dschungel. "Could be, could be," she laughed. "So sensitive." She went on to recall how she had watched the band flower in Berlin. "Martin and the band felt comfortable in Berlin because Berlin was not a fake city," she said. "The people were real ... they were saying what they think and I think Depeche Mode liked that. They could relax in Berlin, even though they were having massive hits in Germany, because Berlin was totally different from the rest of the world. It was this island ... the people who lived there, who moved to Berlin, were either men who didn't want to go to the army – naturally left-wing people – students, or pensioners. It was a different atmosphere altogether. You couldn't compare it with the feeling in London. I know from all these so-called pop stars who came to Berlin, they really liked it because it was so real. Even David Bowie was hanging around. People didn't care.

"We always called it grey," she continued. "In the 80s, Berlin was really, really poor. It was a sick city; there was no industry happening, it was an in-between state; there was money pumped in so that it could survive. For me, the first time I saw a normal businessman was when I went to New York. We didn't have that in Berlin. Now we do. Back then they didn't exist. We were just discussing female history, relationship stuff, politics, anarchism, artist communes, new ways to live together, and this kind of stuff – that was what was going on in Berlin. It was a whole different atmosphere. Everybody had an opinion."

▭–▭–▭

The first Depeche Mode release from these new Hansa sessions was the August 1984 single 'Master & Servant', Gore's most overt fetish song – a metaphor for life, he suggested. It was not just the subversive lyrics that broke the teen-pop mould but the hard, aggressive instrumentation.

There had been much talk about the BBC banning the single, while its controversial subject matter meant that it faired poorly in most European territories, but it still reached Number Nine in the UK and Number Two in Germany. The band promoted the record with Gore dressed in full-on fetish wear: leather, bondage harness, black nail varnish. It was all about the sex.

The 12-inch mix of the single was an even more radical reworking by Adrian Sherwood. "I flew to Berlin to do 'Master & Servant'," he told me. "Gareth was in the top room and I was in the room underneath. The lads kept coming in. I'd have some of the band with me at any given time, and to start with Gareth couldn't understand why I was being brought in until he heard I was making it drastically different to his version, at which point he was really into the idea. Gareth's a really brilliant engineer. I think he thought: why has Dan brought Adrian in? Is he going to do my job? That wasn't the case at all. I was doing a mad mash-up version on the floor beneath where they were doing the other stuff."

Sherwood found the band completely open to his ideas. "They were all lovely lads," he said. "They were spending a lot of time in Germany so they were checking out all the history of the German electronic stuff. Daniel himself was a mad fan of all that. The biggest thing to me is Dan should have kept producing, working a lot more in the studio – not just with Depeche Mode but also with other bands. In my mind he wasted a lot of time running the label, being a businessman, where he could have had a lot more fun doing music, because he's very talented. At that time, Daniel was responsible for a lot of the sounds they were using: he'd bought the Synclavier; he had all his old analogue effects. He was really into all the noises.

"There's a Jamaican saying: each one, teach one. I got inspired by [Pop Group founder] Mark Stewart, who was also into the noisy school of European stuff, also the American collage stuff. Mark was pushing me to go mad. Depeche would have checked out what we were doing. Neubauten, Test Department, Throbbing Gristle were all experimenting with noise. I came from the Jamaican end so I was using dub techniques.

Each person inspired another. I pushed the boat out a bit on 'Master & Servant' and that made them go a bit madder on other approaches to stuff. Each one pushes another."

The link-up with Sherwood was good for Miller. Mute would soon be working with Mark Stewart & The Maffia. It was a busy time. Just as the huge success of Madonna had allowed Seymour Stein to expand Sire, the success of Depeche Mode and Erasure had provided the funds for Mute to grow. Miller had a hit on his hands with 'Darling Don't Leave Me', a Robert Görl single featuring Annie Lennox on vocals, and Görl's excellent solo debut, *Night Full Of Tension*. Nick Cave & The Bad Seeds (featuring Blixa Bargeld) had risen out of the flames of The Birthday Party to release a single, 'In The Ghetto', and an album, *From Her To Eternity*. Miller also signed the British electronic duo I Start Counting to the label and released an album by his old pal from Wire, Bruce Gilbert, called *This Way*.

*Some Great Reward* followed hot on the heels of 'Master & Servant' in September 1984. It was a monster, selling over a million copies in Europe; the inclusion of 'People Are People' helped. It hit Number Three in Germany and reached the Top Ten in Sweden, Switzerland, and the UK, as well as the Top 20 in Austria and Holland.

The album's tag line was *The World We Live In And Life In General*. Although it featured only nine songs, in terms of melodies and textures – both hard and soft – it was the band's masterpiece of the period. The subject matter was interesting and suggested that some of the songs dated back to an earlier period, since amid Gore's usual/unusual treatises on sex and relationships, the overarching theme was: Basildon. The opening track, 'Something To Do', is about boredom in a town where drink is the only release. 'People Are People' could be interpreted as a reaction to the town's narrow-minded views on race; 'Blasphemous Rumours' as an exploration of the church scene he'd grown up around. Even Wilder's song, 'If You Want', could be seen as a hymn to the drudgery of life on the industrial estates. Gahan's vocals had never been better and there was a dark, subtle humour to many of the songs. Most critics, however, focused on the sex, the pervy overtures of many of the songs: 'Master & Servant', obviously, but also the references on other tracks to cross-dressing, infidelity, and lust. The album's working title had been *Perversions*, and in that respect Gore had done his fair share of soul-bearing. But he'd also revealed an appealingly tender, vulnerable side – one that struck a chord with the band's growing fan base – particularly on the almost excruciating 'Somebody', on which he took over lead vocals.

The album cover was again shot by Brian Griffin, but what the image of a bride and groom in a steelworks revealed was unclear. Griffin had shot it in his hometown of Lye in the West Midlands, where the Round Oak steelworks was about to be closed down. He'd worked there briefly as a student. "They were talking about this wedding in a factory," Griffin recalled, homing in on a very Basildon concept. "I should have done it much better. I was emotionally overtaken by the fact they were going to demolish that steelworks, which they did do to develop a shopping centre there. I was into lighting places at that time, being a bit of a megalomaniac, I think. And I chose to do it there."

Griffin recalled how Miller had finally moved out of his mum's place and bought an apartment in Rotherhithe close to Griffin's studio. "He was growing stronger all the time, growing bigger all the time," Griffin said. "I went up to his apartment in Abbey Street, before the railway bridge, only a mile from where I live here in Rotherhithe. He moved into my territory. It was quite a good place – top floor of an old factory. Daniel's apartment was like a synthesizer museum: a history of synthesizers that were working, set out in a big 'U' shape. Extraordinary."

"*Some Great Reward* was another thing where Brian had kind of sold the idea to Daniel," designer Martyn Atkins told me. "It was kind of an ego trip in a sense because he wanted to go back to a factory he had worked in on the summer holidays or something. It was more about him going back to this factory as a photographer and shooting it. When they told me the idea I said we should do it more like the film *Saturday Night & Sunday Morning* – there's this great scene where Albert Finney and Shirley Anne Field go up the hill. It's like the classic Northern thing: he goes up on the hillside, which overlooks the town, they're looking down on the town, and they're talking about the future; he's not really listening to her and she's saying: oh, yeah, we can get a nice little terraced house. And you can tell he's just thinking: fuck – it's like this whole thing of your life being ahead of you, all this future to look forward to, but you live in this shitty little town with these belching chimneys and really the only future is you're going to go down the pit. I did actually go to the *Some Great Reward* shoot and tried to direct it a bit but it was such a specific thing … I don't think that album cover does anything that is endearing or enhances their image.

"What was weird was we were doing all the different things for the singles, and the singles were much stronger looking than the album cover," Atkins continued. "I was kind of used to everything radiating from the album cover. That's like the jewel in the crown. It just seemed like at that time things were getting a little disjointed. The cover for 'Master & Servant' had the chain on it. The good thing about that was it was really impactful for ads and posters and T-shirts. It really gave them a hard kind of image, which in some way did something to readdress what people had said about the band's music and look."

Atkins was growing closer to the band and would from here on take almost complete creative control over the band's visual imagery. "I'd go down to the studio in London or they'd be recording in Berlin and I'd fly over for a few days and we'd go though some ideas and go to some clubs and have some drinks as well," he recalled. "I think we were very aware that whatever we created had to work on so many more levels than graphics for record covers in the past. Everything was for sale; everything was becoming merchandise. This was the beginning of branding as we know it today."

Alongside the fetish gear, Martin had started wearing the Iron Cross and various German military uniforms. "I never got the feeling that any of that stuff was to do with being into the Nazis," Atkins said. "It always seemed to me like Keith Moon dressing up in an SS uniform. I thought he was just having fun with it. I never asked him about that, either. It just seemed normal to me. Also, the whole thing of dressing up like a woman – it's almost like a cliché in English bands. All the glam bands used to have one guy in them that dressed up as a woman, so I just thought it was the same thing."

▭▭▭

Although they were spending a lot of time in the city, Depeche Mode had not entirely decamped to Berlin. Gore kept his Maida Vale flat and Fletch and his girlfriend Grainne had moved out of her parents' home in

Basildon and into their own London apartment, also in Maida Vale. Matt Fretton was a regular visitor to both places. "We'd meet up and we'd go to the Maida Arms," he recalled. "We'd just go and drink beer and hang out like normal people in a pub. Fletch was always a mystery. There's a sense of humour which is particular to those Basildon guys, Martin, Fletch, and Dave. They will take the piss out of each other, and Fletch was kind of teased for this kind of banana-fingered bass playing, and it was alluded to regularly that he didn't really do anything. It was never sadistic, it was just teasing. I think it was more about knocking people down to size."

For the final months of 1984, just as in the previous two years, the band toured their new album. This time they played their biggest UK and European tour to date, stretching over three months. The UK leg climaxed with four nights at the Hammersmith Odeon. In October, a third single was pulled from *Some Great Reward*. If 'Master & Servant' had pushed the envelope, 'Blasphemous Rumours' was outrageously provocative. Perceived by some to be an attack on God, the single peaked at Number 16 in the UK and went largely unnoticed in Europe. The *Top Of The Pops* performance – for which Gore wore a leather skirt, a girl's see-through slip, and bondage harnesses, while playing a bicycle wheel – provoked a barrage of complaints.

With this, the UK mainstream – particularly Radio 1 – all but decided that enough was enough with this band. There would be no more heavy radio play for the singles and, as a result (and with rare exceptions), no more big Top Ten singles. Not everyone was happy. "As the music grew darker, Dave Gahan would complain that certain radio DJs, such as Steve Wright, would introduce their records with something along the lines of: this band are so depressing," plugger Neil Harris recalled. "In the period where Martin was getting into bondage and all that kind of stuff, it didn't cause me any problems at all. I thought it was great. If anything, it added more interest and it gave more gravitas to the band. It helped in a way to take away the lightweight view the media had of them. I thought it was very positive. I also thought Martin looked great in a leather skirt."

The provocative, harder sounding, ultra-hip, and connected Depeche Mode were still not getting much in the way of recognition from the rock critics. They were still being covered by teen mags such as *Bravo* in Germany and *Record Mirror* in the UK, while their only UK cover story during this period came from *Smash Hits*, with Gore to the fore in his leather skirt and silk slip. *Melody Maker* was largely supportive but the *NME* waited until December to give the band a fairly tame feature.

"They felt they had to work for the press," PR agent Chris Carr told me. "Other bands just got it automatically." Carr and Miller worked hard on getting the band the dues they deserved, but to limited success. Carr had been to Berlin to see the band record and suggested the *NME* come along to see the process. "I said to Daniel: listen, we're going to have to embed somebody and show them what actually happens. People were still enthralled by the Stones' way of recording, and Depeche's wasn't that dissimilar. Daniel had a budget and he would do deals with the studios and there would be hours where there'd be trying to get a sound from something, much like Keith just sitting on the floor and jamming away."

The *NME*'s Danny Kelly saw something interesting in these working-class boys from Essex, but it was a slow process. In Berlin, however, the band received the credit they deserved. "Generally, they were in a more adult world in Europe and were treated with due respect," Carr said. "I think they felt slightly cowed when they came back to the UK, especially within the social circle, because there were other bands with a higher cool quotient. They had the Berlin cool crowd and then kickback from the techno scene in the States. There was a girl called Nanni Froelich and her group of friends – all of a sudden, statuesque German models were hanging with the band and going from one place to another. It gave them something, whereas if they walked into a club over here ... Steve Severin had a fair bit to do with helping the band develop their quotient of cool over here, but more in an inadvertent social thing. He could understand where they were coming from, and for a while he hung with them. That kind of gave them their London cool."

Carr also observed the band's strong connection to Basildon. "The whole Basildon crew – I don't know any other artist who I've worked with over the years that has actively fostered a relationship with mates of theirs that are not in a financial bracket to compete," he recalled. "But they didn't drop those people. In fact, they embraced them; there would be summer parties at people's houses where they would all be invited. I don't know any other band that has done that. The people from Basildon weren't in the same financial bracket but they kind of manoeuvred around that with some dexterity so people didn't feel as if it was charity."

The touring team for *Some Great Reward* was tight-knit, too. Alongside Daryl Bamonte, tour managers Andy Franks and J.D. Fanger had already clocked up four band tours. Both men would become key members of the live setup, even to the extent of having a vote on certain decisions within the band democracy. They, like Dan Silver, were part of the 'family'.

Even on the Some Great Reward tour, Depeche Mode were still playing 'New Life', 'Ice Machine', 'Photographic', and 'Shout', and encoring with 'Just Can't Get Enough'. They also played all the singles, apart from 'Get The Balance Right', and most of new album. One of the band's Hamburg shows was filmed and released on video as *The World We Live In And Live In Hamburg*.

The set designer behind the Some Great Reward tour was Jane Spiers, later described by Andy Fletcher as "the most amusing girl of the entourage". She designed a moving factory set with scaffolding and metal sheeting for Gore and Wilder to bang with hammers. At a time when it was unusual to have a woman in control of a live tour, hiring Spiers was another groundbreaking move for this still-managerless, all-electronic band.

"I actually joined on the Construction Time Again tour," Spiers told me from her home in New Zealand. "I was a freelance lighting designer. There were probably two other women involved in touring in the world when I started. It was very much a male orientated business. Most of the companies still don't have any. I suppose it's because you have to start at the bottom loading trucks and all that sort of thing. Most girls don't want to get into that side of it."

Prior to working with Depeche Mode, Spiers had done the lights for The Police, Squeeze, Bob Marley, Peter Tosh, and Selector. "Some Great Reward was a massive tour," she recalled. "The stage was like a big 'M' with ramps that used to lift up. Alan was really put in charge of the artistic side of it. He was the one who was talking to me about what concepts and ideas we had." Spiers would present her ideas directly to the band; Miller, she said, "would not have a big say" in this aspect of the band's career.

"They used to give me incredible license to do whatever I liked," she continued. "I don't think I ever put an idea to them that they didn't actually just do. They'd sometimes say to me: I want a few extra screams – we were always looking for different things, moving things, that would make the whole place just go off at the press of a button. That's what they liked best: the audience reaction to whatever I could pull out of the hat.

"I always felt I had enough of a budget to do what I wanted, whatever you wanted to do, whatever it was going to cost," she said. "I don't think anybody told me what it was supposed to be worth or what the budget was. The money was never mentioned; it didn't seem to have any relevance at all. I'd just listen to the album and come up with some ideas. They'd say the more 'wows' we can get, the better. They wanted to be as slick as humanly possible."

On this tour, Franks and Fanger tried to separate the band from the crew because there was far too much drinking and high-jinx going on. "It was definitely a lively bunch of guys on the road," Spiers laughed. "We'd think nothing at all of doing a load-out and finishing at two in the morning and then going to a club until seven in the morning and then going straight back to do the load-in for the next one. We seemed to have incredible stamina. The band, at that stage, were put into different hotels.

"Live, Dave was always really dynamic," she noted. "He was fantastic. The lightshow did have a big part in it. The show, in the end, became quite iconic. People just loved going to Depeche Mode shows because they did get incredible value for money. The shows were monumental. Even if you don't like the albums, you couldn't not like the live show. It just had incredible energy. Dave would have to run miles on those big stadium stages and he managed to do it night after night. I don't think they got sick of playing 'Just Can't Get Enough'. There was never any of that. I don't think anybody got sick of it – if it came on in a club when we were in a club we'd actually all get up and dance to it.

"It was a very strange lifestyle for them. It was great that Dave, Fletch, Martin, and Alan all had lovely partners that were really supportive. I think that was a big part of them keeping their feet on the ground. All of them liked having a good laugh. We would be amused about Martin's stage wear. I'd see him going around dress shops and things, and he'd ask my opinion on what he was going to buy. Every now and again somebody would raise their eyebrows at some of the strange outfits he wore. They were pretty out-there. But everybody was quite proud of his style, and everybody would very much stick up for him."

Spiers also recalled a 'drastic' incident during one of the band's German dates. "Somebody let off a tear-gas bomb in the middle of the crowd just in front of the lighting desk," she said. "I saw the cloud go up, and we were all on cans talking during the show, so I yelled to everybody on the truss to get down as fast as they could. The smoke went across and hit the stage, so suddenly you heard all the music go wonky. I ran up to the high stands – a mistake because tear gas rises – and at that stage I couldn't see or breathe, so I managed to crawl back down and crawl out of the stadium. There were just people all over the ground, people vomiting. Absolute mayhem. Horrendous." This incident aside, Spiers found the Depeche Mode crowd to be quite well behaved. "Everybody was up for a good time."

ㅁ-ㅁ-ㅁ

After the UK and European legs, the Some Great Reward tour was due to hit the USA and Canada in March 1985 for the band's first American gigs in two years, followed by four dates in Japan. Before heading out to the USA the band went to Hansa to record a new single, 'Shake The Disease'. Following the pattern of recent years, the single was intended as the start of a new album. But when the single stalled at Number 18 on the UK chart the album sessions were abandoned.

Depeche Mode's commercial appeal may have been waning in the UK but they still had massive support across Europe. The Some Great Reward tour had been a huge success in Denmark, Sweden, Norway, Italy, Switzerland, France, and of course Germany. Reports filtered back to the UK about how popular the band were in Europe via interviews in magazines such as *No 1* and in an article for *The Face* in which the author went to great lengths to justify her liking for a band that most people thought were naff.

The USA was also starting to open up to Depeche Mode. 'People Are People' had been a slow-burning club hit in late 1984. It was nothing compared with Sire's biggest act, Madonna, who had recently scored a huge Number One hit with 'Like A Virgin', but it had sold a reasonable amount. Sire boss Seymour Stein was still broadly supportive of the band and the label released an inventive compilation album made up of tracks from the band's second and third LPs, *People Are People*, to capitalise on interest in the single. Even so, Depeche Mode weren't a top priority for Sire, which was also now pushing The Smiths, kd lang, The Cult, and new product from Talking Heads and The Ramones as well as Madonna.

"In terms of America, a couple of times Daniel got me to call Seymour to say: this band are huge, get your finger out," Neil Ferris recalled. "I remember ringing Seymour and saying: Seymour, you're like an art collector; you come to England to collect pieces of art to hang on your wall. Depeche Mode cannot hang on your wall – you've got to get out there and make them happen. And Seymour said: I know Neil, I know – for God's sake, I believe in this band."

Supported by the live dates, 'People Are People' continued to sell well and became the band's first US hit, peaking at Number 13. Having all but written off the USA, Depeche Mode now found themselves part of a new 'alternative' subculture that included bands such as REM, The Smiths, New Order, The Cure, U2, Psychedelic Furs, and Echo & The Bunnymen.

Depeche Mode's 1985 US tour was patchy but promising. They were noticeably huge in California: in Los Angeles, they sold out the 5,000-capacity Hollywood Palladium in 15 minutes, halving Billy Idol's previous sales record. A gig booked at the University of Southern California was so oversubscribed that the band were forced to move to the much larger Irvine Meadows arena, for which they sold 7,000 tickets in 30 minutes. Elsewhere, in places such as New York City, Washington DC, and Dallas, it was more about rebuilding the brand. *Some Great Reward* scraped into the US Top 50 selling half a million copies. It was a first indication of how vast and lucrative a territory the USA would become.

Betty Page joined the US tour for a *Record Mirror* cover story (once again, only Gore featured on the cover). The article was titled 'The Last Of The Futurists' and included a report on a show played to 15,000 people in Orange County. "In that article I asked why no one was taking them seriously, because look at what they'd done: it's amazing what they'd achieved," Page said. "One of the things that surprised me the most was that Americans loved Depeche Mode so much, considering what else was going on at the time, musically, in America; that they would embrace a synthesizer band – an electronic band – when America was supposed to be all about rock.

"I think their success in America was two things," Page continued. "Firstly they were prepared to put in the work, because the only way you could break America was just by going to play there incessantly and get radio stations to play your music; and secondly all that early electro-pop music that came out of this country in the early 80s was hugely influential on hip-hop and early rap. Hugely. They missed out in that first wave but they caught up with it later and probably capitalised on it more than anyone else. I also think they just understood that you had to do those cheesy TV shows and interviews if you wanted to maintain your success. A lot of bands were like: no, I'm not doing that shit. Depeche just understood how the business worked."

In the summer, the final leg of the Some Great Reward tour took the band to Belgium, France, and Greece. Depeche Mode also became the first band to tour behind the Iron Curtain in Hungary and Poland. These gigs were not lucrative but they were vital in terms of building the market that would explode once the Berlin Wall came down.

"What's really interesting is, when you look into East Germany, they were really the only pop band which was totally accepted in the East," Gudrun Gut told me. "For all the young people I met after the Wall came down from East Germany, one band stood out: Depeche Mode. It was really *the* band. The people from the East looked really closely at their social behaviour: are they real, are they a fake band? And Depeche Mode is not a fake band. They are modern, they represented that whole generation of East Germans."

"They were accessible at a time when a lot of other people weren't," Chris Carr recalled. "They had that work ethic. When they did Eastern Europe – I was born and bred in Kenya and I always thought the English were so parochial, whereas Depeche had a thirst to get out and see. For most English bands it was like: we'll go to Holland because we can go and smoke pot, or we can drink beer in Germany, so we'll do that, but some of these other places are just not worth doing … OK, your loss. For [booking agent] Dan Silver it was a big adventure as well. He was making fair bit of money, to say the least."

In the UK, however, success in Europe or the USA counted for little. Depeche Mode were still seen as outsiders; they were not invited to play Live Aid, for instance. Future *NME* editor Danny Kelly was refused entry to Poland, where he had been due to report on the band's huge impact in Eastern Europe, so instead he interviewed the band in London. He was impressed by the 12-inch monster remixes by Adrian Sherwood but still spent half his article questioning the band's credibility.

Depeche Mode had played 80 dates in nine months on the Some Great Reward tour. They were exhausted. Arguments arose over Gore's new material. 'Shake The Disease' had a familiar Gahan/Gore contrasting vocal, as heard on hits like 'Everything Counts' and 'People Are People', but "disease" was not a very pop word. The rest of the material Gore had been working on for the abandoned album was even darker, touching on death and depression – it was so morose, in fact, that the band's marketing people were starting to freak out.

Gore freaked out in turn and went missing for a while. When he returned, the arguments over the direction the band should take continued. They were on the verge of breaking America and the question of artistic growth versus commercial success weighed heavily on his shoulders. How much further could the band take their audience without losing them? Depeche Mode was now an industry with an ever-growing team to support. There was pressure.

The differences in the band-members' lifestyles were also growing ever more prominent. Dave had married Jo and was talking about babies; Martin was growing wilder; Alan was planning a solo album. Abandoning the album sessions left them all with time on their hands to pick at these disputes, until a split seemed almost inevitable. It also left a gap in the release schedule – particularly problematic for a European market that demanded feeding.

The band regrouped to record a stopgap single, 'It's Called A Heart', at Martin Rushent's Genetic Studios. Gareth Jones was not available to co-produce the single; Daniel Miller was there with the band but the end result was a dead session, a dead single – the sound of a band running out of ideas and enthusiasm.

'It's Called A Heart' was included on a greatest hits package, *The Singles 81–85*, released to fill the spot where a new album should have been. It was a triumphant compilation that managed at once to paper over the cracks in the band's internal division, while also suggesting, perhaps, that this could be the end. It reached Number Six in the UK charts and picked up good reviews in the *NME, Smash Hits, No 1*, and *Record Mirror*.

Unsurprisingly, the album sold better in Germany than anywhere else. It was re-titled *Catching Up With Depeche Mode* in the USA but made little headway in the charts, a sign of the work the band still needed to do over there – if they could find the will.

## CHAPTER 13
# BLACK & BLUE

**D**ave Gahan was 23, a year younger than Gore and Fletcher. He had his Porsche and he and Jo were happy in their big house in Basildon. Yes, he was rich: the unique profit-sharing deal Depeche Mode had agreed with Mute saw to that. But was he happy? Band relations were at an all time low, leading Gahan to consider his future. He was the frontman, the focus of the live shows, but from a musical perspective he was being sidelined.

Dave was a man in a band who wanted to rock'n'roll but couldn't. Was he too reliant on Martin? Gore was the one exploring new musical worlds, new clubs – having fun, taking over the band. Yet how come Dave was the one wheeled out for these naff TV shows to explain the meanings behind the songs – meanings Martin wouldn't even explain to him? Gahan was mouthing words he didn't understand, often to songs he didn't particularly like. He was a man in chains. He thought a lot about the band. He was the last one left in Basildon. He thought a lot about Martin. What if Gore didn't deliver new hits? Or what if Martin did deliver – more odd, dark, depressing songs he couldn't fathom and that didn't exactly move him?

Martin looked at Dave, fishing in Basildon, and then looked away again. He was now what he had always dreamed of being: a millionaire pop star. Just like Vince, who as the band's primary songwriter benefited from the publishing royalties in the early days, Gore was reaping the vast rewards of the band's success. His personal earnings vastly outstripped whatever the others were making.

Rod Buckle had signed Martin and Vince to three-year music publishing deals in 1980, retaining the use of the songs they delivered in those three years for a period of 25 years. It was, Buckle told me, "the standard music publishing deal at the time". The deals were good: they were structured in such a way that overseas deals – traditionally a cutthroat area – were weighted in the songwriters' favour.

Once the initial three-year deal had run down – and "despite all sorts of advice from managers, accountants, tour managers" – both Vince and Martin signed new publishing agreements with Buckle at Sonet. They were put on a better royalty rate, and the timespan on ownership of the songs was reduced to 15 years. "Three years later, Vince re-signed with me again," Buckle added. "Martin was the same." On this third re-signing, the Sonet ownership of the songs was reduced again, by a further five years to just ten. Gore and Clarke were both sitting on fortunes that basically meant they never need work again. In 1990, when they eventually left Sonet deals, both men signed new publishing agreements elsewhere. Gore was rumoured to earn around £15 million from his deal with EMI; Clarke reportedly brought in around half of that amount.

Writing the songs was where the money was. Dave wasn't stupid. He knew that. But he wasn't writing any songs. His money came from record sales and touring. If either of those dried up he was in trouble. Martin, who had recently bought himself a bigger flat in Maida Vale – big enough for a pool table – could live off the songs.

Gahan found himself increasingly preoccupied with this sort of thing. The band's recent singles collection had drawn a line under the first phase of their career. They were split over what direction to take next, their future prospects dulled by the fractured nature of inter-band relations. Under a cloud of doubt, recrimination, and jealousy they began work on a new album. This was purely a business decision; there was a massive tour planned and they needed a new album to keep the machine on the road.

There was not much excitement within the band. The demos Gore had delivered to the others a while earlier, which were considered at the time to be too depressing, formed the bulk of the material. Depeche Mode began recording at Westside Studios in London at the end of 1985. Perhaps to give the whole thing fresh impetus, Daniel Miller suggested recording the album in one continuous session that stretched over four months like a Werner Herzog film production. It was an intense way of working.

"Daniel had the idea, inspired by Herzog, that with *Black Celebration* we would 'live' the album," co-producer Gareth Jones told me. "From the moment we started recording it until the moment we finished it we did not have a single day off, and we all got severe cabin fever as part of that process. We took no time off at all. We got up, we went into the studio, we slept, we came back to the studio; the only time we didn't do that was the one day we moved from London to Berlin, and then we went straight to the studio and started setting up. The whole of *Black Celebration* was cinematically conceived, if you like.

"The music compounded the cabin fever," Jones added. "It wasn't like cheerleading every day or going to the gym; clearly we fed back into the atmosphere of the album, and the atmosphere of the songs affected us greatly as we were making it. It got pretty crazy at times. Claustrophobia as well … there's a lot of great beauty in *Black Celebration*, but also a kind of claustrophobic sadness as well … a claustrophobic depression."

The big decision to be made was whether 'Stripped' should be the album's first single. "We brought Neil Ferris into the studio to play it to him," Jones recalled. "We sat him down, turned the lights down, and turned the speakers up, and he was really excited about it as well because he'd not had that treatment before. We were all waiting with bated breath, really, because we were convinced it was the first single but we needed him to love it as well."

As it transpired, Ferris was "really moved" by the song. "Neil's obviously a professional," Jones recalled. "He's not going to come in and go: that's shit. I've stayed in touch with Neil as well and I have a lot of respect for his positive energy and focus and his love of music, so as well as being a total professional and a hyperactive 80s plugger – a very successful one as well – he was also a music lover, and it did hit him. It's an amazing record: it starts off with the incredible sample of the motorbike turning over and the Porsche engine kicks in and it's all throbbing and dark."

Dark was the key word. *Black Celebration* was the culmination of the drive that had started at the Garden, at the beginning of *Construction Time Again* – a drive to get darker and weirder, be more moody and more reverberant. With *Black Celebration* the band were celebrating, in the title of the album, what they were trying to do: celebrating the darker side of life.

The album was again completed at Hansa in Berlin. "At the end of *Black*

*Celebration* everyone was really burnt out," Jones said. "Martin's got more focused since then on sonically sculpting his records, but at that time, basically, when Martin had done the demo he was almost done. He was like: well, that's it, now can we move on. Obviously sometimes he was involved, but he's got a quicksilver mind and he didn't enjoy sitting around in the studio for hours tweaking sounds. Really, that was me, Alan, and Daniel.

"Daniel and I got a bit obsessed with the album," Jones added. "But that was part of it: part of the philosophy of the project was to get obsessed. Everyone committed to that at the beginning. We didn't have a group hug at that stage but we were all committed: OK, we're going to live the album, we're not coming out until it's finished."

'Stripped' was released in February 1986; just as Gore intended, it was heavy, bleak, and dark. It reached Number Four in Germany, went into the Top Ten in Sweden and Switzerland, and peaked at Number 15 in the UK. The band put in a terrifyingly odd performance on the BBC's mainstream TV show *Wogan*, with the band in black, Gore in full-on cross-dressing fetish-wear, and the song a move away from the overtly commercial. It wasn't that great, either – it was thrillingly awkward, yes, but in many ways it did not go far enough. 'Stripped' sounded best in the context of the album. The band had finally made a record that could be listened to as a whole rather than just as a collection of songs, however brilliant they might have been. The whole was stronger than the individual parts. The band gamely promoted the single around Europe on yet more mainstream TV shows, but they were now completely at odds with the format.

The video for 'Stripped' was shot in Berlin by Peter Care, who had previously worked extensively on visuals for Cabaret Voltaire in the late 70s and early 80s, including the cult film *Johnny YesNo*. (He has since been working on an updated version of the film, with new music by Richard H. Kirk, for Mute.) He also directed the famous video for the band's 1984 single 'Sensoria', which enjoyed a seven-month run on MTV and was among the first three music videos procured by the Museum of Modern Art in New York. Care had been a key part of the Sheffield industrial/electronic music scene, which included The Human League, Clock DVA, Hula, and ABC, and had also shot the videos for Depeche Mode's two previous singles, 'Shake The Disease' and 'It's Called A Heart'.

"They were very much at that transition point when I started working with them," he told me. "Fletch and Alan were very nice to me: they befriended me and talked to me more. They were more comfortable with me as a person. My frustration was that, because they were just very nice guys from Basildon, they didn't have an attitude – when they walked or moved around or did something that wasn't playing their instruments, they didn't have the charisma I was used to capturing with people like Cabaret Voltaire or ABC."

Care remembered the moment Gore walked onto the set. "He was in his Berlin transvestite/industrial kind of look: eye makeup on, leather skirt and leather apron, and shorts," he recalled. "He looked great in one way and completely startling and strange in another, and of course the crew … you're hiring guys who are taxi drivers by nature, so it must have been really horrible for him to have these guys who are macho idiots making rude comments and laughing behind their hands.

"The music to me didn't have much oomph to it until I moved to LA and I saw how popular they were and how their music fitted America. It was a revelation for me. It just seemed so wrong at the time and perfect in other ways. Listening to their music driving around in LA made a lot more sense than listening to it on the Tube or in a taxi in the middle of London."

Care remembered Daniel Miller as the driving force behind the band's videos. "We had a meeting for 'Stripped'," he recalled, "and Daniel spoke 90 per cent of the time: listen to the music, we want you to do this, do that – and then we just started to shoot it in Berlin. Who wants to be lifting a 20-foot-high piece of canvas for a projection screen on the Berlin Wall at three in the morning? But they did it, and it was quite glamorous in a way – the roads were empty, everything was empty. I had to get some stuff for the projections, just portraiture, where I wanted them to be up against abstract landscapes: streets or concrete, walkways, bridges. Alan really enjoyed it. He was the one who was saying: can you make us look like Cabaret Voltaire? It was very sweet, almost."

Working with Care was another brave step for the band. Nobody was quite sure what they'd end up with. "There was one video where I remember getting a call from a record guy really high up, like the chairman of A&M, who said: Peter, we don't want that fucking art, don't do that art shit that you do, this a music video for nine-year-olds, Saturday morning, just get on with it, make it look good," he recalled. "That was my message. I think Depeche Mode liked the videos I did with them, but I remember there was a bit of a hoo-ha with 'Stripped'. We were cutting it and we got this message that Dave Gahan wanted an image from a concert of everybody lighting up their cigarette lighters and waving them, and at the time I thought that was hugely cornball. I remember calling somebody and saying: this has got nothing to do with the video, why do you want it in? I just got this message saying: put it in, fuck off. So we cut it in for a short insert, and that must have really annoyed him, because the message came back that said it had to be in for a total of two seconds. It was a strange moment."

*Black Celebration* was released in March 1986. The album's core themes – death, depression, shame, guilt, sex – were played out with a less industrial, more textured sound. It was an album that did many different things for many different people. There was romance – humour even – to be found amid the exhausting desperation. It was a record for outsiders, a cult record, even an existential record. The album's dry tag line was *Life In The So-Called Space Age*.

Gore sang four of the eleven tracks. This was truly his album. But the idea of this being the band's dark masterpiece played better in the USA than it did in the UK. The album suffered in trying to balance the relentless sense of hopelessness suggested by the songs with a commercial appeal: it came up short on both counts. Nonetheless, it was the first work the band had produced since *A Broken Frame* that you could immerse yourself in, alone in the dark, with headphones on. Gore's voice was not exactly threatening; the sounds on the songs were often too pleasant, the innuendo perhaps too pronounced. Maybe if Dave had truly been involved it would have been harder. His voice and the heavy throb the band had mastered were severely under-used. In retrospect it still sounds desolate, but not in a good way. *Black Celebration* was the sound of business, of a band aware of their responsibilities and uncertainties, asking all the right questions but coming up with none of the answers. It was the last album they recorded in Berlin, a city whose dancing partner was, appropriately, said to be death.

The devoted Depeche Mode fan base sent the album to Number Three in the UK. It was also incredibly popular across Europe: Number One in Switzerland, Number Two in Germany, Number Five in Sweden, and Number Eleven in France, with over one and a half million copies sold. It was panned by the *NME* but received support from the usual sources: *Record Mirror*, *No 1*, *Just 17*, and *Smash Hits*. Depeche Mode were no closer to gaining credibility.

The cover art was also a disappointment. "The idea for the *Black Celebration* album cover was mine," Martyn Atkins told me. "It was basically supposed to be a building and we were going to put these big black banners hanging off it, almost like the Nazi banners, but we were just going to do it with huge black banners that didn't say anything on them. We'd have this modern office block – an almost neo-classical office block – and we would hang these huge drapes and do a photo of it. Then somehow that idea got talked around, through Brian [Griffin] talking to Daniel, that Brian could build a model and he could build this model in his studio and we could photograph that. It sounds like *Spinal Tap* – we could photograph that model and it would be like my original idea. And it would be a lot cheaper, I guess, although with Brian shooting it I don't know. I was fucking horrified when I went down to Brian's studio and he had this model on this table … I didn't know whether to laugh or cry. Fuck, man. It was just so amateurish."

*Black Celebration* marked the end of Griffin's relationship with Depeche Mode. "I never did any cover work ever again after that album," he told me. "I think I probably screwed it up a bit. The model-maker I was working with, although extremely talented, was questionable in his consumption. I think it was a poor show by me. I tried to make it work but it was awful."

Atkins and his colleagues at his design company, Town & Country Planning, had been developing logos for each individual song on the album. He used them to rescue the cover. "The thing was: at that time, everything was really tight, time-wise," he said. "You couldn't change anything because everything was in place: plugging, interviews, distribution. You couldn't change the release date. We'd be putting together the album cover two weeks before it was released. It was like you were on this train and you couldn't get off, so we just came up with a concept of cropping the photo down and making more of all the logos that we'd been working on for each song. They were all embossed on the cover. The cover actually looked OK in the end because it had this tactile thing to it that you didn't see until you moved it in the light."

*Black Celebration* was also the last Depeche Mode album to feature the production team of Jones and Miller. Mute Records was growing at a rapid rate, moving offices again to the larger 86 Harrow Road in London W10, and Miller had many responsibilities. Vince Clarke's new band, Erasure, was starting to take off; there were singles and albums from Crime & The City Solution, Nick Cave & The Bad Seeds, Frank Tovey, I Start Counting, various Wire projects, and new acts He Said and Diamanda Galás. Miller had also started to fund other small labels such as Blast First, Cooking Vinyl, and Rhythm King.

"Harrow Road was massive," Atkins recalled. "When Mute moved there it was just like: fucking hell, these guys have made the big time. It was like an office building. It wasn't like a couple of rooms in a building. They took over a whole building on Harrow Road."

Atkins would go on to take complete control of the band's visuals for their next album, *Music For The Masses*, and would also start dating Martin Gore's soon-to-be-ex-girlfriend, Christina Friedrichs. "When I dated Christina, the money had come in and Martin bought another flat in Maida Vale, round the corner from the old one," Atkins recalled. "She was in the old flat, and then not long after that he bought a house in the country as well. Do you remember that band Bros? They lived next door to Martin, and there were always school kids hanging around outside on the street. I used to go out all the time with Martin and his posse and he always used to be having parties at his house. I did more hanging out and partying with him than ever before."

▭▬▭

The Black Celebration tour would run for six months and saw the band playing their biggest UK dates yet, including two nights at Wembley Arena and the 6,000-capacity Birmingham NEC. John Peel reviewed the Wembley show and came away a fan. The Jane Spiers-designed stage set was loosely based on Leni Riefenstahl's film of the 1936 Olympics. It featured inflatable plastic, smoke machines, lasers, fluorescent ultraviolet paint, projections behind the band, and massive stage curtains. "That's the stage design I liked the best," Spiers recalled. "The big inflatable stage set. All the risers had internally lit stripes in them. Then we had these giant inflatable fan-shaped things that used to come up in the middle of the shows. Martin was quite interested in Hitler's architect, Albert Speer. He said he liked all the pomp and ceremony that went with that look."

Once again, J.D. Fanger did the front-of-house sound, Daryl Bamonte was on the backline, and Andy Franks – who later had to be taken off the tour after suffering a brain haemorrhage – was on monitors. Future manager Jonathan Kessler was the tour accountant, part of a 40-strong crew.

Support for the tour was provided by Sheffield band Hula, who had recently recorded an impressive album, *Murmur*, using cut-ups, weird rhythms, and paranoid vocals, all blended together into a unique white-funk sound. As was usual for Depeche – but not for the rest of the business – the band and Miller had asked Hula to play, rather than selling the support slot to the highest bidder.

"I don't know if there was a specific record of ours they liked," Hula's Mark Albrow told me. "Everybody in the independent area was always checking out each other's work. I know it was mentioned that a 12-inch of ours, 'Walk On Stalks Of Shattered Glass', had some stuff on it they said they found interesting – a tape thing going through a noise gate, triggered by something else. I think there must have been a recognition of similar creative interests. Depeche Mode were all very down to earth. They all gave the impression of being a democratic unit – no overbearing leaders. But Dave Gahan would be off the bus in a separate car from the rest of the group. He didn't mix as much as the others. At one gig – at the Brighton Conference Centre, I think – some jealous boyfriend managed to lob a pint of beer over him mid-performance. Afterward, Dave was upset and focussing on it. It struck me as strangely vulnerable.

"I think they had some palm trees in their backstage area – probably synthetic ones. There was a Japanese woman who followed them everywhere – she was known to the group and invited backstage at each gig. It was more like a civilised drinks party, not wild and not drunk. There was always a very orderly atmosphere backstage – an immensely professional team of riggers, stage managers, security people. It was all very civilised. Doing a show, energy-wise, is a big thing and has quite an effect on people. Some people can unwind by drinking too much alcohol. But the Depeche Mode operation was slick – disciplined without being oppressive. Just very, very professional."

At the Brighton gig, Hula's manager, Pete Marchetto, remembered the two bands taking advantage of all the empty floor space to have an impromptu 'them versus us' football match. "The strangest vision was Martin Gore playing with skin-tight trousers with handcuffs dangling from his belt and proving himself an alarmingly adept player," he recalled. "Largely thanks to him, Hula were trounced."

Mark Albrow watched Depeche Mode every night and described Andy Fletcher as "quite an endearing presence" during the show. "It works in the same way as Phil Oakey picking up the two girls – because they were just ordinary girls," he said. "How that dynamic worked on stage for them was the same – everyone can identify with the girls, and Fletch, because they were just normal. The feel of the group doesn't get too polished and too distant from the audience."

Albrow was also impressed by the more avant-garde aspects of the show. "They had this tubular sculpture thing, a bit like a sound sculpture, that Martin would bing and bong," he said. "That, again, made things a bit more interesting – it made you think these guys are aware of Test Department, Einstürzende Neubauten …

"I remember I felt sympathy for what I perceived as a creatively tight situation," he added. "They had to work really hard because they have to work within such tight pop parameters – they've got so many interests and they have to compress it all within these tight parameters. In a way, if you're in a successful pop group and you suddenly want to be Test Department, you can't do that without throwing your career down the pan. But you can integrate it, which is very smart."

In April, as Depeche Mode moved from the UK to an enormous tour of Europe for 24 arena dates, a second single was pulled from *Black Celebration*. 'A Question Of Lust' featured Gore singing lead vocals; Gahan stood at the back and bashed a drum for TV performances. The single peaked at Number 28 in the UK but went into the Top Ten in Germany.

With his bleached-blonde hair and penchant for German army uniforms, Gore was now looking like a Young Nazi.

"Depeche were taken more seriously in Europe and the US," the band's PR, Chris Carr, told me. "And they were going though that stage where any criticism hurt them. Dave, for instance, was like: fuck them, what's the point of talking to them, they're just going to slag us off. That would be echoed by Fletch. Martin wouldn't say anything and would just sort of go: I've got nothing to say to them. I remember being at Wembley Arena, watching them with Daniel, and Dave just conducted that audience. It was a Nuremberg kind of thing; it was bizarre. If he had told the crowd to riot, they were all going to, blindly."

Carr also saw Miller take a professional step back from the band. "Around the time of *Black Celebration*, he was also involved in The Bad Seeds records, and Mute had grown to such a size that I think Daniel realised he was getting stretched," Carr said. "His stamina was pretty immense but I think he thought it was time for them to stand on their own. It was mutual. Daniel felt he couldn't be totally hands-on. The band were growing. That was all part of an integral thing that Daniel instigated at the beginning: the territory comes with responsibility. He gave them the opportunity to learn.

"Daniel's a fairly astute political animal. Whenever people would ask about doing interviews with Daniel, I'd go and see him and he'd say: Chris, you know the only publication I want to talk to is *Marxism Today* ... and by and large he was serious, at the time. Not so much that he was Marxist, but his idea was to put back in what he earned. I remember Roger Ames at London Records trying to buy Mute. Daniel just wouldn't entertain it whatsoever. Daniel was steadfast about his independence."

Carr also observed the inter-band dynamic. "Fletch and Martin were joined at the hip," he said. "Martin would do whatever Fletch did. They became a limited company and they used to vote. If they wanted to do something they'd have a vote on it: the band and [tour managers] J.D. and Franksy. Whatever Fletcher voted, Martin would follow."

The band's growing stardom was also starting to become overbearing. "I remember being on the road with them in Europe and just chatting to fans and they'd say they learnt English from Depeche Mode," Carr recalled.

"I remember being in Rimini, Italy, after the show ... police cars taking the bus back. We go into the hotel and Mart says the party's in his room. And suddenly they had two security guards at Martin's door ID-ing everyone that came into the room. I'd been with all different size bands and never witnessed that stuff. At the end it was chucking out time and Mart goes: Chris, help me, go and look in the bathroom and go and look on the balcony. There were two girls, one in the bathroom, one on the balcony, trying to be the last to leave or not to leave at all ...

"I think part of why they lasted so long is down to a social dysfunction between Martin and Dave," Carr continued. "There's a mutual respect, but Martin isn't wired to be that confrontational. They both leave gaps inadvertently for one another. Dave was obviously very conscious of not being able to write songs; when he did write songs, they were going to be compared to Mart's, and that's not fair. Dave is more conventionally wired to a certain extent. With Martin there's very little confrontation that's visible. It's there and it manifests itself; it's there but he won't confront it, he'll bide his time and let things decay, or whatever. Somehow, through their mutual dysfunction, Dave and Mart each get their own way, whereas with most other bands it's just combustion."

▭▬▭

After Europe, the Black Celebration tour hit the USA and Canada for Depeche Mode's most extensive North American dates yet: 29 shows in total, with three at New York's Radio City Music Hall and two at Laguna Hills in Irvine Meadows, California. 'Stripped' had not even been released as a single, and *Black Celebration* had barely limped into the Top 100, but these shows and this visit to the USA were massively successful, with crowds of up to 17,000 fans singing along to every word.

Depeche Mode were still a cult but a very popular one. Some US critics felt the "throbbing loneliness and confusion" of the band's songs reassured a younger generation that they are not alone. Others felt that this appeal could be explained by the Mute connection, or the fact that the band self-managed and seemed to have a distaste for anything corporate. Either way, from their stronghold in California, Depeche Mode took America.

The support act for the US and European legs of the tour was Book Of

Love, a new band also signed to Sire Records whose singles 'You Make Me Feel So Good' and 'I Touch Roses' were underground dance hits. They had also played support to the band on their previous US tour. "Between the two tours it was really, really different," the band's singer, Susan Ottaviano, told me. "The Some Great Reward tour was spotty in some parts of the country, like when we were in Middle America. They were never empty and the shows were never weak but maybe they weren't sold out. I don't think we sold out the Forum in San Diego, for example. They could be slightly uneven because that's what it's like when an artist is not successful across the board. I sort of got on the game with them, too. Depeche Mode never really got any press in the US. They were very sort of mysterious and invisible – they weren't one of the bands people wrote about a lot. They were not getting any commercial radio but we were hearing them in clubs or on college radio.

"To watch the support building over the two tours: you could see it, it was amazing," she said. "All of a sudden, at every hotel we stayed at, there'd be a group of girls in black – the little goth girls, you knew exactly who they were – they'd all be outside, or in the hallways, looking. It was crazy how the whole thing just sort of happened. The Black Celebration tour was just massive. We played a stadium that had held a mass rally – it had a secret entrance underneath. I don't know if that was Berlin or wherever; the places were just getting larger and larger. We played in every single place in Germany you could imagine. All the shows in Germany were huge: those are the ones that were 10, 15, 20,000 people. I had trouble with the big crowds and Dave told me very early on to say you're the person with the microphone – you have to take that on. It was good advice. I grew a set of balls and tried to deal with the crowd.

"Dave was a little bit more fragile on the Black Celebration tour than he was before," Ottaviano continued. "But they were definitely a different kind of band – they didn't act like pop stars. The whole Basildon thing was very, very clear and very strong, especially then. So many of them were from Basildon. I felt like that was a really strong presence. I knew it was a big working-class town. It was a clique in that way, something that kept them together."

Ottaviano also knew what was going on at Depeche Mode's US label

Sire. "Craig Kostich was the head of the dance department at the time," she recalled, "but I would still go back to Seymour as the person who had the biggest influence. Howie Klein was the Vice President at Sire – another big influence. He was doing us and Erasure. Sire's head office was located in New York and probably only six people worked there. Depeche were really spoiled by Daniel Miller. Things like that don't exist in the USA. Seymour Stein was the closest thing to that and he was still attached to a big corporation. Daniel really took good care of them."

Rod Buckle observed a key change in the band on the Black Celebration tour. "They moved away from being The Bay City Rollers and became U2, in a nutshell," he said. "When we did *Black Celebration*, I pretty much set up the processes and introduced them to the right people: J.D. Fanger and Andy Franks, all the other roadies who became tour managers. I'd done a tour with George Thorogood and become friendly with J.D. and Franksy on that tour. Probably Ferret [Neil Ferris's PR company] introduced them to [tour agent] Dan Silver or maybe the guys at Rough Trade. Dan Silver was a good, honest broker. He was a good guy and he worked very hard. I fought with him because the record companies were pushing me and I'd say: we've got to do France first, or it's the half term holiday, the kid's have got money ...

"The Black Celebration tour had a global gross of $100 million and Depeche walked away with profit of about $40 million," Buckle continued. "At the same time, The Cure were touring America. On a Wednesday we'd play Red Rocks in Denver and on a Friday The Cure would play Red Rocks. On a Thursday we'd play Tower Theatre in Philadelphia and on a Sunday The Cure would play. It was absolutely the same audience, the same demographic. The Cure, same weeks, same number of shows, same size audience, had had to borrow $11 million from Polygram to pay their touring costs at the end of their tour because it was so run so loosely. They should get credit: Fletch, Dave – and Martin, laconically – for surrounding themselves with pretty good people."

Howie Klein, Sire's 36-year-old General Manager, had previously worked as a DJ on KUSF, a small but influential college radio station based at the University of San Francisco. The station had played Depeche Mode fanatically, long before they were accepted by the mainstream. "In the early stages, before the band broke, the alternative stations that were playing them a lot were WLIR on Long Island, in the suburbs of New York City; WHFS in Washington DC; WRAS in Atlanta; WBCN in Boston; KROQ in Pasadena/Los Angeles; and WXRT in Chicago," Klein recalled.

In the early 80s, there were no alternative stations on the commercial dial in the USA. KUFS was one of the biggest radio stations in the Bay area and became very influential – not just locally but also nationally – in helping to popularise alternative music. Depeche Mode were one of the first bands to break out through that process. "We started playing them and then KMEL adopted it as well," Klein recalled. "KMEL was a big powerhouse, dance-orientated pop station with a gigantic signal, a giant San Francisco station that reached a lot more people."

Klein recalled one of the first discussions he had with the band as General Manager of Sire. "They said: now that you're here, we hope that we're going to be the priority, and it's not always going to be Madonna, or Van Halen," he told me. "They listed a bunch of big bands that [Sire distributor] Warner Bros had that always had records that came out at the same time as Depeche Mode records. Those bands and artists always became the priority, and DM always had to take a back seat. What they were saying to me was: are you going be the person who is going to make us the priority?"

Klein was already a huge fan of the band but he didn't have the power to do that on his own. Part of the reason New Yorker Seymour Stein hired him, however, was so that the label would have a voice in Burbank, Warner Bros' home in Los Angeles, and be able to ensure that its acts were prioritised. "Depeche Mode was the band that Seymour and I decided would be the first of those bands," Klein recalled, "and between Seymour and I, we were able to get enough of a coalition of people inside of the company to get behind the band, and believe in the band, and be willing to spend resources on the band in terms of time and money to break them. They were already big in England and throughout Europe, and our argument was that there was no reason this band shouldn't be gigantic in America as well. To be honest with you, the thing that really broke Depeche Mode more than anything was their live touring: they became a much bigger band from touring than from record sales at first.

"Still, the fact of the matter was that Seymour and myself consciously made the decision to push Depeche Mode and insisted they be prioritised, which is what the band had asked us to do – and was what we both wanted," Klein continued. "Seymour was in New York, he didn't have the attention that was needed to be there on top of every little decision that gets made, like including them in an ad, or including them on a compilation – he just wasn't always there for that. That's why he hired me. We totally, 100 per cent saw eye to eye that Depeche Mode had to be our top priority for Sire, and that we would push them at all expense and just concentrate on breaking them in America. Once we saw that work and realised the formula of how to do that, the next band we chose to do the same thing for was Erasure.

"The other thing people overlook, which is important, is that Depeche Mode had so many unsuccessful records on Sire before they finally broke," he laughed. "Once they broke and once the first record went Gold, suddenly they became gigantic at Warner Bros because all these records that had only sold like 10,000 or 20,000 copies ... well, they were there and all these new fans of the band who started buying them went back to the catalogue.

"I can't emphasise to you how important that is for a label. In those days, in order to successfully market a new record, it could cost as much as five dollars a record to break a new band, market it, get it on the radio, and pay everybody. It would cost a fortune per record sold, so the profit margins were very low. To market a catalogue record – for all those four or five records that hadn't sold any copies that we had in our catalogue – it cost a penny, one cent. Suddenly, the profits from Depeche just started cascading, so internally they became one of the most powerful bands on Warner Bros – just like they wanted."

The first US Top 40 radio stations to pick up on Depeche Mode were in surprising locations: Phoenix, Arizona, and Houston, Dallas, and San Antonio, Texas. But perhaps there was a reason why these were the places where the band was breaking: years later, Klein realised that these were the cities where ecstasy use was exploding in almost epidemic proportions.

"Eventually, all of the stations started playing them and they became gigantic Top 40 hits," Klein recalled. "But you always have to have some stations that get it started, and it was breaking out of Texas more than other places in terms of Top 40. It's odd, because people think of Texas as being this reactionary, backward place – which it is, politically – but when it came to breaking DM or Erasure, they were way ahead of the game."

All along, Depeche Mode had wanted to be as big inside Sire/Warner Bros as Madonna, Van Halen, and ZZ Top. Now they were. "It was a little joke between us, because those acts were silly," Klein recalled, "but Depeche Mode had always been told: we really like your record, but we are really working ZZ Top now ... or Rod Stewart, or whatever garbage the label was going after instead of them. But they became as big as any of those acts because of this massive catalogue explosion. That doesn't happen in a normal situation. But when you have as many records as they did, and they all start catching on, suddenly the momentum becomes so big that everyone – even people in our corporate headquarters, above the record level – was suddenly noticing: wow, there's this really big band Warner Bros have called Depeche something-or-other."

It wasn't just Klein and Stein: several other people at the label were completely dedicated to Depeche Mode, including Stephen Baker, who later became the President of Warner Bros but who at the time was a product manager, and Craig Kostich, who was Sire's dance-promotion guy. "Those two people were also what Warner Bros used to call rabbis," said Klein. "A rabbi is kind of a tongue-in-cheek phrase, but they would be the people who were the main advocate of the band, who would be pushing them and pushing them. We would have these meetings, these ceaseless meetings – all the time at every different level there'd be meetings – and at every meeting there always needed to be someone pushing Depeche Mode to the front and getting them the most attention. Craig Kostich, Stephen Baker, myself, and Seymour formed a little coalition of people who would always say it had to be Depeche Mode. We were up against people who had different priorities. There were definitely people who felt it had to be Rod Stewart. If there was something good happening, they wanted it to go to Dire Straits or whatever they believed in."

Huge success in America also brought problems for Depeche Mode – particularly in relation to Daniel Miller. "One of the problems for the band was they didn't have management in the US," Klein recalled. "It was a funny situation. In effect they were self-managed, or Daniel was managing them. But Daniel was looked at in America as the head of Mute, which is what he was. In the US, you can't be both – in fact, it's illegal. You can't be both a manager and a record label – they have to be separate, and that's because there's a history in the US of record labels ripping off artists; the feeling was that you have to have someone independent of that whose loyalty would be strictly toward the band and not the label.

"There's a law – certainly in California and New York – where there has to be that separation. So it was a confusing situation, and Daniel also had other responsibilities – even though Depeche Mode were his number one priority, he was trying to break other bands and records were being released all around the world. We felt that, once Depeche Mode started breaking, we very much needed someone who would be an advocate solely for them and not care about anything else and not be drawn in other directions and not do anything except try to break Depeche. And Bruce Kirkland was that someone."

New Zealander Kirkland, who would go on to become CEO of EMI, had his own artist representation and marketing company, representing such acts as Kraftwerk and Peter Gabriel. He would become a key figure in the next stage of the band's career as they renegotiated their original five-album deal with Sire.

"It was a combination of Daniel and the band who decided on Kirkland," Klein recalled. "Daniel had clout with us – the type of clout you give to someone you respect and admire – but the people in the American music industry are looking for a different kind of clout. They're looking for clout that has to do with having some kind of financial power and business power. These people didn't know who Daniel Miller was and couldn't have cared less if he was a creative genius. It didn't matter if he was a visionary – that isn't something that goes into the equation. It was felt that someone was needed who could really be pushing the band 24/7 forever and just concentrating on Depeche Mode and doing whatever it took to make sure, first of all, that the entire label kept focus on them – and also to make sure the music industry kept focused on them. Daniel was in no position to do that. No one based in England could do that. It was impossible. You have to be in America."

After finally securing huge success in America, Depeche Mode played three hysteria-soaked dates in Japan and then eight final Black Celebration dates in the stadiums and arenas of France, Italy, and Denmark. It was August 1986; Fletch and Martin had just turned 25. The band's setlist still featured the ghost of Vince – 'Photographic', 'Boys Say Go!', and the encore, 'Just Can't Get Enough' – but they were their own men now.

For the final leg of the tour the band chose Eyeless In Gaza – another Cabaret Voltaire/Throbbing Gristle-inspired group – as the support act. Gore was a fan of the band's Cherry Red albums *Red Rust September* and *Back From The Rains*. Eyeless in Gaza missed the first gig in Italy as they were late arriving at the venue, having just driven all the way across Europe in a Ford Transit van. Taking their place as a last-minute replacement that night was an assortment of Depeche Mode roadies, including Daryl Bamonte, who did a blues jam and got booed off stage. The final show of the tour, in Copenhagen, was an outdoor event with New Order and Talk Talk in support. Depeche Mode had completed 76 dates in six months, playing to a total of more than 300,000 people. They looked tanned and happy in the pages of *Record Mirror* and *Smash Hits*, who sent reporters along to cover the shows, but behind the scenes of this mammoth tour, success, fame, and money had taken its toll.

This time it was not just Dave Gahan suffering. "Andy Fletcher was not speaking to any of the others in the band," Peter Becker of Eyeless In Gaza told me. Gore was the only original member of the band to appear to escape unscathed. Eyeless In Gaza's singer, Martyn Bates, remembered being welcomed warmly to the tour by a smiling Gore who warned him that the European Depeche Mode crowd was notoriously partisan, and that some of their support acts, such as Furniture, had been "pennied" off.

"We spent some time playing guitar together with Martin," Bates recalled. "I said he should play it on stage. He sort of said: no, the fans wouldn't like it; it would be heresy. Fletch was not talking. He was very withdrawn. Wilder was more like I used to be in this sort of rock band: I've got this great gig and I'm having a great time." Before one gig, in Italy, the heavens erupted and water dripped onto the band's equipment. "Martin was laughing, saying: I'm not going on," Bates said. "Dave was the one determined to go on in the rain, like he would have gone on even if he'd got electrocuted."

In September 1986, a third and final single was pulled from *Black Celebration*: 'A Question Of Time'. Its title was confusingly similar to the previous single, 'A Question Of Lust', but this one had Gahan on vocals and a faster, heavier beat. The band's 17th single to date, it stalled at Number 28: Depeche Mode's worst UK chart showing since their debut, 'Dreaming Of Me'. It would have gone largely unnoticed, even among their devout European followers, were it not for the fact that the video was shot by former *NME* photographer Anton Corbijn, who would go on to redefine the look of the band. Corbijn was a crucial and final addition to the 'family' that would surround and provide for Depeche Mode through the remainder of the decade and into the 90s. Everything was now in place for a new chapter in the band's career. Another book.

The Basildon Development Corporation stood down in 1986. Basildon council was left holding the baby and tried in vain to satisfy the growing requirement for rented housing. There were 6,000 people on the waiting list. The Conservative government gave the council £1.9 million to spend on housing at a time when the local authority said it needed £29 million. Basildon was on a collision course for a severe social housing shortage – and at the start of a steep decline due to the subsequent neglect of its once shimmering, clean estates.

Dave would soon move out. Vince was long gone, Martin and Fletch too. But their families and friends stayed, and Depeche Mode would always stay true to the romanticism of the New Town mentality, the socialist ideal. As a social experiment, it gave the world something truly original.

# MUTE RECORDS DISCOGRAPHY 1978-1986

**1978**
MUTE 1    'T.V.O.D.' / 'Warm Leatherette', The Normal

**1979**
MUTE 2    'Back To Nature', Fad Gadget
MUTE 3    'Memphis Tennessee', Silicon Teens

**1980**
MUTE 4    'Judy In Disguise', Silicon Teens
MUTE 5    'Kebabträume', Deutsch-Amerikanische
           Freundschaft (DAF)
STUMM 1   *Die Kleinen Und Die Bösen*, DAF
MUTE 6    'Ricky's Hand', Fad Gadget
MUTE 7    'Soundtracks 1–5', Non/Smegma
STUMM 2   *Music For Parties*, Silicon Teens
MUTE 8    'Just Like Eddie', Silicon Teens
STUMM 3   *Fireside Favourites*, Fad Gadget
MUTE 9    'Insecticide', Fad Gadget
MUTE 10   'Double Heart', Robert Rental
MUTE 11   'Tanz Mit Mir', DAF

**1981**
MUTE 12   'Make Room', Fad Gadget
MUTE 13   'Dreaming Of Me', Depeche Mode
MUTE 14   'New Life', Depeche Mode
STUMM 4   *Boyd Rice*, Boyd Rice
STUMM 5   *Speak & Spell*, Depeche Mode
MUTE 15   'Rise', NON
MUTE 16   'Just Can't Get Enough', Depeche Mode
MUTE 17   'Saturday Night Special', Fad Gadget
STUMM 6   *Incontinent*, Fad Gadget

**1982**
MUTE 18   'See You', Depeche Mode
MUTE 19   'Fred vom Jupiter', Die Doraus Und
           Die Marinas
MUTE 20   'Only You', Yazoo
STUMM 7   *Upstairs At Eric's*, Yazoo
STUMM 9   *A Broken Frame*, Depeche Mode
MUTE 21   'King Of The Flies', Fad Gadget
STUMM 8   *Under The Flag*, Fad Gadget
MUTE 22   'The Meaning Of Love', Depeche Mode
MUTE 23   'Los Niños Del Parque',
           Liaisons Dangereuses
MUTE 24   'Life On The Line', Fad Gadget
BONG 1    'Leave In Silence', Depeche Mode
YAZ 1     'Don't Go', Yazoo
YAZ 2     'The Other Side Of Love', Yazoo
STUMM 10   *Physical Evidence*, NON
MUTE 26   'For Whom The Bell Tolls', Fad Gadget

**1983**
STUMM 12   *You And Me Both*, Yazoo
MUTE 25   'Or So It Seems', Duet Emmo
STUMM 11   *Or So It Seems*, Duet Emmo
MUTE 27   'Mit Dir', Robert Görl
MUTE 28   'I Discover Love', Fad Gadget
MUTE 29   'Mutiny! (EP)', The Birthday Party
YAZ 3     'Nobody's Diary', Yazoo
BONG 2    'Get The Balance Right', Depeche Mode
BONG 3    'Everything Counts', Depeche Mode
STUMM 13   *Construction Time Again*, Depeche Mode
BONG 4    'Love In Itself', Depeche Mode
Tiny 1      'Never Never', The Assembly

**1984**
MUTE 30   'Collapsing New People', Fad Gadget
           With Einstürzende Neubauten
STUMM 14   *Strategies Against Architecture*
           *80–83*, Einstürzende Neubauten
STUMM 15   *Gag*, Fad Gadget
MUTE 31   'Darling Don't Leave Me', Robert Görl
           With Annie Lennox
STUMM 16   *Night Full Of Tension*, Robert Görl
MUTE 32   'In The Ghetto', Nick Cave & The Bad
           Seeds
STUMM 17   *From Her To Eternity*, Nick Cave
           Featuring The Bad Seeds
MUTE 33   'One Man's Meat', Fad Gadget
MUTE 34   'Letters To A Friend', I Start Counting
STUMM 18   *This Way*, Bruce Gilbert
BONG 5    'People Are People', Depeche Mode
BONG 6    'Master & Servant', Depeche Mode
STUMM 19   *Some Great Reward*, Depeche Mode
BONG 7    'Blasphemous Rumours' / 'Somebody',
           Depeche Mode
STUMM 20   *Easy Listening For The Hard Of*
           *Hearing*, Boyd Rice & Frank Tovey

**1985**
MUTE 35   'Still Smiling', I Start Counting
MUTE 36   'The Dangling Man EP', Crime & The
           City Solution
STUMM 22   *Just South Of Heaven*, Crime & The
           City Solution
MUTE 37   'Hypnotized', Mark Stewart & The Maffia
STUMM 24   *As The Veneer Of Demoocrazy Starts*
           *To Fade*, Mark Stewart & The Maffia
MUTE 38   'Tupelo', Nick Cave & The Bad Seeds
STUMM 21   *The Firstborn Is Dead*, Nick Cave &
           The Bad Seeds

| | |
|---|---|
| MUTE 39 | 'Luxury', Frank Tovey |
| STUMM 23 | *Snakes & Ladders*, Frank Tovey |
| MUTE 40 | 'Who Needs Love Like That', Erasure |
| MUTE 41 | 'Only One I', He Said |
| MUTE 42 | 'Heavenly Action', Erasure |
| BONG 8 | 'Shake The Disease', Depeche Mode |
| BONG 9 | 'It's Called A Heart', Depeche Mode |
| Tag 1 | 'One Day', Vince Clarke & Paul Quinn |
| MUTEl 1 | *The Singles (81–85)*, Depeche Mode |

**1986**

| | |
|---|---|
| MUTE 43 | 'Pump', He Said |
| MUTE 44 | 'Luddite Joe', Frank Tovey |
| MUTE 45 | 'Oh L'amour', Erasure |
| STUMM 25 | *Wonderland*, Erasure |
| MUTE 46 | 'The Kentucky Click' / 'Adventure', Crime & The City Solution |
| MUTE 47 | 'The Singer', Nick Cave & The Bad Seeds |

| | |
|---|---|
| STUMM 28 | *Kicking Against The Pricks*, Nick Cave & The Bad Seeds |
| MUTE 48 | 'Pulling 3g's', He Said |
| STUMM 29 | *Hail*, He Said |
| MUTE 49 | 'Catch That Look', I Start Counting |
| STUMM 30 | *My Translucent Hands*, I Start Counting |
| MUTE 50 | 'Just Talk', A.C. Marias |
| STUMM 27 | *The Divine Punishment*, Diamanda Galás |
| MUTE 51 | 'Sometimes', Erasure |
| MUTE 52 | 'The Mercy Seat', Nick Cave & The Bad Seeds |
| MUTE 53 | 'Snakedrill', Wire |
| BONG 10 | 'Stripped', Depeche Mode |
| STUMM 26 | *Black Celebration*, Depeche Mode |
| BONG 11 | 'A Question Of Lust', Depeche Mode |
| BONG 12 | 'A Question Of Time', Depeche Mode |
| STUMM 31 | *1+2*, Recoil |
| STUMM 32 | *Blood & Flame*, NON |

# INDEX

Words in *italics* indicate album titles unless otherwise stated. Words in quotes indicate song titles. Page numbers in **bold** refer to illustrations.

# ACKNOWLEDGEMENTS

What I didn't want to do with this book was use any quotes from old band press interviews, all of which are archived at the excellent sacreddm.net. Extracts from these old cuttings repeatedly appear in the three books already available on the band: *Black Celebration* by Steve Malins, *Some Great Reward* by Dave Thompson, and *Stripped* by Jonathan Miller. It seemed pointless to repeat these well-worn quotes again.

Instead, I wanted to take a fresh look at Depeche Mode by interviewing as many original sources as possible. I thank the band members (particularly Andy Fletcher) who were aware this book was being written and encouraged some of their oldest and closest friends and colleagues to participate.

The biggest thanks go the people I interviewed for this work: Peter Lucas, Gary Turner, Sue Ryder Paget, Pete Hobbs, Phil Burdett, Reverend Chris Briggs, Graham Bonney, Deb Danahay, Vin Harrop, Betty Page, Brian Denny, Richard Seager, Angela Hogg, Seymour Stein, Neil Ferris, Peter Care, Matt Fretton, Martyn Bates, Pete Becker, Robert Marlow, Andy Goode, Nikki Avery, Adrian Sherwood, Rik Wheatley, Jane Spiers, Martyn Atkins, Paul Langwith, Boyd Rice, Genesis Breyer P-Orridge, Mark Albrow, Mark Irving, Gary Harsent, Susan Ottaviano, Brian Griffin, Simone Grant, Robert Gorl, Anne Swindell, Howie Klein, Mark Crick, Mick Nixon, Howard Swindell, Tracey Rivers, Tony Mitchell, Steve Burton, Gareth Jones, Kim Forey, Kevin Walker, Chris Carr, Gudrun Gut, Neil Arthur, Stephen Luscombe, Tony Burgess, Mortiz Reichelt, Rod Buckle, Alison Moyet, and John McCready.

Thanks also to those who agreed to be interviewed but we never quite made it: Gail Forey, Mark Longmuir, Hilde Swendgaard, Stevo, Bruce Kirkland, Suzanne Todd, and Michael Pagnotta.

I was a frequent visitor to the band's official website at depechemode.com, to basildon.com, to mute.com, and to numerous band fan-sites, particularly depeche-mode.com. Key works in print included: *Basildon – Behind The Headlines* by Peter Lucas, *Basildon – Birth Of A City* by Peter Lucas, *Basildon* by Peter Lucas, and *Britain's New Towns* by Anthony Alexander, plus, to a lesser extent: *Arcadia For All* by Colin Ward, *Basildon – Mood Of A Nation* by Dennis Hayes and Alan Hudson, *Documents and Eye Witnesses: An Intimate History Of Rough Trade* by Neil Taylor, *When The Lights Went Out: Britain In The Seventies* by Andy Beckett, *Starmakers And Svengalis* by Johnny Rogan, *Thatcher's Britain* by Richard Vinen, *Zoo Station: Adventures in East And West Berlin* by Ian Walker, *Wreckers Of Civilisation: The Story Of Coum Transmissions & Throbbing Gristle* by Simon Ford, and *Rip It Up And Start Again* by Simon Reynolds.

Michele Newman at the *Basildon Echo* and Jim Worsdale assisted in the tracking down of Peter Lucas. Thanks also to Tom King at the *Basildon Echo* for his continued support.

Also thanks to: Tom Seabrook and Mark Brend at Jawbone, Nannette Elke at Random House, and Kevin Pocklington at Jenny Brown Associates.

Special thanks to: Shirley, Theo, Thalia, and Sylvie.

Dedicated to Andrew Loog Oldham

# PICTURE CREDITS

Other books in this series:

MILLION DOLLAR
BASH: BOB DYLAN,
THE BAND, AND THE
BASEMENT TAPES
by Sid Griffin

ISBN 978-1-906002-05-3

BOWIE IN BERLIN:
A NEW CAREER IN A
NEW TOWN
by Thomas Jerome
Seabrook

ISBN 978-1-906002-08-4

BILL BRUFORD THE
AUTOBIOGRAPHY:
YES, KING CRIMSON,
EARTHWORKS, AND
MORE
by Bill Bruford

ISBN 978-1-906002-23-7

TO LIVE IS TO DIE:
THE LIFE AND DEATH
OF METALLICA'S
CLIFF BURTON
by Joel McIver

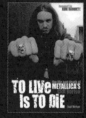

ISBN 978-1-906002-24-4

THE IMPOSSIBLE
DREAM: THE STORY
OF SCOTT WALKER
AND THE WALKER
BROTHERS
by Anthony Reynolds

ISBN 978-1-906002-25-1

JACK BRUCE:
COMPOSING
HIMSELF: THE
AUTHORISED
BIOGRAPHY
by Harry Shapiro

ISBN 978-1-906002-26-8

FOREVER CHANGES:
ARTHUR LEE AND THE
BOOK OF LOVE
by John Einarson

ISBN 978-1-906002-31-2

RETURN OF THE
KING: ELVIS PRESLEY'S
GREAT COMEBACK
by Gillian G. Gaar

ISBN 978-1-906002-28-2

A WIZARD, A TRUE
STAR: TODD
RUNDGREN IN THE
STUDIO
by Paul Myers

ISBN 978-1-906002-33-6

SHELTER FROM THE
STORM: BOB DYLAN'S
ROLLING THUNDER
YEARS
by Sid Griffin

ISBN 978-1-906002-27-5

SEASONS THEY
CHANGE: THE STORY
OF ACID AND
PSYCHEDELIC FOLK
by Jeanette Leech

ISBN 978-1-906002-32-9

WON'T GET FOOLED
AGAIN: THE WHO
FROM LIFEHOUSE TO
QUADROPHENIA
by Richie Unterberger

ISBN 978-1-906002-35-0

THE
RESURRECTION OF
JOHNNY CASH:
HURT, REDEMPTION,
AND AMERICAN
RECORDINGS
by Graeme Thomson

ISBN 978-1-906002-36-7

CRAZY TRAIN: THE
HIGH LIFE AND
TRAGIC DEATH OF
RANDY RHOADS
by Joel McIver

ISBN 978-1-906002-37-4

THE 10 RULES OF
ROCK AND ROLL:
COLLECTED MUSIC
WRITINGS 2005-11
by Robert Forster

ISBN 978-1-906002-91-6

GLENN HUGHES THE
AUTOBIOGRAPHY:
FROM DEEP PURPLE TO
BLACK COUNTRY
COMMUNION
by Glenn Hughes

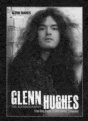

ISBN 978-1-906002-92-3